AF895524

Springer Proceedings in Business and Economics

Springer Proceedings in Business and Economics brings the most current research presented at conferences and workshops to a global readership. The series features volumes (in electronic and print formats) of selected contributions from conferences in all areas of economics, business, management, and finance. In addition to an overall evaluation by the publisher of the topical interest, scientific quality, and timeliness of each volume, each contribution is refereed to standards comparable to those of leading journals, resulting in authoritative contributions to the respective fields. Springer's production and distribution infrastructure ensures rapid publication and wide circulation of the latest developments in the most compelling and promising areas of research today.

The editorial development of volumes may be managed using Springer Nature's innovative EquinOCS, a proven online conference proceedings submission, management and review system. This system is designed to ensure an efficient timeline for your publication, making Springer Proceedings in Business and Economics the premier series to publish your workshop or conference volume.

This book series is indexed in SCOPUS.

Daniel Schallmo · Abayomi Baiyere ·
Frank Gertsen · Claus Andreas Foss Rosenstand ·
Christopher A. Williams
Editors

Digital Disruption and Transformation

Case Studies, Approaches, and Tools

Springer

Editors
Daniel Schallmo
Institute for Entrepreneurship
Neu-Ulm University of Applied Sciences
Neu-Ulm, Germany

Frank Gertsen
Aalborg University
Aalborg, Denmark

Christopher A. Williams
IU International University of Applied Sciences
Augsburg, Germany

Abayomi Baiyere
Copenhagen Business School
Frederiksberg, Denmark

Claus Andreas Foss Rosenstand
Aalborg University
Aalborg, Denmark

ISSN 2198-7246 ISSN 2198-7254 (electronic)
Springer Proceedings in Business and Economics
ISBN 978-3-031-47887-1 ISBN 978-3-031-47888-8 (eBook)
https://doi.org/10.1007/978-3-031-47888-8

© The Editor(s) (if applicable) and The Author(s), under exclusive license to Springer Nature Switzerland AG 2024

This work is subject to copyright. All rights are solely and exclusively licensed by the Publisher, whether the whole or part of the material is concerned, specifically the rights of translation, reprinting, reuse of illustrations, recitation, broadcasting, reproduction on microfilms or in any other physical way, and transmission or information storage and retrieval, electronic adaptation, computer software, or by similar or dissimilar methodology now known or hereafter developed.
The use of general descriptive names, registered names, trademarks, service marks, etc. in this publication does not imply, even in the absence of a specific statement, that such names are exempt from the relevant protective laws and regulations and therefore free for general use.
The publisher, the authors, and the editors are safe to assume that the advice and information in this book are believed to be true and accurate at the date of publication. Neither the publisher nor the authors or the editors give a warranty, expressed or implied, with respect to the material contained herein or for any errors or omissions that may have been made. The publisher remains neutral with regard to jurisdictional claims in published maps and institutional affiliations.

This Springer imprint is published by the registered company Springer Nature Switzerland AG
The registered company address is: Gewerbestrasse 11, 6330 Cham, Switzerland

Paper in this product is recyclable.

Preface

Today's global, digital economy requires a holistic view on digitalization and has become central for all non-profit and for-profit institutions. In this special issue, we address key digitalization challenges from company, institutional, industry, and societal perspectives and how these can create our common innovation future.

This special volume presents current academic research and practical findings, covering the field of digitalization. Included contributions are (1) The Evolution of Digital Transformation; (2) Skills and Knowledges expected in Digital Transformation's era; (3) Digital Transformation of Business Model: The Case of Israeli HealthTech; (4) Digital business models and financial performance: On the importance of business renewal; (5) Digital Innovations and transformation in the Public Sector of Panama; (6) Platform-Based Interorganizational Learning for Business Model Innovation: Case Study AgilHybrid; (7) Data-Driven Foresight in Life Cycle Management: An interview study; (8) Digital disruption – how medical doctors employ influencer marketing strategies; (9) The transformation of the accounting profession within a digitalized economy and the impact on accounting education; and (10) SMEs' Innovation Leveraged by Digital Transformation During Covid-19.

We hope that the Special Issue stimulates an intensive discussion between scientists, lecturers, and students from the fields of digitalization and disruption, and that the content will be used in research and teaching. We wish practitioners from the areas of management, strategic planning, and business development to be able to apply the insights to successfully practice digitalization and thus take advantage of the digital potential within their business model and industry.

The editors will like to thank the Springer team and everyone who was involved in the typesetting and design. In particular, we like to thank Mr. Prashanth Mahagaonkar from Springer, and our research assistant at the University of Applied Sciences Neu-Ulm, Verena Mattes, for their valuable input and for their willingness to be at our side with advice and action at any time.

On behalf of all authors, we wish the readers of the compilation a great deal of knowledge and success in their work on digitalization.

Neu-Ulm, Germany — Prof. Dr. Daniel Schallmo
Frederiksberg, Denmark — Prof. Dr. Abayomi Baiyere
Aalborg, Denmark — Prof. Dr. Frank Gertsen
Aalborg, Denmark — Ass. Prof. Dr. Claus Andreas Foss Rosenstand
Augsburg, Germany — Prof. Dr. Christopher A. Williams
October 2023

Contents

The Evolution of Digital Transformation

Cheng Gong, Xavier Parisot, and Detlef Reis

Abstract The evolution of digital transformation (DT) poses a significant challenge for organizations worldwide, representing both disruptive difficulties and tremendous opportunities for renewing value offerings, business models, and organizational practices. To use DT as an impetus for positive change, however, it is critical that scholars and practitioners have a clear, unified understanding of the concept. We structure our discussion as follows: Sect. 1 of this chapter discusses the confusion around the concept "digital transformation" and its related concepts (i.e., digitization, digitalization). Section 2 presents the etymology of these three concepts', leading to a discussion of the main etymological reasons behind the confusion. In the Sect. 3, we explore the historical use of these concepts in the pertinent literature; we reveal how scholars have interpreted the concepts inconsistently and associated them with a myriad of different realities/phenomena. Section 4 introduces a concept formation and assessment methodology to lay the theoretical foundation of how concepts can be analyzed and assessed. Section 5 offers a collection of existing definitions of digitization, digitalization, and digital transformation that we selected to analyze their defining attributes. We present a detailed example of how we systematically analyzed and assessed digitization's historical defining attributes. We then report the results of the same analysis for digitalization and digital transformation to assuage the "fuzziness" issue associated with these concepts. Section 6 sums up and discusses our findings that we hope will inspire academics and practitioners to use these terms carefully and consistently.

Keywords Digital transformation · Digitalization · Digitization · Concept evolution · Reconceptualization

C. Gong (✉) · X. Parisot · D. Reis
The Institute for Knowledge and Innovation, South-East Asia (IKI-SEA), Bangkok University, Bangkok 10110, Thailand
e-mail: cheng.gong.lisa@foxmail.com

X. Parisot
e-mail: xavier.p@bu.ac.th

D. Reis
e-mail: detlef.r@bu.ac.th

© The Author(s), under exclusive license to Springer Nature Switzerland AG 2024
D. Schallmo et al. (eds.), *Digital Disruption and Transformation*, Springer Proceedings in Business and Economics, https://doi.org/10.1007/978-3-031-47888-8_1

1 Introduction

World Economic Forum (2017) acknowledged digital transformation as one of the world's most pressing challenges for most organizations. Digital transformation (DT) is challenging how organizations can better meet evolving customer expectations, deliver their value propositions, and respond to a changing living and working environment. The growing penetration of digital technologies in the market inevitably drives organizations to rethink their value chain and draw up a roadmap to successfully embark on the "going digital"-journey. While there is general agreement on its growing importance to an organization's success, the inconsistent use of the term "digital transformation" in academia and business practice generates confusion.

On the academic front, the definitional inconsistency of digital transformation and its related terms (e.g., digitization, digitalization) and the theoretical inconsistency of its implications at multiple levels of analysis hamper the betterment of research. The co-existence of numerous conflicting definitions has rendered these terms meaningless. It creates difficulties in developing a consistent stream of research that builds on what has been done before, thus making it more complicated to define and test relationships for digital transformation theory building (Gong and Ribiere 2021). The vagueness in the literature demonstrates a lack of a comprehensive, unified understanding of digital transformation (Goerzig and Bauernhansl 2018; Haffke et al. 2016; Matt et al. 2015; Morakanyane et al. 2017; Van Veldhoven and Vanthienen 2019). This lack of a homogeneous interpretation of the concept is detrimental to research synergy, leading to wildly contradictory and incompatible research findings unfit to guide business practice.

On the practical front, digital transformation appears to be one of the top priorities on business leaders' agendas (Sundblad 2020). However, a McKinsey (2018) study found that the success rate for implementing DT in organizations is less than 30%; moreover, among those organizations reporting a successful implementation, only 23% improved their organizational performance, and in only 7% of cases were these improvements deemed sustainable. The success rates do not exceed 26% in digitally savvy industries (e.g., high tech, media, and telecom) and fall between 4 and 11% in more traditional industries (e.g., oil and gas, automotive, infrastructure, and pharmaceuticals; De la Boutetière et al. 2018). IBM claims that successful digital transformation took around four years and observed that 85% of efforts fail (Gibson 2018). Moreover, Gartner (2019) predicted that through 2021, digital transformation initiatives would take large traditional organizations, on average, twice as long and cost twice as much as initially anticipated.

Leaders and executives using the term DT inconsistently to describe various strategizing and organizing activities (Warner and Wäger 2019) may risk blurring the distinct direction of organizational strategic moves (e.g., aiming for incremental vs. radical changes). Having an unclear DT vision challenges C-suite managers in claiming authority and clearly defining job responsibility for digital-related projects at the organizational level. Having diverse interpretations of DT makes it harder to benchmark one's performance against other organizations and industries on DT metrics and best practices at the industrial level.

2 Concepts' Etymology

Exploring the etymology of a term is crucial in concept formation since it reveals all the historical connotations contained in a particular term and opens up "a whole new understanding of the true reality" (Eriksson 2010, p. 5). Indeed, the origin, derivation, and historical evolution of a term explain the multivalence of its meanings, i.e., the multiplicity of its definitions (Gerring 1999). This definitional plurality generates a halo of meanings that can affect how common people, managers, and scholars understand a concept "at first sight." Therefore, a comparison between the existing meanings and the one retained for the conceptual definition is informative in concept formation studies (Eriksson 2010). It helps discriminate between the terms' historical meanings, the actual meanings shared in common languages, and the meaning chosen by scholars. Moreover, the diversity of accepted meanings in the common language helps understand the size and scope of the term's "halo effect" (Dumez 2011) chosen to denominate the concept. The meaning of the term(s) chosen in the seminal definition(s) also determines what kinds of empirical cases the concept applies to, how far this application should go, and where it should stop. In other words, the concept's meaning determines its empirical domain of validity.

The words digital and digitize share a common Latin root: "digit." This term emerged in ancient Latin (1st Century BC) *digitus* originally means "finger or toes," and evolved into modern Latin (since about 1500) *digitalis* means "fingers." The modern use of the term "digital" as an adjective, meaning "of signals, information, or data: represented by series of discrete values (commonly the numbers 0 and 1), typically for electronic storage or processing" started from 1940 (OED 2010). George Stibitz first used the term in 1942 in the expression "digital computer" as a counterpart to the analog (Aspray 2000). "Digital" also means "of a computer or calculator: that operates on data in digital form; (of a storage medium) that stores digital data" (since 1945); "of technologies, media, etc.: involving digital data; making use of digital computers or devices" (since 1948; OED 2010). These historical meanings of the word "digital" laid the foundation of the modern use of the verb "digitize," referring to "converting into a sequence of digits in computer programming, moving from analog number to electronic digits" (since 1953; "Online Etymology Dictionary" n.d).

Etymologically, the word "digitization" is clearly rooted in the verb "digitize," while the word "digitalization" comes from the same Latin root "digital," which serves as one component of the concept "digital transformation." This etymological word commonality inevitably generates confusion between the meanings of these terms, which leads to an interchangeable use of the different terms in both academia and practice. All the concepts discussed above are using common language terms for their concept formation. The multivalent meanings of these terms also blur the

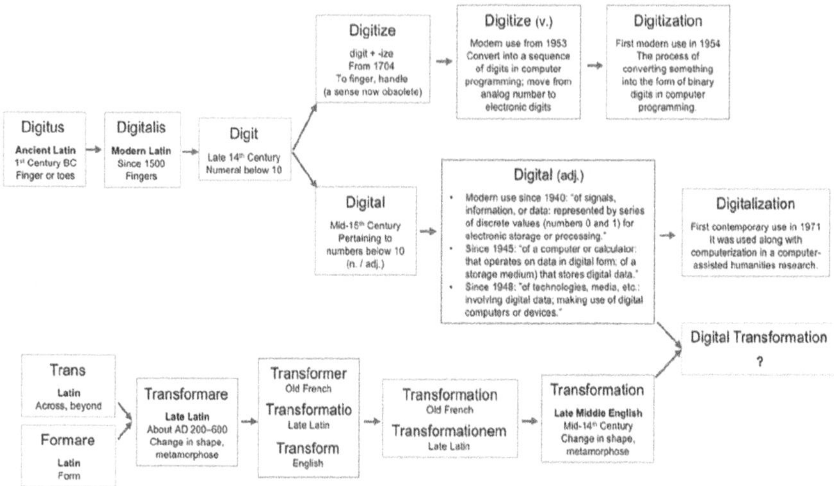

Fig. 1 Etymology of digitization, digitalization, and digital transformation (*Source* Own illustration)

specificities of each concept. Therefore, discrimination between digitization, digitalization, and digital transformation is more challenging to achieve from a common language perspective. While this common denomination strategy improves these terms' familiarity, it decreases the ability to discriminate the concepts. The following exploration of the intension and extension of each of these concepts could solve that matter.

We present a summary of the etymology of the terms digitization, digitalization, and digital transformation (see Fig. 1). A more detailed etymological analysis of these terms can be found in section Appendix 1.

3 The Historical Use of the Concepts

Understanding the history of a concept's formation is critical to recognize the evolution of its scope and limits of application. This history starts with the seminal definition(s) of the concept and continues with the evolution of that definition when confronted with multiple empirical realities. As for digitalization and digital transformation, this historical analysis is critical to explaining the sources of confusion that resulted in the shared common etymological roots. It reveals the definitional overlap and distinctions between these three terms and allows to retrace the chronological emergence of their associated core attributes and auxiliary hypothesis (Lakatos 1978).

3.1 Digitization

The Oxford English Dictionary (OED) traces the first modern use of the term "digitization" jointly with computers to the mid-1950s (OED 2014). According to the OED, digitization refers to "the action or process of digitizing; the conversion of analog data (especially in later use images, video, and text) into digital form." Some scholars refer it to the technical process of converting analog data into a digital format: an array of zeros and ones stored in a way that makes them readable by computers. With the technological development, the creation, storage, communication, and consumption of information and non-digital products are all being gradually digitized (Press 2015). The development of digital technologies and their implications in different fields have compelled scholars and practitioners to explore digital technologies' potential, extending from the technical process to their impact on different entities (i.e., organizations, businesses, industries, societies).

A Google Trend search by Seibt et al. (2019) indicates that the term digitization used to be more popular in English-speaking countries, while the term digitalization has been more frequently searched for in continental Europe. No distinction is widely represented in dictionaries, such as the Oxford dictionary, which offers the same definition for both terms. The Encyclopedia Britannica ("Encyclopedia Britannica" n.d.) and sociological dictionaries (Bruce and Yearley 2006; Scott and Marshall 2009; Swedberg and Agevall 2016; Turner 2006) do not define the terms digitization and digitalization. However, both terms are applied in business contexts, public debates by media (Seibt et al. 2019) with correlated meanings that have been causing a great deal of confusion.

In the academic literature, no single seminal scientific definition that all the authors agree upon can be found for each of these concepts. Moreover, all the definitions of digitization are rooted in common language, not in systematic scientific conceptualization. Digitization and digitalization terms are often applied to signify the same objects/phenomenon. The same overlap exists between the use of the term digitization and the term digital transformation. Some authors use different terms interchangeably consciously or unconsciously; others may differentiate one concept while using the other two terms as equivalents implicitly or explicitly. Such confusion or lack of a common conceptual basis makes it impossible to ensure cumulative and sustainable knowledge creation (Sparrowe and Mayer 2011). Consequently, this lack of clarity leads some authors to distinguish these three terms and their associated definitions in their articles to attach one specific term to one specific object/phenomena (e.g., Mergel et al. 2019; Verhoef et al. 2019).

3.2 Digitalization

The first contemporary use of the term "digitalization" along with computerization appeared in Wachal's (1971) essay that discusses the social implications of the digitalization of society in computer-assisted humanities research (Brennen and Kreiss 2016). In general, digitalization refers to "the use of digital technologies" (Srai and Lorentz 2019, p. 79). It "loses its more technical aspects to digitization while maintaining the vague ideas of restructuring social life or business, and all the normative connotations they entail" (Seibt et al. 2019, p. 10). Dijk van Jan (2006) noted that digitalization "allows a considerable increase in the production, dispersion, and consumption of information and the signals of communication" (p. 193), and "produces a culture of speed because creative production is assisted by the power of accelerated processing and distribution in computers and networks" (p. 209).

Digitalization is often used as a synonym of digital transformation when describing changes brought by the adoption of digital technologies in society and organizations. Besides, Seibt et al. (2019) argued that the discussion around the digitalization of industry is a debate that got labeled "Industries 4.0," which is the most prominent field of the industrial application of digitization, digitalization, and automation (Schumacher et al. 2016). Bloomberg (2018) noted that "automation is a major part of the digitalization story, whether it be shifting work roles or transforming business processes generally" (p. 4).

The implementation of IT tools/software in organizations, such as MRP (Material Requirements Planning), Manufacturing Resource Planning (MRP II), ERP (Enterprise Resource Planning), and BPR (Business Process Reengineering), leads to the first generation of digitalization processes. During the 1970s and 1980s, with computer hardware and software development, MRP and MRP II emerged, driven by the need for stronger integration between the functional enterprise silos, the suppliers, and the customers. From the 1990s, ERP (i.e., the adoption of standard software packages) and BPR (i.e., business management initiatives striving for process efficiency supported by IT) started to emerge and spread. ERP is a "framework for organizing, defining, and standardizing the business processes necessary to effectively plan and control an organization so the organization can use its internal knowledge to seek external advantag*e*" (Blackstone and Cox 2005, p. 38). This dictionary definition resonates obviously with the expected outcomes of digitalization. The common aim/goal is to optimize organizations' existing business processes through efficient coordination between routines (Pagani and Pardo 2017). Organizations may undertake a series of digitalization projects to automate processes and increase process efficiency (Bloomberg 2018).

For the practitioners, digitalization refers to "the use of digital technologies and data (digitized and natively digital) to create revenue, improve business, replace business processes (not simply digitizing them) and create an environment for digital business" (i-scoop 2016), and "using digital technologies to automate processes for better outcomes and to optimize value" (NCMM 2020). For scholars, digitalization refers to "the adoption of Internet-connected digital technologies and applications by companies" (Pagani and Pardo 2017, p. 185), and "a means to fulfill customers' needs more effectively, adapt to changes in the sector and increase their competitive advantage" (Rachinger et al. 2019, p. 1150).

In digitalization, digital technologies serve as enablers for organizations to change their existing business processes (Verhoef et al. 2019), including communication

(Ramaswamy and Ozcan 2016; Van Doorn et al. 2010) and distribution (Leviäkangas 2016). To achieve such goals, organizations may use ERP or other digital technologies to support the digitalization process. The changes ERP introduced are primarily limited to business processes within organizational boundaries in efficiency improvement, cost reduction, and business process optimization (Ash and Burn 2003; Kauffman and Walden 2001), mainly focusing on deploying internal management information systems (Boersma and Kingma 2005). ERP and BPR put effort into exploiting IT software packages to improve organizational processes, focusing on production effectiveness and efficiency internally. Digitalization emphasizes the change process as a whole to achieve economic-driven outcomes through ERP or BPR and other digital technologies.

3.3 Digital Transformation

There is no common consensus regarding the seminal scientific definition of digital transformation in the literature. Historically, the ideas of digital products, services, and mediums can be traced back to the 1990s and 2000s (Auriga 2016; Schallmo et al. 2017). Morton (1991) noted that organizations experience fundamental transformations for effective IT implementation. This idea gave birth to a research stream studying IT-enabled organizational transformation, which may be seen as one of the scholarly roots of DT research (Nadkarni and Prügl 2020). It initiated DT's discussion with a strong IT focus as a catalyst of the information revolution (Gates et al. 1995) in the context of the Information Society's age and global competition. Therefore, at the early stage, a strong emphasis was put on the "digital" part – the use of digital technologies, providing a limited understanding of the "transformation" part of an entity. Thus, oftentimes, the concept of DT was used, or probably misused, synonymously with the one of digitization (the technical process) and digitalization (the installation process). With the accelerating development of digital technologies since the 1940s, industrial changes and societal developments throughout the previous decades could be witnessed, thus giving more importance to the transformational part of DT.

People then started to associate DT with the changes that digital technologies cause or influence in all aspects of human life (Stolterman and Fors 2004). The "transformation" part of DT, which was undervalued, gradually came back to attention. As different research streams started to emerge, some scholars gradually realized that DT is more than just a technological shift (Henriette et al. 2015). Apart from technology, it requires "actors" (Nadkarni and Prügl 2020) and the alignment of strategy and other factors, such as culture, mindset, talent development, and leadership (Goran et al. 2017). In recent years, some researchers have been concentrating on identifying DT's dimensions and drivers (Liere-Netheler et al. 2018a, b; Verhoef et al. 2019) as follows:

- **External drivers encompass:** (1) innovation push and market pull generated by the adoption and development of digital technologies (Nambisan et al. 2017; Sambamurthy et al. 2003); (2) increasing volume of data (Kouroubali and Katehakis 2019; Pappas et al. 2018; Zaki 2019); (3) accelerating customer behavior changes (Rogers 2016; von Leipzig et al. 2017; Westerman et al. 2014); and (4) laws/government policies adjustments (Gong et al. 2020; Nambisan et al. 2019), etc.
- **Internal drivers include:** (1) strategic imperative, such as, process and workplace improvement (Henriette et al. 2016); (2) vertical and horizontal integration (Camarinha-Matos et al. 2019; Gölzer and Fritzsche 2017; Borangiu et al. 2019; Liere-Netheler et al. 2018a, b); (3) management support (Matt et al. 2015; Vukšić et al. 2018); and (4) cost reduction (Liere-Netheler et al. 2018a, b), etc. Some other scholars focus on the positive and negative impacts of DT.
- **Positive consequences contain** (1) decision making improvement (Heilig et al. 2017; Roedder et al. 2016); (2) competitive advantage creation (Korhonen and Halen 2017; Schwertner 2017); (3) value creation enhancement, e.g., optimize customer experiences (Rogers 2016), etc.
- **Negative consequences cover** Cybersecurity (Möller 2020) and privacy (Mendhurwar and Mishra 2019), etc.

Beyond these new research directions, debates regarding the true nature of DT are ongoing. The controversy may be fundamentally founded in the fact that the range of DT definitions vary from: a slight technology-enabled change such as implementing a new ERP System (Chanias 2017) to a more radical and evolutionary process that takes place over time (Janowski 2015; Loebbecke and Picot 2015; Wang et al. 2018) or the economic and societal effects of digitization and digitalization (OECD 2018). While some researchers associate DT with business models (Berman 2012; Bharadwaj et al. 2013; Gassmann et al. 2014; Schallmo et al. 2017) and strategy (Bharadwaj et al. 2013; Henriette et al. 2015; Matt et al. 2015; Rogers 2016; Westerman 2018), others view DT as a paradigm or as a process (Berman 2012; Janowski 2015; Wang et al. 2018). As a result, the growing diversity of research fields associated with the concept of DT complexifies its clarification.

3.4 Synthesis

Historically, the three terms digitization, digitalization, and digital transformation are interconnected and describe different objects or phenomena. Digitalization with a longer history of use in the literature than digital transformation inevitably encompasses the early discussion of digitization's social impact and the later discussion of digital transformation's result. The absence of prevalent academic definitions for these three concepts is rooted in their ontogenesis, which was multivalent and parallel. Then, the multiplicity of connections between these concepts and others leads to a broad diversity of parallel theorizations. While this situation enriches the spectrum of digital transformation research programs (Lakatos 1978), it does not clarify the concepts.

Multiple theorizations based on multiple conceptual definitions hinder the scientific community's ability to better define and connect all the objects involved in digital transformation, i.e., to standardize and generalize their research strategy. Therefore, the possibility of comparing different results from different studies is very limited in the current situation. It implies that authors of academic papers should first consider the connections applied between the chosen terms, the definitions, and the objects or phenomena under scrutiny.

Apart from its truly intended meaning, digitalization has also been used to describe digitization in some cases and digital transformation in other cases. Some authors such as Verhoef et al. (2019) view the terms in a sequential order (digitization → digitalization → digital transformation) with digitalization bridging and connecting the other two terms; other scholars disagree with this view. The situation is further complicated when linguistically translating digitalization and digital transformation as one word in some languages to explain the change and its end-results of using digital technologies, not the technical process.

Digitalization is used to depict a state of being digitalized and the process whereby the entities are affected by the action of "going digital." Today's consensus seems that digital transformation is more than digitization (Haffke et al. 2016; Iansiti and Lakhani 2014; Yoo et al. 2012). According to a scoping review of Verhoef et al. (2019), most of the literature subscribes that digitization and digitalization imply more incremental phases to attain the most pervasive phase of digital transformation (Loebbecke and Picot 2015; Parviainen et al. 2017a, b). However, the inconsistent use of digitalization and digital transformation still exist in a broad range of academic and practitioner literature. And a disconcerting limitation of the existing literature is the failure to distinguish them properly.

4 The Concept Analysis Methodology

Based on Ogden and Richards (1923) semantic triangle (i.e., symbol, thought/reference, referent) and on Sartori's (1984) work (i.e., term/word, meaning, referent/object), Gerring (1999) proposed eight in-depth criteria of conceptual goodness: familiarity, resonance, parsimony, coherence, differentiation, depth, theoretical utility, and field utility. Gerring (1999) supports Ogden and Richards (1923) view that concepts are good when they attain a proper alignment between the three dimensions of intension, extension, and term (pp. 357–358) (see Fig. 2):

- **The term** refers to the words allocated to a concept as a label covering both the intension and the extension. It impacts the level of familiarity, resonance, and field utility of the concept.

Criteria	Explaination	Rating Scale					
		0	1	2	3	4	5
Familiarity	The degree to which a new definition "makes sense," or is intuitively "clear," depends critically upon the degree to which it conforms/clashes with estabilished usage.	Definition clashes with established usage					Definition conforms with established usage
Resonance	The "cognitive click" of a given term.	No "cognitive click"	Low	Fair	Nomal	High	Max "cognitive click"
Parsimony	The length of the definition (number of defining attributes) while concisely defining a concept.	≥ 15 attributes	13~14	11~12	9~10	7~8	≤ 6 attributes
Coherence	The sense in which the attributes that define that concept, and the characteristics that actually characterize the phenomena in question, "belong to one another."	Attributes are not logically or functionally related					Attributes are logically or functionally related
Differentiation	It refers not only to semantic space (i.e., the degree to which a concept's definitional borders are clear) but also to physical space (i.e., the degree to which a concept's borders in time and space are clearly demarcated).	No clear boundaries from/overlap with other concepts					Clear boundaries from other concepts; the concept is sufficiently bounded
Depth	The depth and utility of a concept is enhanced by its ability to "bundle" characteristics. The greater the number of properties shared by the phenomena in the extension, the greater the depth of a concept.	Limited number of properties shared by the phenomena					A great number of properties share by the phenomena
Theoretical utility	The concept's usefulness in theory formulation (i.e., to formulate new theories or refine existing).	Useless in theory formulation					Usefull in theory formulation
Field utility	The disruption that concept formation can do to the rest of the "semantic/phenomenal field" in which academic work.	Damage the semantic field the concept enters					Enrich the conceptual quality of existing concepts in the field

Fig. 2 Concept goodness assessment rating scale (*Source* Own illustration). *Notes* The eight criteria of concept goodness are adapted from Gerring (1999)

- **The intension**, i.e., connotation, meaning, definiens, or definition, refers to the properties or attributes that define a concept. The attributes specifically chosen to define the concept establishes its level of parsimony and internal coherence.
- **The extension**, i.e., denotation, referent, object, definiendum, refers to the object, event, or phenomenon to be defined and the referent or referents to which a concept applies. It determines the nature of the empirical cases a concept applies to and impacts the concept's theoretical utility and depth. It determines a concept's level of differentiation.

Exploring the evolution of definitions reveals: (1) the multiplicity of definitions proposed in the literature; (2) to what extent their defining attributes overlap between the three concepts: digitization, digitalization, and digital transformation; (3) the plurality of conceptual boundaries and therefore of realities under scrutiny. It allows specifying the core and peripheral defining attributes used to define the three concepts. The defining attributes can then be grouped to analyze their logical alignment (internal coherence) as well as their external differentiation. Hence, such an analytical process facilitates a qualitative evaluation regarding the connections between the three dimensions of the semantic triangle and assesses the conceptual goodness of the targeted concepts using a rating scale adapted from Gerring's (1999) framework (see Fig. 2).

5 The Defining Attributes Analysis and Conceptual Assessment of the Relevant Terms in the Literature

5.1 Digitization

Definitions of digitization are collected until saturation/repetition of the defining attributes is observed. This process ensures that most of the applied defining attributes are identified. Saturation was achieved with 11 definitions. These key definitions of digitization evolved over the past two decades since the first definition was proposed in 1995 (and are presented in Appendix 2).

We summarize the 27 defining attributes of digitization and their frequency in Table 1. Based on the accumulated frequency of these attributes, the first five defining attributes are the core defining attributes (most frequent); the following 3 defining attributes are the peripheral (average frequency); and the rest are the outsiders (low frequency).

The analysis shows that digitization refers to a technical process of converting analog data/information[1] into digital forms. It is a process that has both symbolic (i.e., converting analog data into bits represented as 0 s and 1 s) and material (i.e., artifacts used to store and communicate digitized information) dimensions. Hence, through digitization, data is deconstructed and encoded as strings of 0 s and 1 s that "can then be expressed in many different ways, on many different types of materials, and in many different systems" (Brennen and Kreiss 2016, p. 2) as information. The ultimate characteristic of being stripped of errors, repetitions, and static allows digitized data and information to be easily stored, transferred, manipulated, and displayed, thus reducing paper clutter and improving efficiency. Digitization makes physical products programmable, addressable, sensible, communicable, memorable, traceable, and associable (Yoo 2010). Traditional physical products embedded with digital technologies, such as cameras (Tripsas 2009), phones (Ghazawneh and Henfridsson 2013), magazines (Nylén et al. 2014), and automobiles (Svahn et al. 2017), can provide a much wider range of functionality than non-digital products (Holmström 2018). The essence/essential meaning of digitization is presented in Fig. 3.

Based on the concept goodness assessment rating scale, digitization's concept goodness is discussed as follows:

Familiarity: Digitization is rooted in the modern use of the verb "digitize" and refers to "the action or process of digitizing, i.e., the conversion of analog to digital forms." If "digitization" as a whole word is not always very familiar for common people, the root "digit" and the suffix "-ization" are separately familiar. Such a level of familiarity here is enough to grasp the "conversion" nature of the term easily. However, in English, constructing a noun out of a verb by adding an "-ization" generates a double meaning (Taylor 2000). The new term will denote either the process described by the original verb or the end-state that results from the culmination of such a process (Buller and Gamble 2002). Therefore, common people can

[1] Note that data and information are used as synonyms in these definitions.

Table 1 Digitization's defining attributes and frequency

Concepts	Digitization												
Defining attributes	Negroponte (1995)	Yoo et al. (2010)	Katz and Koutroumpis (2013)	OED (2014)	Brennen and Kreiss (2016)	Legner et al. (2017)	Gölzer and Fritzsche (2017)	Schallmo and Williams (2018)	Bloomberg (2018)	Verhoef et al. (2019)	Gartner's IT glossary, n.d	Attributes frequency	Attributes repetition
Analog	✓	✓	✓	✓	✓	✓		✓	✓	✓	✓	0.37	10
Digital form/bits	✓	✓	✓	✓	✓	✓	✓		✓	✓	✓	0.37	10
Process	✓		✓	✓	✓	✓		✓	✓		✓	0.30	8
Data/information	✓	✓	✓	✓	✓		✓		✓	✓		0.30	8
Conversion	✓		✓	✓	✓	✓				✓		0.22	6
Encoding		✓					✓		✓			0.11	3
Technical	✓					✓						0.07	2
Action				✓						✓		0.07	2
Transmit									✓			0.04	1
Change											✓	0.04	1
Digitize				✓								0.04	1
Physical artifacts								✓				0.04	1
Store									✓			0.04	1
Social			✓									0.04	1
Transformation			✓									0.04	1
Techno-economic environment			✓									0.04	1

(continued)

Table 1 (continued)

Concepts	Digitization												
Defining attributes	Negroponte (1995)	Yoo et al. (2010)	Katz and Koutroumpis (2013)	OED (2014)	Brennen and Kreiss (2016)	Legner et al. (2017)	Gölzer and Fritzsche (2017)	Schallmo and Williams (2018)	Bloomberg (2018)	Verhoef et al. (2019)	Gartner's IT glossary, n.d	Attributes frequency	Attributes repetition
Socio-institutional operation			✔									0.04	1
Digital communications			✔									0.04	1
Digital application			✔									0.04	1
Signals					✔							0.04	1
Material					✔							0.04	1
Implementing								✔				0.04	1
Business processes								✔				0.04	1
Acquire knowledge								✔				0.04	1
Create new value								✔				0.04	1
Stakeholders								✔				0.04	1
Computers									✔			0.04	1

(*Source* Own illustration)
Note Attributes frequency equals the number of attributes repetition divided by the total number of defining attributes identified (27)

Fig. 3 The concept of digitization (*Source* Own illustration)

interpret the combination of "digit" and "-ization" in three different ways: process, result, or both. The multiplicity of possible interpretations decreases the accuracy of describing the phenomenon.

Resonance: Digitization first resonates with "digit," "digital," and "digitize." The cognitive click between "digitization" and "digital" is relevant and increases the level of the catchiness of the label/term. However, the connection between the label/term and its formal meaning is not that obvious. There is clearly a rhyming scheme in the label/term, which also increases its catchiness.

Parsimony: 5 core and 3 peripheral attributes are recurrently applied to define digitization. The number of attributes at the core meets the parsimony criteria as expressed by Gerring (1999): "[no more than] a half-dozen attributes" (p. 371).

Coherence: Digitization has a high level of internal coherence. The 5 core defining attributes (e.g., analog, digital form/bits, process, data/information, conversion) convey the essential meaning of a conversion process from analog data/information to digital form/bits. Taking the peripheral (e.g., encoding, technical, action) into consideration, the essential meaning of the action "digitize" is further strengthened. They depict a technical process of "encoding [analog] into zeroes and ones so that computers can store, process, and transmit such information" (Bloomberg 2018). The instances and attributes used to define this concept are internally consistent and logically related (see Fig. 4). To achieve a more precise elaboration, we differentiate data and information from a knowledge management perspective. Data refers to the facts and statistics collected together for reference or analysis, whereas information to "any non-random pattern or set of patterns" (Bennet et al. 2015) conveyed or represented.

Differentiation: The main challenge of defining digitization is to establish clear borders within a field of similar terms (e.g., digitalization, digital transformation). However, based on the defining attributes' analysis, this concept's definitional borders are relatively clear in the technical sense as demonstrated in coherence, thus allowing a good operationalizability.

Depth: The clear boards of digitization in the technical sense, on the other side, lower the level of its depth to cover the number of properties shared by this object/

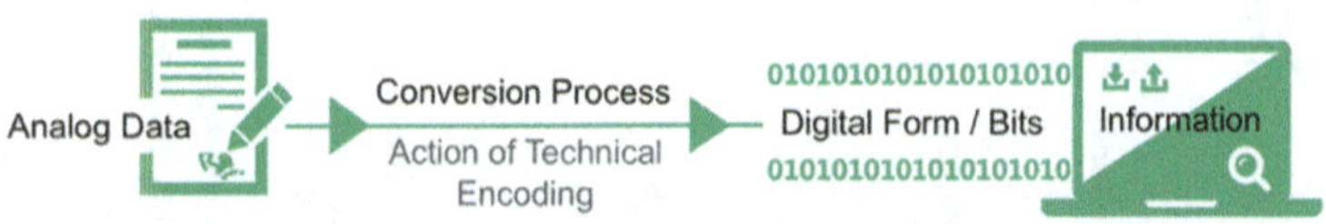

Fig. 4 The visual presentation of reconceptualized digitization internal coherence (*Source* Own illustration). *Note* Attributes "Action of Technical Encoding" are peripheral defining attributes

phenomena in its extension. In other words, poor ability of bundling characteristics. However, according to the definitions in Appendix 2, digitization is not a residual concept (i.e., define a concept by what it isn't).

Theoretical utility: Digitization was first used jointly with computers, then extended from the technical process to its impact on the development of digital technologies and their implication. It is not theory-driven since its concept inception comes from a technology implication perspective, which limited this concept's theoretical utility from its position within a narrower array of terms. Especially in computer science, digitization is used to describe the technical process of converting numerical or other information represented in a form suitable for processing by computers. However, with the unclear conceptual definitions (mixing the process and result) in the early years, this concept was used to mobilize the meanings of its related terms as they share the same roots. Simply using them interchangeably without a solid theorization process may increase this concept's theoretical utility but destroy other criteria (e.g., coherence, differentiation) and formulation of theories.

Semantic field utility: Digitization has a relatively high semantic field utility as it does not destroy these words used to define it. Digitizing the analog data does not change the understanding of converting or encoding them into digits (0 s and 1 s). None of these neighboring terms are hurt while conceptualizing digitization. By contrast, it establishes a very good relationship with them and increases their utility in the semantic field.

In short, several conclusions emerge from this evaluation: the concept of digitization performs quite well on the parameter of the term (i.e., familiarity, resonance, field utility) and intension (i.e., parsimony, coherence), and moderately on the parameter of extension (i.e., depth, differentiation, theoretical utility) concerning a lower score of theoretical utility. Digitization meets the criteria of depth and differentiation well in the technical sense. Figure 5 presents the overall result of our assessment of the term digitization on the eight criteria with the help of Gerring's framework (as shown in Fig. 2).

5.2 *Digitalization and Digital Transformation*

While digitization appears to be a distinct concept that refers to the technical process of converting analog data into digital formats, defining attributes of digitalization and digital transformation overlap. Therefore, a systematic analysis of digital transformation's concept formation and conceptualization evolution constitutes a prerequisite for further theorization and modelization. To achieve better readability, the authors decided to present these two concepts together to show the commonality and difference.

Gong and Ribiere (2021) reviewed 134 digital transformation definitions to provide insights into six core defining primitives of this concept. They found that the challenge and need to develop a sustainable nomenclature of digital-related terms

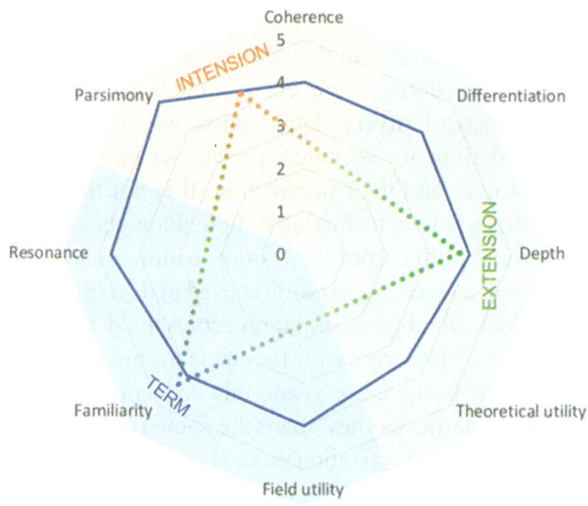

Fig. 5 The concept assessment result of "digitization" (*Source* Own illustration)

and concepts is an urgent and important problem to tackle, especially the difference between digitalization and digital transformation.

This chapter further discusses these two distinct, yet interrelated concepts through a diachronic analysis of their definition attributes based on empirical evidence. Thus, a search query for empirical papers studying digitalization and digital transformation was performed in the EBSCO database, and full-text papers were downloaded and screened for their eligibility. Thirty-six definitions were extracted based on empirical evidence, including 24 definitions of digital transformation and 12 definitions of digitalization. The defining attributes and their frequency for each term are listed in Appendix 3 to clearly show their similarities and differences.

In total, there are 41 defining attributes for digital transformation and 30 for digitalization, which indicates a high level of discrepancy among the available definitions and the issue of conceptual stretching in these definitions. Regarding the etymological and historical issues discussed in Sects. 2 and 3, it is not surprising that around 36% (15 out of 41) of digital transformation's defining attributes overlap with digitalization. Taking a closer look at these attributes, the internal coherence and external differentiation are debatable. No single definition that encompasses all or most of the core and peripheral defining attributes also supports this view. Such diversity of attributes either indicates the multiplicity of meanings attached to one concept or suggests there should be two or more concepts to better discriminate the meanings based on logical internal coherence and external differentiation. The choice made here will also affect the theory-building associated with these terms in the long run.

Having a clear boundary for each concept will determine what reality is effectively attached to a particular concept and benefit the empirical research to obtain consistent and comparable results. To achieve such aims, a deep analysis of all these defining attributes (of the concepts *digitalization* and *digital transformation*) in the context of the papers from which the definitions were extracted is needed. The same methodology used to analyze the concept *digitization* was applied again to analyze the core and peripheral attributes for assessing the concepts of *digitalization* and *digital transformation* based on Gerring's (1999) framework. However, we decided not to present our analysis in all its details here to avoid content repetition and overextending the scope of this chapter.

Digitalization. Looking at all the defining attributes of digitalization, the following points can be drawn:

- Firstly, digitalization refers to the change process of adopting and using digital technologies, whether these changes occur in individuals' connection and their behaviors (Gimpel and Röglinger 2015), or the manifold socio-technical changes in broader individual, organizational, and societal contexts (Legner et al. 2017). This variety of change in the context of digitalization indicates a contextual hierarchy in these definitions.
- Secondly, the outcome of digitalization is more focused on describing the consequences that implementing digital technologies may have on offerings (i.e., products and services) and the quality of the organization's relationships with others (e.g., increased simplicity, efficiency, speed, competitiveness, etc.). It focuses on the change of existing socio-technical structures that were previously mediated by non-digital artifacts (Thorseng and Grisot 2017) and the potential changes in the processes beyond the mere digitizing of existing processes, forms, and work products (Parviainen et al. 2017a, b). That is, it is beyond the technical process of digitization. In contrast, digitalization is the main driver that affects the business environment and inter-functional coordination in particular (Ruiz-Alba et al. 2019) to integrate the functional silos. It is a means to fulfill customers' needs more effectively (Rachinger et al. 2019) and makes businesses act rapidly in a short time frame (Sehlin et al. 2019). It has accelerated the shift from product-based to service-based businesses, affecting fundamentally how firms compete for and transact with customers (Hänninen et al. 2018). It changes the relationships into ones that are mediated by digitized artifacts and relationships with newly embedded digital capabilities (Thorseng and Grisot 2017).
- Thirdly, digitalization may be a source of an organization's competitive advantage through increased efficiency. It improves the organization's effectiveness and influences its internal structures by reinforcing interdisciplinary collaboration (Rachinger et al. 2019).

Figure 6 presents the identified defining attributes of digitalization. It reveals that there are several dimensions included in this concept, some of which overlap with digital transformation. This overlap is rooted in the etymological confusion as discussed in Sects. 2 and 3, leading to an unclear border with digital transformation. A further explanation to realign these dimensions is needed to increase its internal coherence and external differentiation to understand this concept better.

The concept of digitalization is woefully debatable. In the case of picking out one phenomenon among other phenomena, this concept generates confusion by linking its neighboring concepts with their overlapping attributes in reference to various objects/phenomena. That is, an undifferentiable conceptual definition may contribute to digitalization's familiarity, resonance, and depth; however, it largely diminishes its

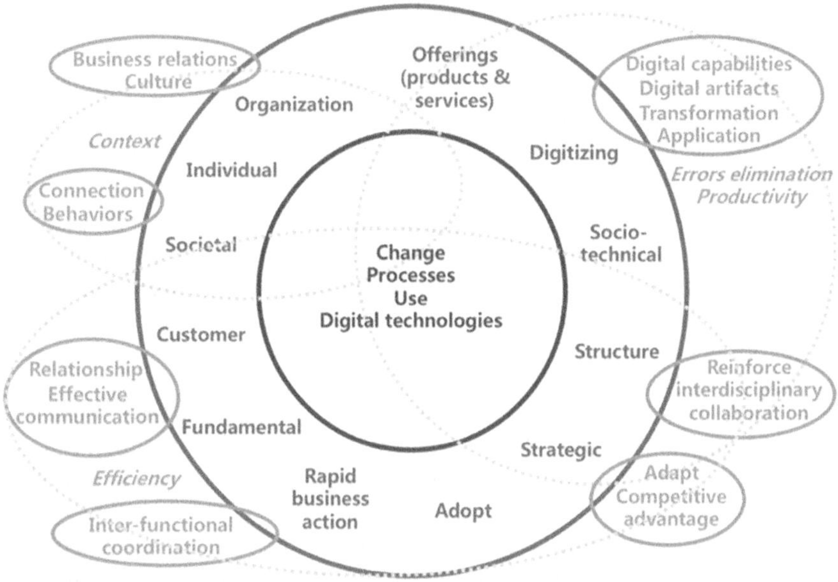

Fig. 6 The core and peripheral defining attributes of digitalization (*Source* Own illustration). *Note* The defining attributes away from the bullseye in the small circles are the outsiders (low frequency) compared to the core defining attributes in the inner ring and peripheral in the outer ring

level of differentiation and blurring its boundaries from other neighboring concepts. Without a clear boundary specifying digitalization's nature, such confusion will continuously damage the semantic field utility and connect phenomena whose shared properties are not related in some manner. Therefore, a reconceptualization with a high level of coherence and differentiation is needed for this concept to perform better in extension and intension.

Digital Transformation. In a different vein, looking at the defining attributes of digital transformation (DT), the scope and the expected outcome of digital transformation are different from that of digitalization:

- Firstly, digital transformation refers to a transformation (i.e., fundamental change) process of using digital technologies rather than a non-fundamental change process. Liu et al. (2011) defined digital transformation as "an organizational transformation that integrates digital technologies and business processes in a digital economy" (p. 1730) based on their qualitative case study of CBC Bank's global e-banking project. Digital technologies are used to transform the customer value proposition and organizing operations to create new business models (Berman 2012). It changes a business model in how the organization creates value for its customers (i.e., customer value proposition) and how it captures that value (i.e., how it makes money) (Iansiti and Lakhani 2014). Kane et al. (2015) confirmed digital transformation as an organizational transformation, where digital technologies transform the business models and processes, based on their survey of more than 4,800 business executives, managers, and analysts in 129 countries and 27 industries, as well as interviews with business executives and technology vendors. Such transformation of business activities, processes, models, competencies, operational routines, and organizational capabilities to fully leverage the changes and opportunities brought by digital technologies is profound and fundamental in nature (Demirkan et al. 2016; Li et al. 2018). It encompasses the networking of actors such as businesses and customers across all value chain segments and applying digital technologies (Schallmo et al. 2017). Hence, these aforementioned attributes resonate with the emerging notion of business model innovation, which has received massive practical (Pohle and Chapman 2006) and theoretical (Schneider and Spieth 2013, 2014; Zott et al. 2011) interest in recent years. Its broad definition as "the implementation of a business model that is new to the firm" (Björkdahl and Holmén 2013, p. 214), and its main dimensions of value creation, value proposition, and value capture (Baden-Fuller and Haefliger 2013; Clauss 2017; Johnson et al. 2008; Massa and Tucci 2014; Morris et al. 2005; Zott and Amit 2013) fit the expected end results where digital transformation is heading to at the strategic level.

- Secondly, the end result of digital transformation is a significant *transformation* (i.e., a redefinition of mission and purpose to reflect a new direction), rather than a simple *realignment* (i.e., a change to the way of doing things that do not involve a fundamental reappraisal of the central assumptions and beliefs within the organization) from a change management perspective (Balogun et al. 2015). Digital transformation generates radical improvement (Westerman et al. 2011). It is a holistic effort to revise core processes and services, which results in a complete revision of the existing and the creation of new digital products and services (Mergel et al. 2019). Digital transformation goes beyond just technological shift (Kane et al. 2015); it also involves the process of strategic renewal and dynamic capabilities development of an organization (Warner and Wäger 2019) to address the opportunities and risks that originate from digital technologies (Singh and Hess 2017). It affects employees' operational work routines (Chen et al. 2014) at the operational level, and also managerial processes (Iansiti and Lakhani 2014) and human relations (Mićić 2017) at the managerial level. Redefining the organization's value propositions may be shaped by customer interaction and collaboration (Berman 2012) and customer engagement (Schuchmann and Seufert 2015). Digital transformation can influence organizational culture and capabilities (Li et al. 2018; Tan et al. 2015) and "lead to highly dynamic markets, pressuring employees to continuously adapt to new situations and increasing the need for agility and lifelong learning" (Schwarzmüller et al. 2018, p. 126). While top executives set and drive the digital agenda, it's crucial that they also put a focus on employees and talent engagement to achieve digital maturity (Kane et al. 2015).
- Thirdly, while 11 definitions out of 24 studies explicitly acknowledge organizations as the entity (i.e., the unit of analysis affected by digital transformation), few studies also include industry and society as entities. Digital transformation is the integration of digital technologies into business, resulting in fundamental changes in the way the world does business and communicates (Mićić 2017).

Digital technologies are rapidly transforming the fundamental nature of a broad range of organizations and revitalizing their digital business models across industries (Demirkan et al. 2016). Such a holistic form of business transformation is accompanied by fundamental economic and technological changes at the organizational and industry-level (Chanias et al. 2019) and unfolds their impact across society in a strategic and prioritized way (Demirkan et al. 2016). This indicates a multiplicity of the entity affected by digital transformation.

- Lastly, using "digital economy" and "digital maturity" to define digital transformation raises the issue of conceptual stretching, which refers to the distortion that occurs when a concept does not fit the new cases (Collier and Mahon 1993; Sartori 1970). These two terms themselves remain unspecified in the literature. Utilizing them to broaden digital transformation's connotations can stretch digital transformation to "cover instances that lie quite a bit outside their normal range of use" (Gerring 1999, p. 360).

Figure 7 shows the identified defining attributes of digital transformation.

In short, several conclusions emerge from this evaluation. It is noteworthy that the concept of DT performs quite well on several criteria: it is familiar and resonant and seems to be sufficiently parsimonious and highly theoretically useful. Therefore, as noted above, it is little wonder that the concept gained popularity so quickly, which has put it at a risk of turning into a buzzword. However, with a reconceptualization that better connects the essence of defining attributes, the overall concept assessment results improve. The concept DT performs quite well in its term, extension, and

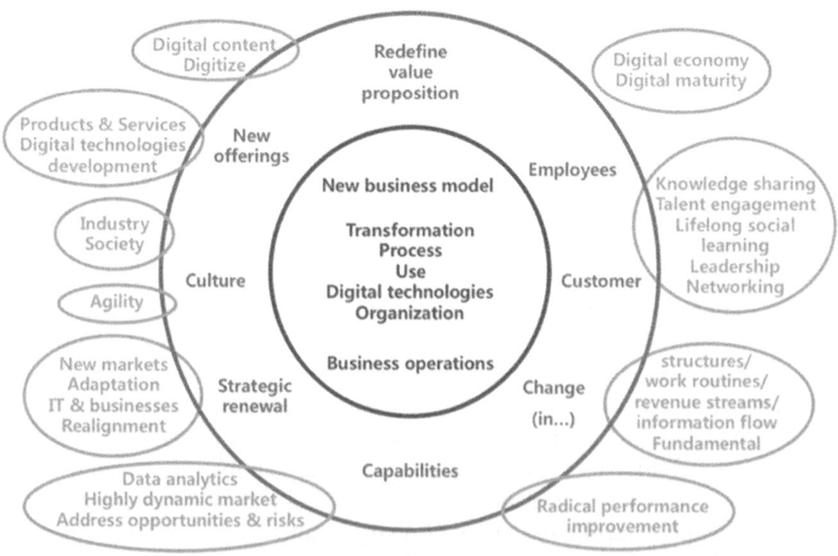

Fig. 7 The core and peripheral defining attributes of digital transformation (*Source* Own illustration). *Note* The defining attributes away from the bullseye in the small circles are the outsiders (low frequency) compared to the core defining attributes in the inner ring and peripheral in the outer ring

intension: high resonance and theoretical utility; good depth, familiarity, coherence, and differentiation; moderate parsimony, and field utility to some extent.

5.3 Synthesis

Following all the discussion in this section, there are some overlaps of digitalization and digital transformation: both terms acknowledge the change process enabled by digital technologies. Yet, they are emphasizing the different scope and end results of this change process. Indeed, both digitalization with the suffix "-ization" and digital transformation using the term "transformation" indicate that the deep nature of these concepts is a process, more specifically, a change process. However, in general, the existing literature is not sufficient to differentiate digitalization from digital transformation.

Only considering core defining attributes, the critical attribute to distinguish these two concepts is "change" (digitalization) versus "transformation" (digital transformation). Such difference in terms of the scope of the change to further differentiate these two concepts is evident in the domain of change management but may not be obvious in common language. From a change management perspective, this core defining attribute for each concept already indicates the different nature of the process enabled by digital technologies and the expected end-result they may achieve. Regarding the scope of change, digitalization is an incremental or continuous change that involves installing digital technologies needed to keep an organization on its chosen path with improved efficiency. This change may not necessarily be small, even involve significant commitments of resources, time, people, and money. However, it has not fundamentally altered the organization's core (i.e., the organization's central assumptions and beliefs), such as the structures, missions, visions, cultures, etc. On the contrary, digital transformation encompasses a fundamental shift in the organization's business model, touching all structural, cultural, and procedural aspects. It is an all-encompassing metamorphosis (transformation) of an entity (organization). This entity affected by such fundamental change is included in digital transformation's core defining attributes, but not mentioned in digitalization's definitional core.

Extending to digitalization's peripheral attributes, there is a contextual hierarchy of the entities affected by this change (i.e., individual, organizational, and societal). A similar hierarchy can be found in digital transformation's defining attributes (i.e., organizational, industrial, societal). Moreover, if the digital transformation definitions were extracted from both conceptual and empirical papers, the entities affected by digital transformation would encompass an organization, a business network, an industry, or society (Gong and Ribiere 2021). Hence, this hierarchical perspective is one dimension that needs further research.

If we only consider organizations as the entity, we propose that digital transformation focuses on transforming the organizations' business operations to create new business models. In contrast, digitalization focuses on the installation of digital technologies, so that they can be used to achieve economic-driven outcomes (e.g., improve efficiency and productivity, or error elimination). It is a means to help the organization reinforce its existing value proposition efficiently and effectively, i.e., a change to the way of doing things with the deployment of digital technologies in place. It does not involve a fundamental reappraisal of the organization's central assumptions or a paradigm shift of its organizational identity or business model. Therefore, based on our comprehensive analysis, we conclude that digital transformation is not equivalent to digitalization, and recommend the two concepts to be kept distinct at the conceptual level.

6 Discussion

The growing penetration of digital technologies in the market with the associated changes inevitably drive organizations to rethink their options to digitally transform themselves.

To better understand the evolution of digital transformation, this chapter discussed the confusion around the DT concept and its related concepts (i.e., digitization, digitalization) following a systematic methodological approach. Firstly, we presented the etymology of the three concepts, leading to a discussion of the main etymological reasons behind the confusion. Secondly, we discussed the historical evolution of these concepts, thereby revealing their inconsistent use in the existing literature; here, we also offered a synthesis of what realities/phenomena these terms are associated with. Thirdly, we introduced the concept formation and assessment methodology of Gerring (1999) to lay the theoretical foundation of how concepts can be analyzed and assessed. Finally, we collected existing definitions of digitization, digitalization, and digital transformation, and then systematized these based on a defining attributes analysis. Next, we performed and presented a detailed example of how digitization's historical defining attributes were analyzed and assessed based on Gerring's eight criteria. The results of the same analysis for digitalization and digital transformation were presented as well. To our best understanding, these three concepts are interrelated, yet they should be kept distinct at the conceptual level to describe various strategizing and organizing activities in practice and different implications at multiple levels of analysis in research. Based on our comprehensive analysis, we propose differentiating the three concepts as follows:

- ***Digitization*** is the technical process of converting analog into digital formats.
- ***Digitalization*** is the change process of installing digital technologies to reinforce the organization's existing value proposition.
- ***Digital transformation*** is a fundamental change process of an organization enabled by exploring the use of digital technologies to redefine its business models.

On the academic front, this chapter offers a solution to solve the definitional and theoretical inconsistency in the extant literature regarding digital transformation and its related terms. It potentially contributes to developing a consistent stream of research with differentiable concepts for theory-building and compatible research findings to guide business practices.

This chapter also reveals the reality/phenomenon of these concepts on the practical front, providing a clearer guideline for practitioners to develop differentiable strategic plans for organizations to "go digital." Leaders, executives, and employees can use these concepts consistently while referring to specific strategizing and organizing activities for different entities (individual, team, organization, industry, and society). Having a clearer understanding of these phenomena' essence helps to claim authority and job responsibility for digital-related projects at the organizational level and makes it easier to benchmark one's performance against other organizations and industries on digital transformation metrics and best practices at the industrial level.

In conclusion, the evolution of digital transformation offers an opportunity of renewal for many organizations all over the world. Outlining the etymological and historical reasons behind the confusion around digital transformation and analyzing the existing literature, we proposed a solution to differentiate these concepts for the goodness of both academic and practitioner communities. We hope that our work will assuage the "fuzziness" issue associated with these concepts and inspire academics and practitioners to use these terms more carefully, discriminatively, and consistently.

Disclaimer Selected portions of this chapter have previously appeared in the author's work and are used with permission.

Gong, C., & Ribiere, V. (2023). A historical outline of digital transformation. In *Digital Transformation in Healthcare in Post-Covid-19 Times* (pp. 3–25). Academic Press, Elsevier.

Gong, C., Parisot, X., Reis, D. (2023). Die Evolution der Digitalen Transformation. In: Schallmo, D.R.A., Lang, K., Werani, T., Krumay, B. (eds) Digitalisierung. Schwerpunkt Business Model Innovation. Springer Gabler, Wiesbaden.

Appendix 1: The Etymologies of the Terms Digitization, Digitalization, Transformation, and Digital Transformation

Terms	Etymologies
Digitization	The origin of "digitization" is rooted in the modern use of the verb "digitize" (digit + -ize), which is used in reference to computer programming, meaning "the process of converting something into the form of especially binary digits" from 1954 (Merriam-Webster n.d)
Digitalization	The origin of "digitalization" is rooted in the adjective "digital" from ancient Latin *digitus* and modern Latin *digitalis*. It has been used in reference to "using numerical digits" from 1938, especially "of computers which run on data in the form of digits (opposed to analog)" after c. 1945; and "recording or broadcasting" from 1960 ("Online Etymology Dictionary" n.d)

(continued)

(continued)

Terms	Etymologies
Transformation	The origin of "transformation" is rooted in Old French *transformation* (14c.) and directly from the Latin Church *transformation* (nominative *transformation*) "change of shape" (transitive), noun of action from past participle stem of *transformare* "change in shape, metamorphose," from *trans* "across, beyond" + *formare* "to form." Intransitive sense "undergo a change of form" is from the 1590s ("Online Etymology Dictionary" n.d)
Digital transformation	This concept consists of two terms, "digital" and "transformation." The denomination strategy of compounding two words together combines the halo effect of these two words' meaning in the common language and creates a new meaning in the scientific language (Dumez 2011). Since no single seminal definition specifies the original scientific meaning of digital transformation, the confusion existing between scholar's divergent definitions is added to the one connected to the combination of halo effects in the common language. That is, while the meaning of "transformation" and its established usage within practitioners' everyday language and academic' specialized language are clear in the common language, the meaning of the shared root "digital" is generating confusion for the concept digital transformation. A screening by Mertens et al. (2017) produced a list of over 2,500 different terms associated with "digital" in recent scientific literature and financial press. This list includes almost all facets of modern social and economic life. Such finding of diversified common meanings of "digital" also supports the view that "digital" is the troublemaker that causes the combined term "digital transformation" unclear

Appendix 2: The Definitions of Digitization

Authors	Definitions of digitization
Negroponte (1995)	"The conversion of analog to digital information and processes in a technical sense" (p. 15)
Yoo, Henfridsson, and Lyytinen (2010)	"The encoding of analog information into digital format" (p. 725)
Katz and Koutroumpis (2013)	"Digitization, per se is the process of converting analog information to a digital format. Digitization, as a social process, refers to the transformation of the techno-economic environment and socio-institutional operations through digital communications and applications" (p. 314)
OED (2014)	"The action or process of digitizing; the conversion of analog data (esp. in later use images, video, and text) into digital form"
Brennen and Kreiss (2016)	"The material process of converting analog streams of information into digital bits" (p. 1)
Legner et al. (2017)	"The technical process of converting analog signals into a digital form, and ultimately into binary digits" (p. 301)

(continued)

(continued)

Authors	Definitions of digitization
Gölzer and Fritzsche (2017)	"The encoding of data in digital formats" (p. 1334)
Schallmo and Williams (2018)	"Digitally enabling analog or physical artifacts for the purpose of implementing into said artifacts into business processes with the ultimate aim of acquiring newly formed knowledge and creating new value for the stakeholders" (p. 5)
Bloomberg (2018)	"Taking analog information and encoding it into zeroes and ones so that computers can store, process, and transmit such information"
Verhoef et al. (2019)	"The action to convert analog information into digital information" (p. 891)
Gartner's IT Glossary (n.d.)	"The process of changing from analog to digital form. It takes an analog process and changes it to a digital form without any different-in-kind changes to the process itself"

Appendix 3: Digital Transformation and Digitalization's Defining Attributes and Frequency

	Research Types	Qualitative study								Qual. case study					Case study				Quan.		QQ	Examples				Concepts	
	Authors	Westerman et al., 2011	Hess et al., 2016	Singh & Hess, 2017	Li et al., 2018	Gimpel et al., 2018	Schwarzmüller et al., 2018	Warner & Wäger, 2019	Mergel et al., 2019	Liu et al., 2011	Schuchmann & Seufert, 2015	Pagani & Pardo, 2017	Chanias et al., 2019	Ivančić et al., 2019	Iansiti & Lakhani, 2014	Schallmo et al., 2017	Heilig et al., 2017	Al-Ruithe et al., 2018	Fitzgerald et al., 2014	Sousa & Rocha, 2019	Kane et al., 2015	Berman, 2012	Demirkan et al., 2016	Mićić, 2017	Moroz, 2018	Digital transformation	
#	Defining Attributes	4	7	5	13	7	6	8	6	5	3	8	5	4	6	9	9	4	5	5	7	9	10	11	6	Freq.	24
1	Processes		✓		✓			✓	✓	✓		✓		✓	✓	✓	✓			✓	✓		✓		✓	0.58	14
2	Digital technologies	✓	✓	✓	✓	✓		✓		✓			✓				✓		✓			✓	✓	✓	✓	0.58	14
3	Organization	✓	✓	✓		✓				✓						✓	✓	✓		✓	✓	✓				0.46	11
4	Transformation				✓				✓	✓			✓				✓				✓	✓	✓	✓		0.38	9
5	Business operations											✓			✓			✓	✓			✓	✓	✓	✓	0.33	8
6	Use	✓			✓			✓								✓	✓		✓			✓			✓	0.33	8
7	New business model		✓			✓		✓			✓				✓	✓			✓				✓			0.33	8
	Frequency	3	4	2	4	3		4	2	4	1	2	2	1	3	4	5	2	4	2	3	5	5	3	4		
8	Customer								✓		✓	✓						✓	✓			✓		✓		0.29	7
9	Change		✓		✓				✓				✓										✓	✓		0.25	6
10	Create new value (proposition)					✓			✓			✓			✓							✓		✓		0.25	6
11	Strategic renewal			✓				✓									✓				✓		✓			0.21	5
12	New offerings (products & services)		✓						✓			✓				✓										0.17	4
13	Employees						✓					✓					✓				✓					0.17	4
14	Culture							✓						✓			✓							✓		0.17	4
15	Capabilities (development)				✓			✓								✓							✓			0.17	4
	Frequency		2	1	2	1	1	3	4		1	4	1	1	1	2	3	1	1		2	2	3	4			
16	Networking/relationship/connection							✓								✓								✓		0.13	3
17	Radical performance improvement	✓														✓		✓								0.13	3
18	Fundamental				✓								✓											✓		0.13	3
19	Digitize											✓			✓										✓	0.13	3
20	Change in work routines				✓	✓																		✓		0.13	3
21	Adaptation				✓	✓	✓																			0.13	3
22	Realignment between IT & businesses				✓						✓													✓		0.13	3
23	Lifelong social learning						✓													✓						0.08	2
24	Digital maturity													✓							✓					0.08	2
25	Digital economy									✓		✓														0.08	2
26	Change in structures		✓		✓																					0.08	2
27	Capture value/revenue streams					✓									✓											0.08	2
28	Address opportunities & risks			✓																			✓			0.08	2
	Frequency	1	1	1	5	3	2	1		1	1	2	1	1	2	2		1		1	1		2	4	1		
29	Talent engagement																				✓					0.04	1
30	New markets				✓																					0.04	1
31	Leadership																✓									0.04	1
32	Knowledge sharing																			✓						0.04	1
33	Industry												✓													0.04	1
34	Digital technologies development													✓												0.04	1
35	Digital content																			✓						0.04	1
36	Data (Analytics)															✓										0.04	1
37	Change in information flow				✓																					0.04	1
38	Beyond functional thinking			✓																						0.04	1
39	Agility						✓																			0.04	1
40	Highly dynamic market						✓																			0.04	1
41	Society																						✓			0.04	1
	Frequency			1	2		2						1	1		1	1			2	1		1				

Concepts		Research Types	Qualitative					Qualitative cs				Workshop		
Digitalization		Authors	Gimpel & Röglinger, 2015	Mergel et al., 2019	[illegible] et al., 2019	Ruiz-Alba et al., 2019	Rachinger et al., 2019	Pagani & Pardo, 2017	Thorseng & Grisot, 2017	Parviainen et al., 2017	Hänninen et al., 2018	Legner et al., 2017	Riedl et al., 2017	Srai & Lorentz, 2019
Freq.	12	Defining Attributes	7	3	4	4	9	3	6	5	4	7	3	2
0.58	7	Change	✓	✓	✓		✓			✓	✓		✓	
0.42	5	Digital technologies	✓					✓				✓	✓	✓
0.33	4	Use	✓									✓	✓	✓
0.33	4	Processes		✓						✓		✓	✓	
		Frequency	3	2	1		1	1		2	1	3	4	2
0.17	2	Offerings					✓				✓			
0.17	2	Organization						✓				✓		
0.17	2	Rapid business action			✓	✓								
0.17	2	Customer					✓				✓			
0.17	2	Strategic			✓	✓								
0.17	2	Digitizing		✓						✓				
0.17	2	Societal	✓									✓		
0.17	2	Structures					✓		✓					
0.17	2	Socio-technical							✓			✓		
0.17	2	Individual	✓									✓		
0.17	2	Fundamental								✓	✓			
0.17	2	Adopt						✓				✓		
		Frequency	2	1	2	2	3	2	2	2	3	5		
0.08	1	Transformation							✓					
0.08	1	Culture			✓									
0.08	1	Adapt					✓							
0.08	1	Digital capabilities							✓					
0.08	1	Effective					✓							
0.08	1	Behaviors	✓											
0.08	1	Interfunctional coordination				✓								
0.08	1	Digitized artifacts							✓					
0.08	1	Competitive advantage					✓							
0.08	1	Reinforce interdisciplinary collaboration					✓							
0.08	1	Connection	✓											
0.08	1	Relationship							✓					
0.08	1	Relations					✓							
0.08	1	Application						✓						
		Frequency	2		1	1	5	1	4					

Note "Qual." and "Quan." means qualitative and quantitative research, respectively. The abbreviation "QQ" means "qualitative + quantitative research," indicating a mixed-method research approach is applied in this paper. The defining attributes were grouped based on their accumulated frequency. The core defining attributes are shown in the first group (i.e., the top 7 for digital transformation and the top 4 for digitalization); the peripheral ones are in the following/second group; the rest are outsiders

References

Ash, C.G., Burn, J.M.: Assessing the benefits from e-business transformation through effective enterprise management. Eur. J. Inf. Syst. **12**(4), 297–308 (2003)

Aspray, W.: Computing Before Computers. 1990 Iowa State University Press, Ames, Iowa 50010 (2000)

Auriga: Digital transformation: history, present, and future trends (2016). https://auriga.com/blog/digital-transformation-history-present-and-future-trends/

Baden-Fuller, C., Haefliger, S.: Business models and technological innovation. Long Range Plan. **46**(6), 419–426 (2013)

Balogun, J., Hailey, V.H., Gustafsson, S.: Exploring Strategic Change, 4th edn. Pearson Education, Harlow, UK (2015)

Bennet, A., Bennet, D., Avedisian, J.: The Course of Knowledge. MQI Press, Frost, WV (2015)

Berman, S.J.: Digital transformation: opportunities to create new business models. Strateg. & Leadersh. **40**(2), 16–24 (2012)

Bharadwaj, A., El Sawy, O.A., Pavlou, P.A., Venkatraman, N.: Digital business strategy: toward a next generation of insights. MIS Q. 471–482 (2013)

Björkdahl, J., Holmén, M.: Business model innovation–the challenges ahead. Int. J. Prod. Dev. **18**(3/4), 213–225 (2013)

Blackstone, J.H., Cox, J.: APICS Dictionary (11E). APICS. Alexandria, VA (2005)

Bloomberg, J.: Digitization, digitalization, and digital transformation: confuse them at your peril (2018). https://www.forbes.com/sites/jasonbloomberg/2018/04/29/digitization-digitalization-and-digital-transformation-confuse-them-at-your-peril/?sh=3ec17af32f2c

Boersma, K., Kingma, S.: From means to ends: the transformation of ERP in a manufacturing company. J. Strateg. Inf. Syst. **14**(2), 197–219 (2005)

Borangiu, T., Trentesaux, D., Thomas, A., Leitão, P., Barata, J.: Digital Transformation of Manufacturing Through Cloud Services and Resource Virtualization, pp. 150–162. Elsevier (2019)

Brennen, J.S., Kreiss, D.: Digitalization. In: The International Encyclopedia of Communication Theory Philosophy, pp. 1–11 (2016)

Bruce, S., Yearley, S.: The Sage Dictionary of Sociology: Sage (2006)

Buller, J., Gamble, A.: Conceptualising Europeanisation. Public Policy Adm. **17**(2), 4–24 (2002)

Camarinha-Matos, L.M., Fornasiero, R., Ramezani, J., Ferrada, F.: Collaborative networks: a pillar of digital transformation. Appl. Sci. **9**(24), 5431 (2019)

Chanias, S.: Mastering digital transformation: the path of a financial services provider towards a digital transformation strategy. In: Paper Presented at the 25th European Conference on Information Systems, ECIS 2017 (2017)

Chanias, S., Myers, M.D., Hess, T.: Digital transformation strategy making in pre-digital organizations: the case of a financial services provider. J. Strateg. Inf. Syst. **28**(1), 17–33 (2019)

Chen, J.E., Pan, S.L., Ouyang, T.H.: Routine reconfiguration in traditional companies' e-commerce strategy implementation: a trajectory perspective. Inf. Manag. **51**(2), 270–282 (2014)

Clauss, T.: Measuring business model innovation: conceptualization, scale development, and proof of performance. R&D Manag. **47**(3), 385–403 (2017)

Collier, D., Mahon, J.E., Jr.: Conceptual "stretching" revisited: adapting categories in comparative analysis. Am. Polit. Sci. Rev. 845–855 (1993)

De la Boutetière, H., Montagner, A., & Reich, A.: Unlocking success in digital transformations. (2018). Retrieved from https://www.mckinsey.com/businessfunctions/organization/our-insights/unlocking-success-in-digital-transformations

Demirkan, H., Spohrer, J.C., Welser, J.J.: Digital innovation and strategic transformation. IT Prof. **18**(6), 14–18 (2016)

Dijk van Jan, A.: The Network Society. Social Aspects of New Media. SAGE Publications, London–Thousand Oaks–New Delhi (2006)

Dumez, H.: Qu'est-ce qu'un concept? Le Libellio d'AEGIS **7**(1, Printemps-Supplément), 67–79 (2011)

Encyclopedia Britannica (n.d.). https://www.britannica.com/

Eriksson, K.: Concept determination as part of the development of knowledge in caring science. Scand. J. Caring Sci. **24**, 2–11 (2010)

Gartner.: Gartner top strategic predictions for 2020 and beyond. (2019). Retrieved from https://www.gartner.com/smarterwithgartner/gartner-top-strategicpredictions-for-2020-and-beyond/

Gassmann, O., Frankenberger, K., Csik, M.: The Business Model Navigator: 55 Models that will Revolutionise your Business. Pearson UK (2014)

Gates, B., Myhrvold, N., Rinearson, P., Domonkos, D.: The Road Ahead. Viking Penguin, London (1995)

Gerring, J.: What makes a concept good? A criterial framework for understanding concept formation in the social sciences. Polity **31**(3), 357–393 (1999)

Ghazawneh, A., Henfridsson, O.: Balancing platform control and external contribution in third-party development: the boundary resources model. Inf. Syst. J. **23**(2), 173–192 (2013)

Gibson, D.: Digital transformation takes around four years and 85% of them fail, says IBM. (2018) Retrieved from https://www.thedrum.com/news/2018/12/04/digital-transformation-takes-around-four-years-and-85-them-fail-saysibm#:~:text=Waite%20added%3A%20%E2%80%9CAny%20digital%20transformation,'t%20want%20to%20share.%E2%80%9D

Gimpel, H., Röglinger, M.: Digital transformation: changes and chances–insights based on an empirical study. Fim Res. Center Finance Inf. Manag. 1–10 (2015)

Goerzig, D., Bauernhansl, T.: Enterprise architectures for the digital transformation in small and medium-sized enterprises. Procedia Cirp **67**, 540–545 (2018)

Gölzer, P., Fritzsche, A.: Data-driven operations management: organisational implications of the digital transformation in industrial practice. Prod. Plan. Control **28**(16), 1332–1343 (2017)

Gong, C., Ribiere, V.: Developing a unified definition of digital transformation. Technovation **102**, 102217 (2021)

Gong, Y., Yang, J., Shi, X.: Towards a comprehensive understanding of digital transformation in government: analysis of flexibility and enterprise architecture. Gov. Inf. Q. **37**(3), 101487 (2020)

Goran, J., LaBerge, L., Srinivasan, R.: Culture for a digital age. McKinsey Q. **3**, 56–67 (2017)

Haffke, I., Kalgovas, B.J., Benlian, A.: The role of the CIO and the CDO in an organization's digital transformation. In: Paper presented at the Thirty Seventh. International Conference on Information Systems, Dublin (2016)

Hänninen, M., Smedlund, A., Mitronen, L.: Digitalization in retailing: multi-sided platforms as drivers of industry transformation. Baltic J. Manag. (2018)

Heilig, L., Lalla-Ruiz, E., Voß, S.: Digital transformation in maritime ports: analysis and a game theoretic framework. NETNOMICS: Econ. Res. Electron. Netw. **18**(2–3), 227–254 (2017). https://doi.org/10.1007/s11066-017-9122-x

Henriette, E., Feki, M., Boughzala, I.: The shape of digital transformation: a systematic literature review. In: MCIS 2015 Proceedings, pp. 431–443

Henriette, E., Feki, M., Boughzala, I.: Digital transformation challenges. In: Paper Presented at the MCIS (2016)
Holmström, J.: Recombination in digital innovation: challenges, opportunities, and the importance of a theoretical framework. Inf. Organ. **28**(2), 107–110 (2018)
i-scoop: Digitization, digitalization and digital transformation: the differences (2016). https://www.i-scoop.eu/digitization-digitalization-digital-transformation-disruption/
Iansiti, M., Lakhani, K.R.: Digital ubiquity: how connections, sensors, and data are revolutionizing business. Harv. Bus. Rev. **92**(11), 19 (2014)
Janowski, T.: Digital Government Evolution: From Transformation to Contextualization. Elsevier (2015)
Johnson, M., Christensen, C., Kagermann, H.: Reinventing your business model. Harv. Bus. Rev. **86**, 57–68 (2008)
Kane, G.C., Palmer, D., Phillips, A.N., Kiron, D., Buckley, N.: Strategy, not technology, drives digital transformation. MIT Sloan Manag. Rev. **14**(1–25) (2015)
Katz, R.L., Koutroumpis, P.: Measuring digitization: a growth and welfare multiplier. Technovation **33**(10–11), 314–319 (2013)
Kauffman, R.J., Walden, E.A.: Economics and electronic commerce: survey and directions for research. Int. J. Electron. Commer. **5**(4), 5–116 (2001)
Korhonen, J.J., Halen, M.: Enterprise architecture for digital transformation. In: Paper Presented at the 19th IEEE Conference on Business Informatics, CBI 2017 (2017)
Kouroubali, A., Katehakis, D.G.: The new European interoperability framework as a facilitator of digital transformation for citizen empowerment. J. Biomed. Inform. **94**, 103166 (2019)
Lakatos, I.: Science and pseudoscience. Philos. Pap. **1**, 1–7 (1978)
Legner, C., Eymann, T., Hess, T., Matt, C., Böhmann, T., Drews, P., Madche, A.,. Urbach, N., Ahlemann, F. (2017). Digitalization: opportunity and challenge for the business and information systems engineering community. Bus. Inf. Syst. Eng. **59**(4), 301–308
Leviäkangas, P.: Digitalisation of Finland's transport sector. Technol. Soc. **47**, 1–15 (2016)
Li, L., Su, F., Zhang, W., Mao, J.Y.: Digital transformation by SME entrepreneurs: a capability perspective. Inf. Syst. J. **28**(6), 1129–1157 (2018). https://doi.org/10.1111/isj.12153
Liere-Netheler, K., Vogelsang, K., Packmohr, S.: Drivers of digital transformation in manufacturing. In: Paper Presented at the 51st Hawaii International Conference on System Sciences (HICSS), Waikoloa, Hawaii (2018a)
Liere-Netheler, K., Vogelsang, K., Packmohr, S., Hoppe, U.: Towards a framework for digital transformation success in manufacturing. In: Paper Presented at the 26th European Conference on Information Systems, ECIS 2018 (2018b)
Liu, D.Y., Chen, S.W., Chou, T.C.: Resource fit in digital transformation: lessons learned from the CBC Bank global e-banking project. Manag. Decis. (2011)
Loebbecke, C., Picot, A.: Reflections on societal and business model transformation arising from digitization and big data analytics: a research agenda. J. Strateg. Inf. Syst. **24**(3), 149–157 (2015)
Massa, L., Tucci, C.L.: Business Model Innovation. In: Dodgson, M., Gann, D., Phillips, N. (eds.) The Oxford Handbook of Innovation Management, pp. 420–441. Oxford University Press, Oxford (2014)
Matt, C., Hess, T., Benlian, A.: Digital transformation strategies. Bus. Inf. Syst. Eng. **57**(5), 339–343 (2015)
Mendhurwar, S., Mishra, R.: Integration of social and IoT technologies: architectural framework for digital transformation and cyber security challenges. Enterp. Inf. Syst. (2019). https://doi.org/10.1080/17517575.2019.1600041
Mergel, I., Edelmann, N., Haug, N.: Defining digital transformation: results from expert interviews. Gov. Inf. q. **36**(4), 101385 (2019)
Merriam-Webster (ed.): Merriam-Webster.com Dictionary (n.d)
Mertens, P., Barbian, D., Baier, S.: Digitalisierung und Industrie 4.0-eine Relativierung. Springer (2017)

Mićić, L.: Digital transformation and its influence on GDP. Economics **5**(2), 135–147 (2017). https://doi.org/10.1515/eoik-2017-0028

Möller, D.P.: Cybersecurity in Digital Transformation: Scope and Applications: Springer (2020)

Morakanyane, R., Grace, A. A., O'Reilly, P.: Conceptualizing digital transformation in business organizations: a systematic review of literature. In: Paper Presented at the Bled eConference (2017)

Morris, M., Schindehutte, M., Allen, J.: The entrepreneur's business model: toward a unified perspective. J. Bus. Res. **58**(6), 726–735 (2005)

Morton, M.S.: Corporation of the 1990s: Information Technology and Organizational Transformation. Oxford University Press Inc., New York (1991)

Nadkarni, S., Prügl, R.: Digital transformation: a review, synthesis and opportunities for future research. Manag. Rev. Q. 1–109 (2020)

Nambisan, S., Lyytinen, K., Majchrzak, A., Song, M.: Digital innovation management: reinventing innovation management research in a digital world. MIS Q. **41**(1) (2017)

Nambisan, S., Wright, M., Feldman, M.: The digital transformation of innovation and entrepreneurship: progress, challenges and key themes. Res. Policy **48**(8), 103773 (2019)

NCMM: Digital transformation creates middle market growth and opportunity (2020)

Negroponte, N.: Being Digital. Vintage Books, New York (1995)

Nylén, D., Holmström, J., Lyytinen, K.: Oscillating between four orders of design: the case of digital magazines. Des. Issues **30**(3), 53–68 (2014)

OECD: Going digital in a multilateral world (2018). https://www.oecd.org/going-digital/C-MIN-2018-6-EN.pdf

OED: Oxford English Dictionary, 3rd edn. (2010). https://www.oed.com/viewdictionaryentry/Entry/52611

OED (ed.): The Oxford English Dictionary (2014)

Ogden, C.K., Richards, I.A.: The meaning of meaning: a study of the influence of thought and of the science of symbolism (1923)

Online Etymology Dictionary (n.d). http://www.etymonline.com/

Pagani, M., Pardo, C.: The impact of digital technology on relationships in a business network. Ind. Mark. Manag. **67**, 185–192 (2017)

Pappas, I.O., Mikalef, P., Giannakos, M.N., Krogstie, J., Lekakos, G.: Big Data and Business Analytics Ecosystems: Paving the Way Towards Digital Transformation and Sustainable Societies, pp. 479–491. Springer (2018)

Parviainen, P., Tihinen, M., Kääriäinen, J., Teppola, S.: Tackling the digitalization challenge: how to benefit from digitalization in practice. Int. J. Inf. Syst. Proj. Manag. **5**(1), 63–77 (2017a)

Parviainen, P., Tihinen, M., Kääriäinen, J., Teppola, S.: Tackling the digitalization challenge: how to benefit from digitalization in practice. Int. J. Inf. Syst. Proj. Manag. **5**(1), 63–77 (2017b). https://doi.org/10.12821/ijispm050104

Pohle, G., Chapman, M.: IBM's global CEO report 2006: business model innovation matters. Strateg. & Leadersh. (2006)

Press, G.: A very short history of digitization (2015). https://www.forbes.com/sites/gilpress/2015/12/27/a-very-short-history-of-digitization/?sh=4e0189e949ac

Rachinger, M., Rauter, R., Müller, C., Vorraber, W., Schirgi, E.: Digitalization and its influence on business model innovation. J. Manuf. Technol. Manag. (2019)

Ramaswamy, V., Ozcan, K.: Brand value co-creation in a digitalized world: an integrative framework and research implications. Int. J. Res. Mark. **33**(1), 93–106 (2016)

Roedder, N., Dauer, D., Laubis, K., Karaenke, P., Weinhardt, C.: The digital transformation and smart data analytics: An overview of enabling developments and application areas. In: Paper Presented at the 4th IEEE International Conference on Big Data, Big Data 2016 (2016)

Rogers, D.L.: The Digital Transformation Playbook: Rethink your Business for the Digital Age: Columbia University Press (2016)

Ruiz-Alba, J.L., Guesalaga, R., Ayestarán, R., Mediano, J.M.: Interfunctional coordination: the role of digitalization. J. Bus. Ind. Mark. Manag. (2019)

Sambamurthy, V., Bharadwaj, A., Grover, V.: Shaping agility through digital options: reconceptualizing the role of information technology in contemporary firms. MIS Q. **27**, 237–263 (2003)

Sartori, G.: Concept misformation in comparative politics. Am. Polit. Sci. Rev. **64**(4), 1033–1053 (1970)

Sartori, G.: Guidelines for concept analysis. In: Social Science Concepts: A Systematic Analysis, pp. 15–85 (1984)

Schallmo, D., Williams, C.: History of digital transformation. In: Digital Transformation Now! pp. 3–8. Springer (2018)

Schallmo, D., Williams, C.A., Boardman, L.: Digital transformation of business models—best practice, enablers, and roadmap. Int. J. Innov. Manag. **21**(08), 1740014 (2017)

Schneider, S., Spieth, P.: Business model innovation: towards an integrated future research agenda. Int. J. Innov. Manag. **17**(01), 1340001 (2013)

Schneider, S., Spieth, P.: Business model innovation and strategic flexibility: insights from an experimental research design. Int. J. Innov. Manag. Innov. Manag. **18**(06), 1440009 (2014)

Schuchmann, D., Seufert, S.: Corporate learning in times of digital transformation: a conceptual framework and service portfolio for the learning function in banking organisations. Int. J. Corp. Learn. (IJAC) **8**(1), 31–39 (2015)

Schumacher, A., Sihn, W., Erol, S.: Automation, digitization and digitalization and their implications for manufacturing processes. In: Paper Presented at the Innovation and Sustainability Conference Bukarest (2016)

Schwarzmüller, T., Brosi, P., Duman, D., Welpe, I.M.: How does the digital transformation affect organizations? Key themes of change in work design and leadership. MREV Manag. Revue **29**(2), 114–138 (2018)

Schwertner, K.: Digital transformation of business. Trakia J. Sci. **15**(1), 388–393 (2017)

Scott, J., Marshall, G.: A Dictionary of Sociology. Oxford University Press, USA (2009)

Sehlin, D., Truedsson, M., Cronemyr, P.: A conceptual cooperative model designed for processes, digitalisation and innovation. Int. J. Qual. Serv. Sci. (2019)

Seibt, D., Schaupp, S., Meyer, U.: Toward an analytical understanding of domination and emancipation in digitalizing industries. In: Digitalization in Industry, pp. 1–25. Springer (2019)

Singh, A., Hess, T.: How chief digital officers promote the digital transformation of their companies. MIS Q. Exec. **16**(1), 1–17 (2017)

Sparrowe, R.T., Mayer, K.J.: Publishing in AMJ—Part 4: Grounding Hypotheses. Academy of Management Briarcliff Manor, NY (2011)

Srai, J.S., Lorentz, H.: Developing design principles for the digitalisation of purchasing and supply management. J. Purch. Supply Manag. **25**(1), 78–98 (2019)

Stolterman, E., Fors, A.C.: Information technology and the good life. In: Information Systems Research, pp. 687–692. Springer (2004)

Sundblad, W.: CEO Insights: Will Digital Transformation Priorities Finally Stick? (2020) Retrieved from https://www.forbes.com/sites/willemsundbladeurope/2020/07/08/ceo-insights-will-digital-transformation-priorities-stick/?sh=2ed5ff641f19

Svahn, F., Mathiassen, L., Lindgren, R.: Embracing digital innovation in incumbent firms: how volvo cars managed competing concerns. MIS Q. **41**(1) (2017)

Swedberg, R., Agevall, O.: The Max Weber Dictionary: Key Words and Central Concepts. Stanford University Press (2016)

Tan, B., Pan, S.L., Lu, X., Huang, L.: The role of IS capabilities in the development of multi-sided platforms: the digital ecosystem strategy of Alibaba.com. J. Assoc. Inf. Syst. **16**(4), 2 (2015)

Taylor, P.J.: Izations of the world: Americanization, modernization and globalization. In: Demystifying Globalization, pp. 49–70. Springer (2000)

Thorseng, A.A., Grisot, M.: Digitalization as institutional work: a case of designing a tool for changing diabetes care. Inf. Technol. People (2017)

Tripsas, M.: Technology, identity, and inertia through the lens of "the digital photography company." Organ. Sci. **20**(2), 441–460 (2009)

Turner, B.S.: The Cambridge Dictionary of Sociology. Cambridge University Press (2006)
Van Doorn, J., Lemon, K.N., Mittal, V., Nass, S., Pick, D., Pirner, P., Verhoef, P.C.: Customer engagement behavior: theoretical foundations and research directions. J. Serv. Res. **13**(3), 253–266 (2010)
Van Veldhoven, Z., Vanthienen, J.: Designing a comprehensive understanding of digital transformation and its impact. In: Paper Presented at the Bled eConference (2019)
Verhoef, P.C., Broekhuizen, T., Bart, Y., Bhattacharya, A., Dong, J.Q., Fabian, N., Haenlein, M.: Digital transformation: a multidisciplinary reflection and research agenda. J. Bus. Res. **112**, 889–901 (2019)
von Leipzig, T., Gamp, M., Manz, D., Schöttle, K., Ohlhausen, P., Oosthuizen, G., Palm, D., von Leipzig, K.: Initialising customer-orientated digital transformation in enterprises. Procedia Manuf. **8**, 517–524 (2017)
Vukšić, V.B., Ivančić, L., Vugec, D.S.: A preliminary literature review of digital transformation case studies. Int. J. Comput. Inf. Eng. **12**(9), 737–742 (2018)
Wachal, R.: Humanities and computers: a personal view. North Am. Rev. **256**(1), 30–33 (1971)
Wang, Y., Kung, L., Byrd, T.A.: Big data analytics: understanding its capabilities and potential benefits for healthcare organizations. Technol. Forecast. Soc. Chang. **126**, 3–13 (2018)
Warner, K.S.R., Wäger, M.: Building dynamic capabilities for digital transformation: an ongoing process of strategic renewal. Long Range Plan. **52**(3), 326–349 (2019). https://doi.org/10.1016/j.lrp.2018.12.001
WEF: Digital Transformation initiative: in collaboration with accenture (2017). http://reports.weforum.org/digital-transformation/wp-content/blogs.dir/94/mp/files/pages/files/dti-executive-summary-website-version.pdf
Westerman, G.: Your company doesn't need a digital strategy. MIT Sloan Manag. Rev. **59**(3), 1–5 (2018)
Westerman, G., Bonnet, D., McAfee, A.: The nine elements of digital transformation. MIT Sloan Manag. Rev. **55**(3), 1–6 (2014)
Westerman, G., Calméjane, C., Bonnet, D., Ferraris, P., McAfee, A.: Digital transformation: a roadmap for billion-dollar organizations. MIT Center Digit. Bus. Capgemini Consult. **1**, 1–68 (2011)
Yoo, Y.: Computing in everyday life: a call for research on experiential computing. MIS Q. 213–231 (2010)
Yoo, Y., Boland, R.J., Jr., Lyytinen, K., Majchrzak, A.: Organizing for innovation in the digitized world. Organ. Sci. **23**(5), 1398–1408 (2012)
Yoo, Y., Henfridsson, O., Lyytinen, K.: Research commentary—the new organizing logic of digital innovation: an agenda for information systems research. Inf. Syst. Res. **21**(4), 724–735 (2010)
Zaki, M.: Digital transformation: harnessing digital technologies for the next generation of services. J. Serv. Mark. (2019)
Zott, C., Amit, R.: The business model: a theoretically anchored robust construct for strategic analysis. Strateg. Organ. **11**(4), 403–411 (2013)
Zott, C., Amit, R., Massa, L.: The business model: recent developments and future research. J. Manag. **37**(4), 1019–1042 (2011)

Dr. Cheng Gong obtained her Ph.D. in Knowledge and Innovation Management from the Institute for Knowledge and Innovation, South-East Asia (IKI-SEA), Bangkok University, Thailand. She received Young Author Recognition certificates during ITU Kaleidoscope 2020 and was inducted into BGS (Beta Gamma Sigma) for academic excellence. She was awarded the Top 50 Most Influential People in Tacit Knowledge Management in 2023 by GO-TKM. Her educational background and work experience in China, Russia, South Korea and Thailand have given her a base to approach many topics. Her research interest is in digital transformation, knowledge management, innovation management, and change management.

Dr. Xavier Parisot was the former Program Director of the Master in Business Innovation (MBI) and an Associate Professor at The Institute for Knowledge and Innovation, South-East Asia (IKI-SEA), Bangkok University. He teaches innovation management, entrepreneurship and strategy, ontology, epistemology, and research design. His research activities focus on dynamic capabilities and open innovation implications in the emergence of bioindustry business ecosystems.

Dr. Detlef Reis is an Innovation Advisor at The Institute for Knowledge and Innovation, South-East Asia, Bangkok University. He is also an Adjunct Associate Professor at Hong Kong Baptist University's School of Business. Dr. Reis is also the Founder and Chief Ideator of the innovation know-how company Thinkergy (www.thinkergy.com). He is the creator of four proprietary innovation methods marketed by Thinkergy: The innovation process method and toolbox X-IDEA; the innovation people profiling method TIPS; the innovation culture transformation method CooL—Creativity UnLimited; and the creative leadership development method Genius Journey.

Skills and Knowledges Expected in Digital Transformation's Era

Antonios Kargas, Elena C. Gkika, Dimitris Papakyriakopoulos, Faidon Komisopoulos, and Spyridon Filios

Abstract Digital transformation involve a series of structural changes in all aspects of businesses' operations and strategies. Moreover, it involves a constant reevaluation of employees' capability to adjust to new conditions and needs. Recognizing existing skills and knowledges is important for businesses viability while cultivation of desired competencies needed for digital transformation is essential for growth and competitiveness. Proposed research uses data, coming from European Skills, Competences, Qualifications and Occupations (ESCO) database, in order to provide information about existing and forthcoming needs in terms of skills and knowledges. Managers' and Professionals' occupations are examined to reveal frequent appearing and interesting skills and knowledges. Results indicate a wide complexity of skills as far as Professionals are concerned, while Managers have an interesting variation of future skills related with supply chain management. Research contributes on understanding which skills and knowledges format Managers and Professionals, two major importance occupations regarding businesses digital transformation and development of future employees.

Keywords Skills · Knowledges · Competencies · Managers occupation professionals occupation' · Digital transformation · ESCO database

A. Kargas (✉) · E. C. Gkika · D. Papakyriakopoulos · F. Komisopoulos · S. Filios
University of West Attica, 250 Thivon Ave., Aegaleo, 122 41 Athens, Greece
e-mail: akargas@uniwa.gr

E. C. Gkika
e-mail: ghelena@uniwa.gr

D. Papakyriakopoulos
e-mail: dpapak@uniwa.gr

F. Komisopoulos
e-mail: fedonk@uniwa.gr

S. Filios
e-mail: sfilios@uniwa.gr

© The Author(s), under exclusive license to Springer Nature Switzerland AG 2024

D. Schallmo et al. (eds.), *Digital Disruption and Transformation*, Springer Proceedings in Business and Economics, https://doi.org/10.1007/978-3-031-47888-8_2

1 Introduction

The choice of applicants that will be successful as employees is a subject of interest among companies' top management. A successful candidate should have characteristics and abilities associated with technical issues indicated by his high intelligence quotient score. These skills are referred as "hard skills" and their nature is mostly cognitive, technical or knowledge based.

In order to be successful, an employee should also have the necessary qualities called "soft skills" that allow him to communicate effectively, to build interpersonal relationships and interact at workplace by applying effective leadership, mediating or negotiating. The effective communication includes the ability of cautious listening and fluently speaking and the demonstration of empathy to others. Soft skills are the traits, the behaviors and the attitudes described as intangible and nontechnical (Seetha 2014). The soft skills are prerequisites to applying effectively technical knowledge and skills in the working area. Schulz (2008) indicated the importance of soft skills in an individuals' personality. All interpersonal traits and attitudes that make an employee distinguish among other employees are the soft skills he possesses (Oladokun and Gbadegesin 2017).

Even though the importance of skills and competencies is wide accepted, the framework under which labor market is structured seems to have changed significantly over the past ten years. First of all, recruitment procedure significantly relies on social media and talent platforms. Moreover, there is an increased mobility, with people changing jobs more frequently than in previous years, while geographical boundaries have been reduced and distance working reshaped what was regarded as occupational standards. So there is a growing need for required skills/competencies recognition accompanied with training procedures for both existing employees and newcomers in labor market. Such a need is further strengthened by employers' tension to move from low-digital skills jobs to new ICT-based ones (European Commission 2022).

Current research work contributes in recognizing most significant skills and knowledges between those occupied as "Managers" and "Professionals". The European Skills, Competences, Qualifications and Occupations (ESCO) database is used to extract patterns about both occupations' characteristics and structured profiles in terms of skills and knowledges, while most frequent mixtures are discussed. ESCO is a European multilingual classification database, describing, identifying and classifying more than 13,000 professional occupations and more than 3000 skills relevant for the EU labour market.

"Managers" occupation was selected as a result of its decision-making nature, leading internal changes and implementing digital transformation or any other business operations. Understanding which skills and knowledges format Managers occupations can reveal which competencies are evaluated as significant in the business world. According to Katz (1974), effective managers should have technical skills, human skills and conceptual skills. Companies train their managers according to company's standards. The conceptual skills of a manager contribute to vision the future, to make plans and come to decisions for the best of the company (Weber et al. 2009). Moreover, "Professionals" are responsible for training future and existing employees, alongside with research and new knowledge development. Proposed occupation is cultivating future labour force's competencies and it is important to enlight its occupational characteristics.

In the next sections, the research theoretical background is presented, alongside with the problem to be addressed and the research issues to be answered. The measures evaluating significance of skills and knowledges are then presented and most significant results are revealed. Finally, practical implications, limitations and future research recommendations are provided.

2 Theoretical Background

Competencies on a working environment are composed of activities, attitudes, skills and knowledge correlated with job performance and are measurable (Sisson and Adams 2013). Employees' working performance is a function of his basic knowledge and the soft skills he possesses (Oladokun and Gbadegesin 2017). Basic knowledge is acquired in higher educational institutions and enhanced through practical experience. This indicates the insufficiency of academic education alone to equip people with skills and competencies required for their effective performance at a working environment (Singh and Jaykumar 2019). The importance of interpersonal skills, of communication skills, of technology literacy skills and of skills for emerging business practices, as sustainability production, will increase in the near future (Krpálek et al. 2021). Flexibility and sensitivity are also important factors affecting employability.

Dynamic changes in digitalization and automation of management procedures requires qualitative knowledge management. "Human" is a key factor in business administration and streamline of the system is required. The requirements of the market for the necessary competencies and soft skills are increasing. Also increases the necessity of interdisciplinary knowledge, digital literacy, and competence-based management (Krpálek et al. 2021).

According to Vroom's "Expectancy Theory" (Vroom 1964) there is a relationship between the effort put at work, the performance accomplished and the expectation of rewards as result of the performance. Someone has a motive to acquire skills or competencies since they believe that a good performance will lead to desired outcomes (Seetha 2014). Bray and Howard (Bray and Howard 1983) focused on managerial competencies by relating the personality and the motives someone has: the motive of advancing faster than the colleagues, and the motive of achieving high standards at work even when these standards exceed the necessary standards to satisfy their superiors (Weber et al. 2009). E-government and digitalization increase the demand for enhanced employee competences in the areas of information and communication technologies. Technical skills and cognitive knowledge are required to entry-level professionals. As their experience increases, the human skills become necessary to upgrade their interpersonal relationships and manage effectively others, to interact with others and invest in team building. Since managers are more qualified and motivated, they exhibit higher levels of consciousness, openness and positive personality traits towards employee management. Stevens and Campion (Stevens and Campion 1994, 1999) developed a measure of "Knowledge, Skills and Abilities (KSA)" for effectively staffing teams at working environment. Between setting organizational goals and employee commitment the tacit knowledge is a valuable mediator.

Hard competencies are a combination of technical and cognitive knowledge and of skills, acquired by education, training and working experience. Soft competencies are behavioral attributes, values, including ethics, attitudes and emotions expressed through effective communication and interaction with others, in leadership, teamwork and interpersonal relations. A competency model is a descriptive measure that identifies all knowledge, skills and behaviors necessary to perform effectively in an organization (Lucia and Lepsinger 1999). Technical skills and abilities are required to entry-level professionals. As their experience increases, the human skills become necessary to upgrade their interpersonal relationships and manage effectively others, to interact with others and invest in team building. They defined five dimensions of competencies such as: "conflict resolution, collaborative problem solving, verbal and non-verbal communication, setting specific goals and performance management, planning and coordinating information and tasks to form role expectations" (Weber et al. 2009).

Boyatzis (1982) was the first author that attempted to make a list of competencies that would relate the managers' performance effectiveness to specific competencies. According to his list of competencies, managers' performance was classified at superior, average and poor. According to Boyatzis, more than 25 per cent of the variance in managers' performance could be attributed to these competencies. Performance leads the earning capacity of an employee. He concluded at six clusters of competencies namely: "goal and action management, leadership, human resources management, directing subordinates, focus on others, and specialized knowledge" (Boyatzis 1982).

According to Sandwith (1993), five areas of managerial competencies were identified, as: 1. Conceptual/creative: consisting of cognitive skills, 2. Leadership: make plans and turn them to actions, 3. Interpersonal: skills to communicate effectively with others, 4. Administrative: skills on the management of the organization, 5. Technical: skills and knowledge on the job (Sisson and Adams 2013). Competencies are talents brought at workplace exceeding rational behavior (Robotham and Jubb 1996; Seetha 2014). Leadership style based on individual competencies requires the implementation of a model capturing all aspects of work in the digital world. According to Krpálek, et al. (2021) the leadership style and the perceived development of employees' skills, have influenced employees' work commitment. Effective management includes professionalism, reliability, information management, coping with uncertainty and working under pressure, dealing with high levels of stress.

By studying the soft skills necessary for each business environment, recruiters have a better chance to match the right candidate ensuring in that way retention of employees. The selection process improves, the training process is easier, the company may apply improved development programs and the performance evaluation is strengthened resulting at an increased profitability (Weber et al. 2009). Ibrahim et al., (2017), on research of managers in Malaysian private companies, resulted that the methodology of training to acquire skills significantly predict the employee work performance. Authors support the "time–space learning" as prominent training methodology to transferring knowledge and skills to employees. Gibler et al. (2020) researched on corporate real estate managers from Australia, Hong Kong, the UK and the USA. He researched on knowledge and skills necessary for effectively practicing corporate real estate management. The factor analysis he performed resulted at eight factors representing the core skills and knowledge including: "strategic management skills, physical property skills, knowledge of external threat, globalization, financial management skills, technology skills in traditional business functions areas and interpersonal skills". Similarly, Tunde Oladokun (2012) concluded that "financial performance skill, corporate strategic planning, productivity skill, space management and customer/employer management skill" are the most important skills required for real estate management surveyors (Oladokun and Gbadegesin 2017).

In the retail industry and in the hospitality industry candidates are expected to have competencies in customer service, in fluent communication, and also have interpersonal and intrapersonal skills and other soft skills, as a basic entry-level requirement. But in the service sector, a gap is observed between the qualified entry level employees and their availability. Employees are lacking not only hard skills but also soft skills necessary for professional success. They lack intrapersonal skills, they are insufficient on customer service, and they have difficulties with time management. According to Singh and Jaykumar (2019), this gap is increasing slowly and steadily in time.

Digital Transformation raise new requirements in all aspects of business life, from business models and new technologies (Acatech 2016), up to new job requirements and unique specialized skills' set needed (Grzelczak et al. 2017; Kergroach 2017). Additionally, it changed job requirements in a direction that expected skills and knowledges being not always obvious (Maisiri et al. 2019). It is wide accepted that a gap exists between existing employees' skills needed before Industry 4.0 (Prifti et al. 2017) and skills required to successfully implement digital transformation (Shvetsova and Kuzmina 2018).

Moreover, new skills and competencies needed are not exclusively technologically oriented (Schallock et al. 2018) but should exceed technological parameters (Cotet et al. 2017) including soft—skills such as life-long learning, deep knowledge of different disciplines, behavioral skills (Prifti et al. 2017), alongside with interpersonal skills, confidence/motivation, ethics/integrity and critical thinking (Foutty 2019).

Such a framework led to the need for skills and competencies recognition (Lorenz et al. 2015; Zinn 2015), as well as to the development of training programs for practical skills, soft skills, values, entrepreneurship capabilities and other competencies (Selamat et al. 2017). Research on the topic should specify which skills and competencies are more valuable in order to facilitate their reaching goals on digital transformation.

3 Problem

Even though Digital Transformation and Industry 4.0 have a strong technological orientation (Baur and Wee 2015), human factor should not be neglected or ignored (Kargas et al. 2022b) as a result of the increased level of skill's/knowledge's complexity required from the workforce of the future (Maisiri et al. 2019). Employees' characteristics, skills and knowledge are gaining research interest as a source of development (Gkika et al. 2022) and as a mean to reach innovation (Kargas et al. 2022a).

Current paper focus on enlightening which are the current needs on skills/knowledges alongside with tensions on skills/knowledges related with innovation development, when it comes with occupations such as "Managers" and "Professionals". Proposed research aims on revealing existing patterns between executives of these two occupations and recognizing in which skills and knowledges does innovation lies between, as a mean to gain a competitive advantage under digital transformation's era.

4 Research Objective and Questions

Research's objectives are to discover frequent or interesting patterns related with the occupations of "Managers" and "Professionals" by using data gathered from the ESCO database. A frequent collection of skills and knowledges (itemset) could indicate the core requirements within the same occupation hierarchy, revealing existing situation in both "Managers" and "Professionals" occupations. Likewise, interesting variations among similar occupations could signal an innovation pursuit leveraged by technological interventions or market advancements at the same occupations.

Research questions answered under current research are:

- Which are the frequent patterns of skills and knowledges when it comes to "Managers" and "Professionals" occupations?
- Which are the interesting patterns of skills and knowledges when it comes to "Managers" and "Professionals" occupations?
- Do exist patterns of skills and knowledges promising a more innovational orientation?

5 Research Design

Research methodology is based on discovering key associations between the various Skills and Knowledges regarding each occupation described in previous sections. Proposed methodology is suitable for exploratory research purposes (Agrawal et al.

1993) and is part of the machine learning field. Association rules used to express patterns between occupations and skills/knowledges are:

- **Support**: is the percentage of groups that contain all of the items listed in that association rule compared to the total items in the category.
- **Lift**: is a measure of importance and express the deviation of the rule from the model of statistic independency between the antecedent (if) part of the rule and the consequence. In other words, a part of the itemset has a positively (favour) into a specific item and empirically when Lift > 2 it is considered as rule for further elaboration.

High support indicates an expected mixture of skills/knowledges regarding the occupations of Managers and Professionals, while high lift value indicates interesting variations which highlight certain areas of innovation. The relationship between the Occupation's collection and the Skills/Knowledges' collections is supported by an intermediate data set listing the occupation, the associated skill and competences and whether a knowledge or skill has essential (or optional) role for an occupation. Analysis conducted reviewed optional skills and knowledge as required in order to in depth study all existing possible relations.

6 Findings

Conducted analysis targeted two distinct occupations, namely "Managers" and "Professionals". Each occupation is described through and occupational profile, containing description, scope and a list of skills and knowledges that are considered as essential on a European scale.

Managers occupations' category involve tasks of planning, organizing and evaluating activities in any type of organization (governmental or enterprises) as a whole or at the level of organizational unit, while as part of the job it is included the formulation/reviewing of rules, regulations or policies as well (European Commission 2022). Proposed occupation is classified into four major sub-groups: (a) Chief Executives, Senior Officials and Legislators, (b) Administrative and Commercial Managers, (c) Production and Specialized Services Managers and (d) Hospitality, Retail and Other Services Managers.

Professionals occupations' category involve tasks of increasing stock of knowledge, applying scientific concepts and theories and teaching about the foregoing (European Commission 2022). Proposed occupation is classified into six major sub-groups: (a) Science and Engineering Professionals, (b) Health Professionals, (c) Teaching Professionals, (d) Business and Administration Professionals, (e) Information and Communications Technology Professionals and (f) Legal, Social and Cultural Professionals.

At a first level of analysis, the twelve (12) most frequent appearing skills/knowledges for both occupations were detected. Table 1 presents these frequent appearing skills/knowledges which are totally different from the one occupation to

Table 1 Most frequent appearing skills and knowledges

A/A	Managers' occupation	Professionals' occupation
1	Manage staff (skill)	Perform scientific research (skill)
2	Manage budget (skill)	Perform project management (skill)
3	Create solutions to problems (skill)	Think analytically (skill)
4	Recruit employees (skill)	Speak different languages (skill)
5	Adhere to organizational guidelines (skill)	Manage personal—professional development (skill)
6	Have computer literacy (skill)	Scientific research methodology (knowledge)
7	Maintain relationship with customers (skill)	Write scientific publications (skills)
8	Use different communication channels (skill)	Mentor individuals (skills)
9	Ensure customs compliance (skill)	Applying teaching strategies (skill)
10	Perform financial risk management in international trade (skill)	Publish academic research (skill)
11	Maintain relationship with supplies (skill)	Think abstractly (skill)
12	Employment law (knowledge)	Teach in academic or vocational contexts (skill)

the other. Such a diversity is the result of each occupation's nature and the different priorities set to effectively perform it.

As far as Managers' occupation is concerned, all items have a relative frequency of more than 20%, while "manage budget" and "manage staff" have an item relative frequency of more than 40 and 60% respectively. In contrast when it comes to Professionals' occupation the twelve most frequent appearing skills and knowledges have a small relative frequency of 0.1%, with "Perform Scientific Research" and "Perform Project Management" exceeding 0.2%. Such a condition indicates that Professionals have a larger variety of skills and knowledges, while there exist no skill or knowledge being decisive for the occupation's formation. Finally, it is worth mentioning, that for both occupations under research, only one item out of the twelve most frequent appearing skills/knowledge represents a knowledge, while all the rest include skills oriented items.

At a second level of analysis and in order to enrich our understanding "Support" measure was investigated. What is valuable with "Support" is that helps identify rules that are worth considering in order to expand our analysis. Such rules can include the number of Skills/Knowledges that form an itemset. In such a case the higher the "Support" the more information can be extracted regarding the relationship between its items. Research put emphasis on investigating itemsets of at least four (4) Skills/Knowledges and the frequency of appearance among all managers' occupations.

When it comes to Managers' occupation, results are presented in Fig. 1, revealing that in the core of the above—mentioned analysis lie Skills/Knowledges such as:

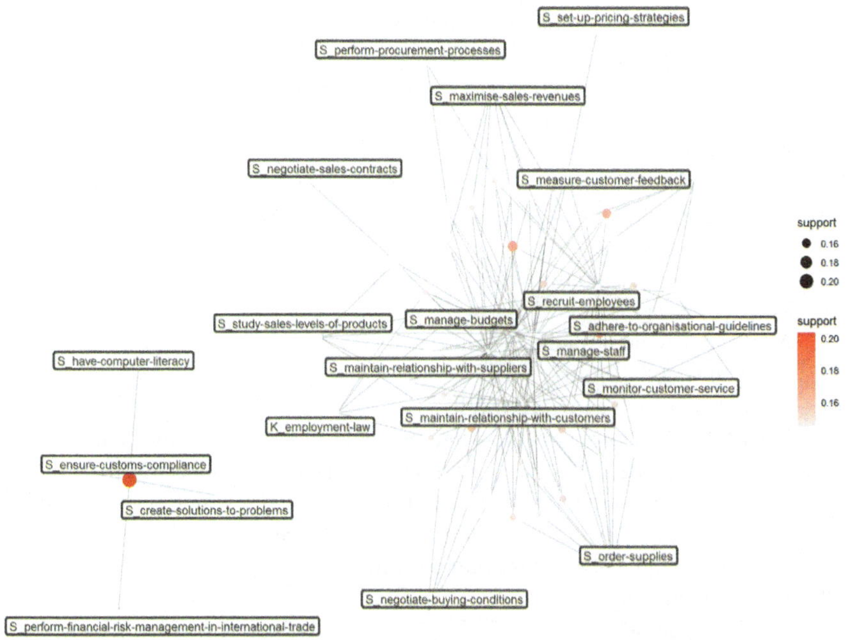

Fig. 1 Managers' support graph

1. Manage Staff (Skill),
2. Manage Budget (Skill),
3. Maintain Relationship with Customers (Skill),
4. Adhere to Organizational Guidelines (Skill),
5. Maintain Relationship with Suppliers (Skill),
6. Recruit employees (Skill)
7. Employment Law (Knowledge),
8. Monitor Customer Service (Skill) and
9. Study Sales—Levels of Products (Skill).

These eight (8) skills and one (1) knowledge are more frequently appearing when itemsets of fours are studied. The first six are also having a high frequency appearance when studied as stand-alone measures, while the rest four seem to be the most frequent appearing supplementary skills (Fig. 1).

At the same time, Professionals' occupation has a large number of skills contributing to its formation. There exist 3 times more skills required in Professionals than in Managers. More precisely there exist thirty-one (31) skills formatting the proposed occupation, while there exist no specific knowledge. Namely, the skills more frequently appearing when itemsets of fours are studied include:

1. Communicate with a non-scientific audience (Skill),
2. Synthesize information (Skill),

3. Promote open innovation in research (Skill),
4. Operate open-source software (Skill),
5. Draft scientific or academic papers and technical documentation (Skill),
6. Promote the transfer of knowledge (Skill),
7. Apply blended learning (Skill),
8. Interact professionally in research and professional environments (Skill),
9. Apply research ethics and scientific integrity principles in research activities (Skill),
10. Manage intellectual property rights (Skill),
11. Manage research data (Skill),
12. Apply for research funding (Skill),
13. Think abstractly (Skill),
14. Evaluate research activities (Skill),
15. Manage findable—accessible—interoperable and reusable data (Skill),
16. Develop professional network with researchers and scientists (Skill),
17. Promote the participation of citizens in scientific and research activities (Skill),
18. Disseminate results to the scientific community (Skill),
19. Conduct research across disciplines (Skill),
20. Think analytically (Skill),
21. Manage open publications (Skill),
22. Manage personal, professional development (Skill),
23. Publish academic research (Skill),
24. Mentor individuals (Skill),
25. Increase the impact of science on policy and society (Skill),
26. Write scientific publications (Skill),
27. Promote inclusion in research (Skill),
28. Demonstrate disciplinary expertise (Skill),
29. Speak different languages (Skill),
30. Teach in academic or vocational contexts (Skill),
31. Perform project management (Skill).

Comparing the above-mentioned skills and the most frequent appearing standalone skills, there exist only two differentiations. "Scientific Research Methodology (Knowledge)" and "Applying Teaching Strategies (Skill)" even though being frequent appearing they seem to be excluded from itemsets of four skills (Fig. 2).

At a third level of analysis, "Lift measure was studies in order to provide evidence about unexpected occurrences of Skills/Knowledges, revealing where innovation exists regarding managers' occupation category. Figure 3 provide such evidence, by revealing most prominent and less expected Skills/Knowledges, when it concerns Managers' occupation. Namely there exist the below mentioned six (6) Skills, while only one (1) Knowledge is included (Fig. 3):

1. Handle Carriers (Skill),
2. Minimize Shipping Cost (Skill),
3. Manage Freight Payment Methods (Skill),

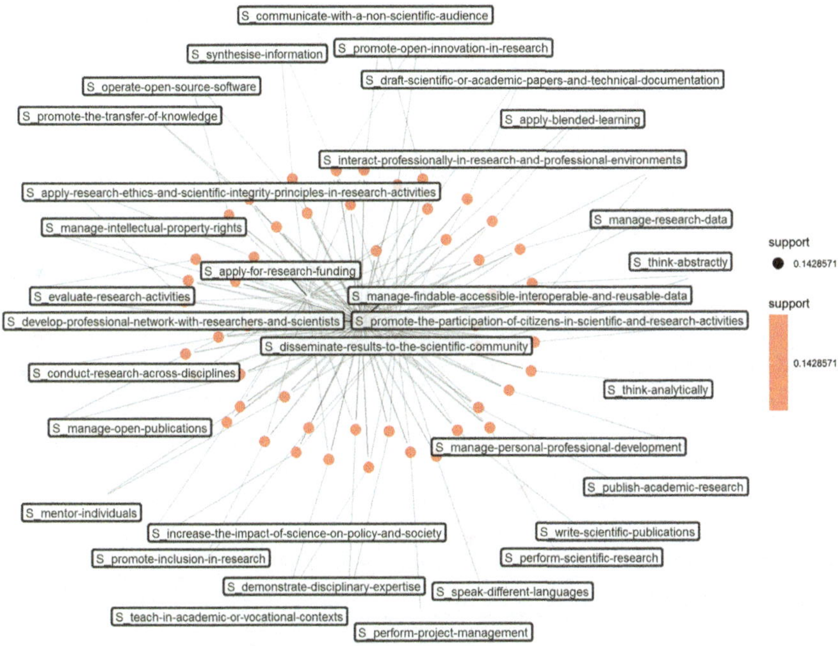

Fig. 2 Professionals' support graph

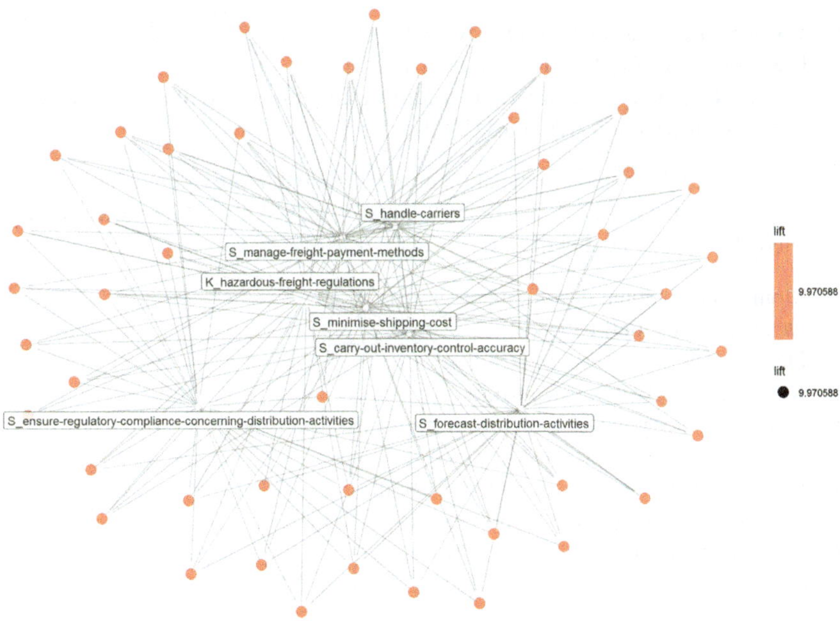

Fig. 3 Managers' lift graph

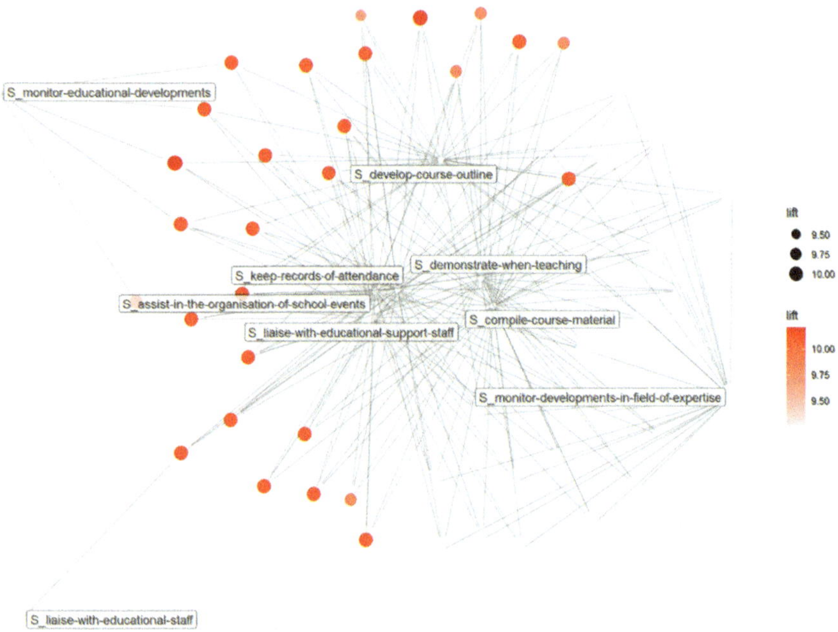

Fig. 4 Professionals' lift graph

4. Hazardous Freight Regulations (Knowledge),
5. Carry out Inventory Control Accuracy (Skill),
6. Ensure Regulatory Compliance Concerning Distribution Activities (Skill) and
7. Forecast Distribution Activities (Skill).

Regarding Professionals' occupation most prominent, less expected, innovational skills are presented in Fig. 4. There exist nine (9) such skills, while no Knowledge is included. Namely these skills are (Fig. 4):

1. Monitor educational development (Skill),
2. Develop course outline (Skill),
3. Demonstrate when teaching (Skill),
4. Keep records of attendance (Skill),
5. Assist in the organization of school events (Skill),
6. Compile course material (Skill),
7. Liaise with educational support staff (Skill),
8. Monitor developments in field of expertise (Skill),
9. Liaise with educational staff (Skill).

7 Contribution

Proposed results contribute to reveal existing and prominent skills and knowledges when Managers and Professionals occupations are studied. Regarding Managers occupation there exist six (6) skills and one (1) knowledge that seem significant in both single view analysis (frequency of appearance) and itemset analysis (itemset of four). Table 2 presents the full list of skills and knowledges under both analyses conducted. Moreover, current research contributes on revealing which skills and knowledges seem more appropriate to help managers meet business operations' needs over a complex network of activities and shared resources. Results indicate a tension of expanding managers' competencies related with supply chain management, which is strongly associated with companies' digital transformation under Industry 4.0 framework, while less emphasis is put on Employees—Suppliers—Customers.

As far as Professionals are concerned, results contribute on understanding the occupation's complexity when it comes to competencies needed. There exist ten (10) Skills, but no Knowledge that seem significant in both single view analysis (frequency of appearance) and itemset analysis (itemset of four). Most of these skills are related with self—competencies and less with mentoring or people management. A totally different view exists when it comes to interesting variations, where most prominent skills are related with supporting activities and teaching. Such a framework indicates the need to transform interaction with audience to a more interactive, digital experience.

Table 2 Managers' significant skills and knowledges

Single view	Itemset view
Manage staff (skill)	
Manage budget (skill)	
Recruit employees (skill)	
Adhere to organizational guidelines (skill)	
Maintain relationship with customers (skill)	
Maintain relationship with suppliers (skill)	
Employment law (knowledge)	
Create solutions to problems (skill)	Monitor customer service (skill)
Have computer literacy (skill)	Study sales—levels of products (skill)
Use different communication channels (skill)	–
Ensure customs compliance (skill)	–
Perform financial risk management in international trade (skill)	–

8 Practical Implications

Results enlight which are the most important and promising skills and knowledges when it comes to Managers and Professionals occupation. Such a contribution can be of high importance in business, academic and training level. In business level results can reveal convergencies/divergencies of existing skills and knowledge between existing situation and optimal condition as described in the paper. Gaps can be covered with training for both existing employees and newcomers. Moreover, promising—interesting skills and knowledges revealed provide valuable information regarding forthcoming tensions when it comes to managers or professionals, indicating areas for future competencies' empowerment.

In academic and training level results enlight areas of existing or future expertise, indicating what market evaluate as significant. Academic and vocational training include both knowledge cultivation and skills raise. Their proportion, the depth of analysis and the areas of expertise under train should be constantly adjust to current and future needs. Especially when it is expected the passing to the digital era, under the Fourth Industrial Revolution (Industry 4.0), such a adjustment it is more and more necessary for national economies in order to maintain their competitive advantage and for employees so that to remain in the labor market.

9 Limitations

Proposed methodology is applied to the most recent data coming from ESCO. This kind of analysis can be characterized as a "snapshot" of current situation when it comes to skills and knowledges of selected occupations. Even though it provides in depth analysis of existing data, it lacks information regarding changes and progresses conducted during the past years. Such a limitation makes difficult to understand which skills and knowledges gained or lose significance while digital transformation passed from research interest to operational implementation in many sectors. Conducting analysis in regular basis, when ESCO's data change, could provide valuable information and restrict proposed limitation's significance.

10 Recommendations for Further Research

As far as future research is concerned, expanding analysis across Atlantic Ocean could provide valuable information. In U.S.A. there exist O*NET OnLine, a database similar to ESCO, that follows a distinct approach and classification. Extracting data and comparing results can provide significant results regarding "interesting" patterns of skills and knowledges that can drive innovation development. It should be taken into account that the structures of these two databases are different, making any comparisons difficult at the point without significant data manipulation in order to homogenize results.

Moreover, as part of future research could be the use of Dominance Analysis (DA) as a mean of predictive modeling, for tensions in skills and knowledges required in the future. It is methodology that can be used to compare the relative importance of each skill and each knowledge in relation to the occupation under research. Dominance Analysis can provide more valuable prediction since it goes beyond just the decomposition of the focal model fit statistic, by producing three distinct results for each skill/knowledge to compare contribution to the proposed occupation as a whole.

References

Acatech, D.A.D.T.: Kompetenzentwicklungsstudie Industrie 4.0. Dortmund (2016) https://docplayer.org/24401230-Kompetenzentwicklungsstudie-industrie-4-0.html (August 26, 2021).

Agrawal, R., Swami, A., Imielinski, T.: Database mining: a performance perspective. IEEE Trans. Knowl. Data Eng. **5**(6), 914–925 (1993)

Baur, C., Wee, D.: Industry 4.0 is more than just a flashy catchphrase. A confluence of trends and technologies promises to reshape the way things are made (2015). https://www.mckinsey.com/business-functions/operations/our-insights/manufacturings-next-act. Accessed 27 2021

Boyatzis, R.E.: The Competent Manager: A Model for Effective Performance. Wiley, New York (1982)

Bray, D.W., Howard, A.: The AT & T longitudinal studies of managers. In: New York, U.S.A. (ed.) Longitudinal Studies of Adult Psychological Development, pp. 266–312. Guilford Press (1983)

Cotet, G.B., Beatrice A.B., Violeta-Carmen Z.: Assessment procedure for the soft skills requested by Industry 4.0. In: 8th International Conference on Manufacturing Science and Education – MSE 2017. 1–8, Trends in New Industrial Revolution (2017)

European Commission.: ESCO Occupations. (2022). https://esco.ec.europa.eu/en/classification/occupation_main. (October 20, 2022)

Foutty, J.: Aspire to lead in Industry 4.0? Hone your soft skills, Wall Str. J. (2019). Available at: https://deloitte.wsj.com/articles/aspire-to-lead-in-industry-4-0-hone-your-soft-skills-01548295337 (Accessed: 26 August 2021)

Gibler, K., Black, R., Moon, K.: Time, place, space, technology and corporate real estate strategy. J. Real Estate Res. **24**(3), 235–262 (2020). https://www.tandfonline.com/doi/abs/10.1080/10835547.2002.12091095. Accessed 5 Jan 2023

Gkika, E., Ntanos, S., Komisopoulos, F., Drosos, D.: The impact of global competition dimensions on economic development. In: ISPIM Connects Athens—The Role of Innovation: Past, Present, Future. LUT Scientific and Expertise Publications, Athens (2022)

Grzelczak, A., Kosacka, M., Werner-Lewandowska, K.: Employees competences for Industry 4.0 in Poland–preliminary research results. In: 24th International Conference on Production Research, ICPR **2017**, 139–44 (2017)

Ibrahim, R., Boerhannoeddin, A., Bakare, K.K.: The effect of soft skills and training methodology on employee performance. Eur. J. Train. Dev. **41**(4), 388–406 (2017)

Kargas, A., et al.: Tracing innovation with skill and competences. In: ISPIM Connects Athens—The Role of Innovation: Past, Present, Future, on 28–30 November 2022. Event Proceedings, 1–11, 2022. Order number in series, vol 110. LUT Scientific and Expertise Publications (2022a). ISBN 978-952-65069-1-3

Kargas, A., Giannakis, A., Foukas, I.: Recognizing skills and competencies required under industry 4.0's framework for achieving business digital transformation. In: Mirjana, P.-B., Çağlar, D. (eds.) Management Strategies for Sustainability, New Knowledge Innovation, and Personalized

Products and Services, pp. 1–34 (2022b). https://orcid.org/0000-0001-6157-1761. Accessed 9 Jan 2022.
Katz, R.: Skills of an effective administrator. Harv. Bus. Rev. **52**(6), 90–102 (1974). https://hbr.org/1974/09/skills-of-an-effective-administrator. Accessed 5 Jan 2023
Krpálek, P., et al.: Formation of professional competences and soft skills of public administration employees for sustainable professional development. Sustainability **13**, 5533 (2021). https://www.mdpi.com/2071-1050/13/10/5533/htm. Accessed 5 Jan 2023
Lorenz, M. et al.: Man and machine in Industry 4.0: how will technology transform the industrial workforce through 2025? (2015)
Lucia, A.D., Lepsinger, R.: The art and science of competency models: pinpointing critical success factors in organizations. Jossey-Bass/Pfeiffer (1999). https://www.wiley.com/en-us/The+Art+and+Science+of+Competency+Models%3A+Pinpointing+Critical+Success+Factors+in+Organizations-p-9780787946029. Accessed 5 Jan 2023
Maisiri, W., Darwish, H., van Dyk, L.: An investigation of industry 4.0 skills requirements. S. Afr. J. Ind. Eng. **30**(3), 90–105 (2019)
Oladokun, S.O., Gbadegesin, J.T.: Adequacy of core knowledge and soft skills in the performance of professional employees of real estate firms in Nigeria. Prop. Manag. **35**(2), 132–149 (2017)
Prifti, L., Knigge, M., Kienegger, H., Krcmar, H.: A competency model for 'Industrie 4.0' employees. In: 13th International Conference on Wirtschaftsinformatik (WI), St. Gallen, Switzerland, pp. 44–60 (2017)
Robotham, D., Jubb, R.: Competences: measuring the unmeasurable. Manag. Dev. Rev. **9**(5), 25–29 (1996)
Sandwith, P.: A hierarchy of management training requirements: the competency domain model. Public Pers. Manag. **22**(1), 43–62 (1993). https://journals.sagepub.com/doi/10.1177/009102609302200104. Accessed 5 Jan 2023
Schallock, B., Rybski, C., Jochem, R., Kohl, H.: Learning Factory for Industry 4.0 to provide future skills beyond technical training. Proc. Manufac. **23**, 27–32 (2018)
Schulz, B.: The importance of soft skills: education beyond academic knowledge. NAWA J. Lang. Commun. 146–154 (2008)
Seetha, N.: Are soft skills important in the workplace? A preliminary investigation in Malaysia. Int. J. Acad. Res. Bus. Soc. Sci. **4**(4) (2014)
Selamat, A. et al.: Higher Education 4.0 Current Status and Readiness in Meeting the Fourth Industrial Revolution Challenges. Redesign. High. Educ. Indus. **1**, 23–24 (2017) Available at: https://pdfcoffee.com/higher-education-40-current-status-and-readiness-in-meeting-the-fourth-industrial-revolution-challenges-1-pdf-free.html (Accessed: 27 August 2021)
Shvetsova, O.A., Kuzmina, A.D.: Development of engineering personnel in the era of the fourth industrial revolution. In: Proceedings of the 3rd International Conference Ergo-2018: Human Factors in Complex Technical Systems and Environments, Ergo 2018, Institute of Electrical and Electronics Engineers Inc., pp. 45–48 (2018)
Singh, A., Jaykumar, P.: On the road to consensus: key soft skills required for youth employment in the service sector. Worldw. Hosp. Tour. Themes **11**(1), 10–24 (2019)
Sisson, L.G., Adams, A.R.: Essential hospitality management competencies: the importance of soft skills. J. Hosp. & Tour. Educ. **25**(3), 131–145 (2013). https://www.tandfonline.com/doi/abs/10.1080/10963758.2013.826975. Accessed 5 Jan 2023
Stevens, M., Campion, M.: The knowledge, skill, and ability requirements for teamwork: implications for human resource management. J. Manag. **20**(2), 503–530 (1994)
Stevens, M., Campion, M.: Staffing work teams: development and validation of a selection test for teamwork settings. J. Manag. **25**(2), 207–228 (1999)
Tunde Oladokun, T.: An evaluation of the training needs of Nigerian estate surveyors for corporate real estate management practice. Prop. Manag. **30**(1), 86–100 (2012)
Vroom, V.: Work and Motivation|WorldCat.Org. Wiley, New York (1964). https://www.worldcat.org/title/work-and-motivation/oclc/243731. Accessed 5 Jan 2023

Weber, M.R., Finley, D.A., Crawford, A., Rivera, D.: An exploratory study identifying soft skill competencies in entry-level managers. Tour. Hosp. Res. **9**(4), 353–361 (2009). https://journals.sagepub.com/doi/10.1057/thr.2009.22. Accessed 5 Jan 2023

Zinn, B.: Conditional variables of "Ausbildung 4.0" – Vocational education for the future. JOTED **3**, 1–9 (2015)

Dr. Antonios Kargas works as an Assistant Professor in the Department of Business Administration in the University of West Attica. He holds a bachelor's degree in economics, as well as a master's degree and a Ph.D. degree from the Department of Informatics and Telecommunications from National and Kapodistrian University of Athens. His research interests include managerial issues related with international business, business management, technological implementation and digital transformation, as well as cost benefit analysis, technoeconomic analysis and applied economics issues. He has more than 30 publications in peer reviewed journals/conferences in the field and more than 190 citations, while he serves as reviewer and co-editor in several international editions.

Dr. Elena C. Gkika is Lab teaching staff in the department of Business Administration at the University of West Attica, Greece. She holds a Bachelor's degree from the Athens University of Economics and Business. She has received a Ph.D. from the Panteion University in adoption of ICTs. She has collaborated with many scholars and she has published within the areas of technology, information technologies adoption and end-user's satisfaction, organizational behavior, entrepreneurship. Her professional experience stems from working at an international bank as consultant and at international companies at Management information systems department.

Dimitris Papakyriakopoulos is Assistant professor at Business Administration department of University of West Attica. He holds a B.Sc. in Informatics, M.Sc. in Analysis and design of information systems and a Ph.D. in Intelligent information system and Supply chain management all from Athens University of Economics and Business. He has more than 20 years working experience in various EU-funded projects, as special advisor in e-government and public reform for the Greek government and technical consultant for major Greek companies. His research interests include business analytics, machine learning and data science. He is member of the DigiT-DSS research lab (University of West Attica) and associate member of ELTRUN (Athens University of Economics and Business). He has also collaborated with initiatives like Efficient Consumer Response (ECR-Hellas) and Wharton Customer Analytics Initiative (WCAI-University of Pennsylvania). His work has been published in several scientific journals including Decision Support Systems, Expert Systems with Applications, Electronic Markets etc.

Dr. Faidon Komisopoulos is a Lecturer in the department of Business Administration at the University of West Attica, Greece. He received a bachelor degree in Technology and Operation Systems another and in Computer Science. On a post-graduate level, he holds a **MBA** from "Haute Ecole Groupe ICHEC—ISC St Louis" (2002), and a **Ph.D**. on Innovation Management. He has been lecturing in several Universities and other institutions in Greece. Before joining academia, he served as commercial director in a multinational Telecom company and he has also worked as Senior Researcher in a recognized research center.

Mr. Spyridon Filios is an academic scholar at the University of Western Attica, an Economics graduate of the Economics Department of the University of Piraeus, and has a master's degree in Regional Economic Development with a specialization in transport from the Panteion University of Social and Political Sciences. From 2019 until today he is an academic scholar at the University of West Attica and teaches the courses, Entrepreneurship and Innovation, Supply Chain Management and Business Strategy. He has participated as an expert researcher in research programs and has published in Greek and international peer-reviewed scientific journals.

Digital Transformation of Business Model: The Case of Israeli HealthTech

Tal Berman, Daniel Schallmo, and Christopher A. Willams

Abstract Exceptional developments in digital technologies have made some of the old theories outdated; hence, there is a need to explore digital transformation through a holistic lens and within various industries and countries. Consequently, we introduced the case of digital transformation of business models as it takes shape in the Israeli HealthTech. We conducted 10 semi-structured expert interviews and complemented these with digital archival data for triangulation. External (e.g. shortage of workforce) and internal (e.g. low digital capabilities) challenges have highlighted the need for digital transformation of business models in healthcare. Thus, we introduce these challenges and the potential value creation in the industry. We also present how Israeli HealthTech start-ups solve challenges and create value in the process. In this way, we contribute to the business model innovation and digital transformation literature. Specifically, in healthcare, we show how value-based healthcare takes place in practice.

Keywords Business model · Business model innovation · Digital start-up · Digital technology · Digital transformation · Digital transformation of business model · HealthTech · Telemedicine · Value capture · Value creation

1 Introduction

For over a decade, digital technologies have played a fundamental role in restructuring, reorganizing, and revamping multiple industries (Fitzgerald et al. 2013; Llopis-Albert et al. 2021) by becoming a driver for the creation and development of new digital products and services (Bharadwaj et al. 2013; von Briel et al. 2018; Yoo

T. Berman (✉)
Johannesburg Business School, 69 Kingsway Ave, Auckland Park, Johannesburg 2092, South Africa
e-mail: 223155414@student.uj.ac.za

D. Schallmo · C. A. Willams
Neu-Ulm University of Applied Sciences, Wileystraße 1, 89231 Neu-Ulm, Germany
e-mail: Daniel.Schallmo@hnu.de

© The Author(s), under exclusive license to Springer Nature Switzerland AG 2024
D. Schallmo et al. (eds.), *Digital Disruption and Transformation*, Springer Proceedings in Business and Economics, https://doi.org/10.1007/978-3-031-47888-8_3

et al. 2010, 2012). Most importantly, they have influenced modern business models (BMs) (Veit et al. 2014; Weill and Woerner 2013) because they have produced many gains upon their implementation (Matt et al. 2015; Westerman and Bonnet 2015), such as improving performance (Srinivasan and Swink 2018) and creating new business opportunities (Teece and Linden 2017). Altogether, their diffusion has assisted with pushing forward digital transformation (DT) throughout the business world (Nambisan et al. 2019).

Similar to digital technologies, DT grants many benefits (Anthony et al. 2019); for instance, it too enhances firms' performance (Tsou and Chen 2021) and offers such novel additions as improving customers' experience (Westerman et al. 2014) and sustaining competitive advantage (Brock and von Wangenheim 2019). Therefore, nowadays, we see ongoing DT processes across many sectors, domains, and industries (Chanias et al. 2019; Matt et al. 2015).

One industry in particular that has been undergoing DT in recent years is healthcare (Kraus et al. 2021). A report by BDO states that 93% of US healthcare organizations have either created a DT strategy or in the process of such creation (BDO United States 2021). Consequently, digital technologies have been diffused by healthcare providers in an attempt to bring about better treatments, diagnostics, and general patient engagement (Marques and Ferreira 2020). The recent COVID-19 pandemic and its ramifications have become a recognized force further accelerating this process (Tortorella et al. 2022) due to the need to maintain social distancing to reduce the spread of the virus (Lee and Lee 2021) and protect medical staff (Baudier et al. 2021).

Nevertheless, in general, adding digital technologies to existing BMs is not an easy task (Caputo et al. 2021). Thus, COVID-19 aside, the implementation of digital technologies in healthcare has been very slow or non-existent (Oderanti et al. 2021) because of the natural risks involved (Kulkov et al. 2021). There are many variables to consider when trying to complete digital technology implementation in this industry, such as passing through heavy regulations (Mathews et al. 2019) and getting physicians and patients to trust the technology enough to use it (Baudier et al. 2021). For these reasons, it remains to be seen whether DT of BMs (DTBM) in this industry can be sufficient to solve its challenges.

The topic of DT in healthcare has resulted in many academic studies (Kraus et al. 2021). However, it appears little is known about which of the new BMs in healthcare are, in fact, effective (Oderanti et al. 2021). Moreover, most research on this topic has not explored the important innovation agents referred to as HealthTech start-ups. Previous research by Garbuio and Lin (2019) classified artificial intelligence (AI)-based HealthTech start-ups according to their value-creation opportunities. Our research is novel, however, because it broadens the outlook to digital start-ups who use varieties of digital technologies and focus on the way they diffuse these to solve the industry's challenges (Nambisan et al. 2019). Predominantly, they do so as part of the entire digital entrepreneurial ecosystem (DEE) (Autio et al. 2018). As a result, we also contribute to the emerging digital entrepreneurship literature (Gehde et al. 2022).

In summary, our research objective is to deliver additional evidence using the Israeli landscape for BM innovation (BMI) and especially DTBM in healthcare, which are enabled by the previously mentioned entrepreneurial businesses referred to as HealthTech start-ups (Beaulieu and Lehoux 2017). In this way, we intend to further advance the field of DTBM.

Our paper progresses as follows. First, we take a thorough look at the relevant BMI and DT literature to learn about current theoretical approaches in general and in healthcare specifically. Thereafter, we explain our qualitative research design and present our findings. Last, we discuss these findings and emphasize our study's contribution to research and practice.

2 Theoretical Background

2.1 Business Model and Business Model Innovation

Although BMs are a fundamental business approach in management practice and research (Alt and Zimmermann 2001), they still lack a unanimous definition (Ritter and Lettl 2018). Nevertheless, while scholars cannot seem to agree on what a BM is (Demil et al. 2015; Schneckenberg et al. 2022), there is a common understanding regarding what it does (Teece 2018)—a BM is a framework for understanding how a firm conducts its business and enriches its stakeholders (Amit and Zott 2012; Zott et al. 2011)—and, equally important, within which boundaries it does so (Doz and Kosonen 2010; Plekhanov et al. 2022; Zott and Amit 2008). Therefore, scholars can now grasp that, while a firm creates value in the form of products and/or services, it captures value in the form of financial revenues in return (Teece 2010, 2018). Another salient component of the BM is the value proposition (VP) (Osterwalder et al. 2015), which is defined as the benefits customers reap when using the firm's products and/or services (Morris et al. 2005).

As previously explained, digital technologies strongly affect BMs (Spieth et al. 2014). Nevertheless, they are no longer sufficient on their own to achieve significant business goals, such as, creating and sustaining a competitive advantage (Baden-Fuller and Haefliger 2013; Chesbrough 2007). Even now, with extraordinary technological advancement (Llopis-Albert et al. 2021), using digital technologies for that goal remains quite challenging (Bonnet and Westerman 2020). Moreover, sometimes digital technologies can add more intricacies into the mix (Nambisan et al. 2017). Therefore, firms these days opt for a different approach of innovating their BMs (Amit and Zott 2020) because such a strategy is deemed to be more effective on one hand (Anwar 2018) and harder to imitate on the other (Amit and Zott 2012).

However, although naturally and closely related to the research topic of BM (Wirtz et al. 2016), in recent years, BMI has become a standalone concept (Schneider and Spieth 2013) that is quite intricate to study (Massa et al. 2017). By and large, as BMI is quite a complexed research concept, it merits strong empirical evidence (Schneckenberg et al. 2022). BM, as previously mentioned, is the way a firm creates and captures value; BMI, then, is considered new ways in which it does so (Casadesus-Masanell and Zhu 2013). Therefore, generally, BMI is defined as new modifications to any of the BM's components, i.e. value-creation, value-capture, value-delivery, VP, and/or what links them together (Foss and Saebi 2017).

As long as they intend to sustain their value creation and capture abilities (Achtenhagen et al. 2013), firms innovate their BMs in reaction to exogenous changes in their environment (Schneider 2019). There are external antecedents for such changes—for example, changes in customers' preferences (Markides 2006)—as well as internal antecedents, such as newly developed dynamic capabilities (DCs) (Teece 2018), which we will define in the next section. Altogether, despite continuous scholarly debate, little is known about the connection between these environmental changes and BMI (Hacklin et al. 2018).

2.2 The Digital Economy

Digital Transformation. As mentioned before, in recent years, DT has become a major research topic (Dąbrowska et al. 2022). Nonetheless, despite its practical usefulness (Anthony et al. 2019), just like BM, it also lacks a commonly agreed-upon definition (Hanelt et al. 2021). Further, the fact that many people use other related trending terms (e.g. 'digitization' and 'digitalization') interchangeably with it has exacerbated this challenge (Ritter and Pedersen 2020). Overall, DT is considered a guide for a much-needed organizational change considering all the digital technological developments (Verhoef et al. 2021) that warrant a holistic perspective (Schallmo et al. 2022). Therefore, for this study, we define DT as a series of actions in which a variety of digital technologies are connected to revamp businesses as a whole and/or specifically their processes (Vial 2019). In sum, DT is suggested to positively influence BM (Berman 2012); hence, these two concepts are interrelated (Kraus et al. 2022). This determination has made DT a significant essence of any modern business (Hess et al. 2016).

Digital Transformation of Business Models. We mentioned the antecedents for BMI in the previous section. Such bearings are predominantly perceived as opportunities to offer customers new and unique VPs (Schallmo et al. 2019). Although, as explained, technology cannot be used on its own to achieve BMI, one cannot underestimate its influence (Rachinger et al. 2018). Therefore, DTBM is defined as the way businesses generate new products, elements, and processes in the BM by utilizing digital technologies (Schallmo et al. 2017). By virtue of being a solid foundation for the holistic digitalization theory, it is strongly recommended that scholars continue analysing DTBM in different sceneries, such as across countries and industries (Schallmo et al. 2022).

Digital Capabilities. Building DCs that assist in driving forward DT is essential for any firm that wishes to reap the previously mentioned benefits (Warner and Wäger 2019). There are many definitions for the DC concept (Barreto 2010); however, because DT influences the way firms interact with their environment (Plekhanov et al. 2022), for this research we define it as how firms react to changes in their environment and create, develop, sustain, improve, and consolidate much-needed and relevant proficiencies, skills, and expertise (Teece 2010, 2018).

A few decades ago, business organizations were occupied with achieving operational excellence (Treacy and Wiersema 1993) by, for example, eliminating mistakes, becoming cost effective, and delivering value in the proper time to their customer base (Hammer 2004). Additionally, at the dawn of the millennium, business organizations, upon understanding the need for information technologies (IT) (Dewett and Jones 2001), focused on achieving a high level of IT capabilities. Such are defined as the capability of firms to employ, implement, and foster IT (Bharadwaj 2000). Lastly, in other related areas, business leaders, other than naturally creating innovative products and services via state-of-the-art processes, also concentrated on hiring the right people and maintaining the right partnerships (Dahlgaard and Dahlgaard 1999). Alas, it is suggested that developing such operational capabilities, e.g. manufacturing, accounting, marketing, finance, etc. (Teece 2007), are insufficient for maintaining competitive advantage. Unfortunately, with today's digital technological developments these are very easy to imitate (Teece 2014).

Therefore, nowadays, firms are expected to become "digital masters" instead (Bonnet and Westerman 2020). Consequently, achieving a high level of digital capability is imperative to firms with success aspirations (Levallet and Chan 2018). Such capabilities allow them to use digital technologies to improve their operations and processes (Bonnet and Westerman 2020). Therefore, digital capabilities are defined as the ability of digital technological systems to bring swift information and results to customers without using external agents (Lyytinen et al. 2016). Digital capabilities assist business leaders to foster the transformative abilities of digital technologies and thus boost their undertakings (Bonnet and Westerman 2020). Nonetheless, these capabilities that enable DT in organizations have stirred little to no scholarly debate so far (Warner and Wäger 2019). However, as such capabilities are developed constantly with the advancement of digital technologies (Bonnet and Westerman 2020), there is a strong need to continue researching them further (Chaudhuri et al. 2022).

Digital Entrepreneurial Ecosystem. As emphasized, digital technologies are used to revamp existing or create new BMs (Casadesus-Masanell and Ricart 2010; Schallmo et al. 2017). Hence, the formerly mentioned boundaries firms used to operate at are, in fact, diminishing (Plekhanov et al. 2022), and such firms become part of complete digital ecosystems (Weill and Woerner 2013).

In the past decade, DT has become a salient force for the creation of digital ecosystems (Plekhanov et al. 2022). An ecosystem in the managerial context evolves when a group of organizations cooperates to create and capture better value (Williamson and De Meyer 2012). Moreover, the focal point in such ecosystems is the ultimate joint VP, which cannot be achieved by any of the firms on their own (Lingens et al. 2021). In the same way, a digital ecosystem is considered a business ecosystem that is engendered by single or several digital technologies (Kopalle et al. 2020). In such digital ecosystems, customers, suppliers, and other actors take part as co-creators (Magistretti et al. 2019).

Further, in recent years, various digital ecosystems have evolved around the concept of industries' technologies, such as financial technologies (FinTech) (Palmié et al. 2020), educational technologies (EdTech) (Hughes 2019), and agricultural technologies (AgTech) (Berman and Schallmo 2021). Such digital ecosystems are referred to as DEEs (Sussan and Acs 2017) and defined as the consolidation of key actors in an area and/or industry who jointly assist with promoting digital start-ups (Du et al. 2018). The goal is to foster the ability of entrepreneurial organizations to assist in solving challenges for regions and/or industries (Silva et al. 2018).

Thus, we understand that the main actors within such DEEs are, in fact, digital start-up companies. These entrepreneurial business entities are defined as new entrants that promote BMI within these mature industries (Babenko et al. 2022) by capitalizing on digital affordances (Autio et al. 2018). Although starting to receive scholarly attention (e.g. Palmié et al. 2021) we still know little about the role of digital start-ups as value creators in such digital ecosystems (Ojaghi et al. 2019; Spadoni et al. 2019).

2.3 *Digital Transformation of Business Model in Healthcare*

Background. As the world's population continues to grow, hospital beds globally have reached a problematic state of deficit (MacIntyre et al. 2019). Even in European countries where the population increase is relatively mild, they suffer the same consequence due to new reforms that resulted in cuts to healthcare budgets (Pecoraro et al. 2021). Further, because of a global aging population (Reynaud and Miccoli 2018), the demand for medical specialists has grown significantly, and the developed world is about to experience a worrying medical personnel shortage in the not-too-distant future (Scheffler and Arnold 2019). Last, the future economic stress caused by expected increases in all health-related expenditures is a worrying trend as well (Oderanti et al. 2021). Therefore, for all these reasons and more, healthcare providers in recent years started revamping their traditional BMs (Deloitte Centre for Health Solutions 2020a) and have been searching for ways to shorten their processes while at the same time achieving better results (Rizwan et al. 2018).

Nowadays, we see an increase in the attempts to use more sophisticated digital technologies on-site (Agarwal et al. 2010). For instance, AI is implemented in areas where there is a significant use of imagery, e.g. radiology (Kulkov 2021); blockchain is used where there is a need to secure delicate medical data (Massaro 2023); and, of course, for many years we have been hearing about the almost science-fiction-like 3D bioprinting of organs for transplantations (Rong et al. 2018), even the ability to print a heart (i24NEWS 2019). However, this is only one side of the picture and just a handful of the digital technologies shaping the medical capabilities of healthcare providers.

Shift in the Industry's Business Models. In many Far East countries, the BM component of value capture in healthcare works in a way that the patient pays the provider as long as they are well (Lentz 2015). Until recently, it was exactly the opposite in the Western world. For example, in the US, providers were getting paid based on their patients' hospitalization time (Schroeder et al. 2013). This BM is similar to that of hotels and originated with an implausible mechanism that incentivized keeping people hospitalized (Cox et al. 2016). Unsurprisingly, the former gives medical agents an incentive to basically do the job they were meant to do. Therefore, in recent years, Western medicine has realized the value of such methods and started concentrating on the concepts of wellness and prevention, i.e. keeping patients as healthy as possible instead of managing their conditions (Vesselkov et al. 2018). This is, by and large, a reaction to changes in policies as well; nowadays, the incentive mechanisms are based on pay-for-performance, i.e. the goal is to reduce hospitals admissions and not vice versa (Cox et al. 2016).

Additionally, as previously mentioned, until a few years ago, most of the digital innovations were on-site (Tortorella et al. 2021) with not enough concern for the way providers communicated with patients (Vesselkov et al. 2018). Nevertheless, patients started taking a more involved and active role in the healthcare process (Leone et al. 2021). Their role has increased so much in recent years (Danaher and Gallan 2016) that they are considered an integral part of many health organizations, i.e. they engage in an employees-like involvement and pertinence (Mende 2019).

The biggest relevant challenge of all, though, is the fact that spending money does not necessarily yield better or even decent results. For example, in the US, although the expenditure per capita is among the highest in the world, the life expectancy is relatively low (Squires and Anderson 2015). Consequently, providers have started to move away from their traditional methods (van Velthoven et al. 2019) and converted to value-based healthcare (VBHC) (Kokshagina 2021; Peters et al. 2015), which is defined as the ratio between the results that patients value and the costs involved in achieving them (Kaplan and Porter 2011; Porter and Lee 2013). Nevertheless, to date, research on how providers can practically shift from traditional models to VBHC is limited (Kokshagina 2021).

It has been motioned that implementing digital technologies may actually improve healthcare services (Laurenza et al. 2018). Therefore, as DT is the improvement of businesses via digital technologies (Schallmo et al. 2019), although still in its research infancy (Garcia-Perez et al. 2023), DT in healthcare is attributed to how using digital technologies one can achieve superior and much more secured medical results (Haggerty 2017), i.e. a significant change in the workflows within all or part of a healthcare provider's landscape (Agarwal et al. 2010).

The Emergence of Telemedicine. One method that enabled the increase in patients' involvement, which is essential for value creation (Dahl et al. 2021), digital ecosystem (Susanto et al. 2021), and VBHC (Randhawa et al. 2021), is telemedicine (Sermontyte-Baniule et al. 2022). Telemedicine is defined as virtual health solutions enabled by sophisticated digital technologies (WHO Global Observatory for eHealth 2010), and it is connected to HealthTech because it solves a medical problem (Moro Visconti 2021). Its emergence has been a gamechanger, using value co-creation via the implementation of complementary digital technologies, e.g. Internet-of-Things (IoT) (Niemelä et al. 2019).

One of the new VPs this development enabled has been the fact that people no longer need to meet their physicians face-to-face in all cases. On the contrary, in most cases, they can do so virtually, instantly, and in any place of their choosing (Baudier et al. 2021). Further, by using various wearables or seamless technologies, they seem to be able to get at least the same results as in person if not better ones (Drago et al. 2023).

It is suggested that telemedicine not only has assisted healthcare providers with delivering better value to their patients but also allows patients to focus on their wellness (Vesselkov et al. 2018). Certainly, this method seems to better adhere to patients' preferences (Hu et al. 1999). For instance, people who live in rural areas can finally gain access to health services or those of a higher degree (Chandwani et al. 2018). Further, by using such technologies, providers can reduce operational costs (Akter et al. 2022) and free much-needed workload from their medical workforce (Sun et al. 2020), who even today suffer from a significant deficit in their numbers (Go Jefferies et al. 2019).

Solutions like telemedicine seem like the epitome of holistic digitalization. Nevertheless, despite all its related advantages, it remains to be seen whether this trend will continue in a post-pandemic world and what its future business impact will be (Lee and Lee 2021).

2.4 Research Questions

Building on the theoretical knowledge brought forward in this section and combining it with our research objective, we aim to answer the following research questions:

RQ1. Which challenges is the healthcare industry trying to cope with these days?

RQ2. How are digital technologies used in healthcare for value-creation?

RQ3. How do HealthTech start-ups use digital technologies to create such value for patients and providers and, at the same time, solve the industry's challenges?

3 Methods

3.1 Research Design

In recent years, a question has been raised about what drives DTBM across countries and industries (Schallmo et al. 2022). Therefore, to promote DTBM research, we elected to investigate the Israeli HealthTech setting. We chose Israel as it is considered a start-up nation (Goldberg 2012) with a very high start-up per capita ratio (Hashai 2015). Further, its HealthTech DEE is vibrating with many digital start-ups (Lovis and Gamzu 2015), and these operate and thrive in many of the fields previously described (Orbach and Ravet 2020). This, in return, has amassed an exceptional amount of venture capital funding, reaching almost $2 billion in 2021 (Start-Up Nation Central 2022).

Further, the area of DT and its complexities (Ivančić et al. 2019), combined with the fact that our research questions are of the "which (what)" and "how" kind (Korstjens and Moser 2017), led us to take an exploratory qualitative research approach (Eisenhardt and Graebner 2007). Additionally, since, as formerly mentioned, there is not enough empirical evidence in the studied field and topics, we opted for a case study methodology (Yin 2017). Consequently, a single case study of the revelatory method was used because DTBM is still considered a new and underexplored concept (Schallmo et al. 2017); thus, it represented a fit (Dremel et al. 2017).

Our predominant goal was to include practitioners in this research to gain valuable empirical evidence for advancing the field of BMI (Schneckenberg et al. 2022) and DTBM (Schallmo et al. 2017) and, as a result, also holistic digitalization (Schallmo et al. 2022). Especially within such research in the sub-field of innovation in healthcare, it is imperative that we broaden our perspective and dig deeper via in-depth interviews (Gehde et al. 2022). For these reasons, we conducted semi-structured expert interviews to gain insights into existing means (Bogner and Menz 2009) as such methodology is the main focal point for any qualitative study (Gioia et al. 2013). Moreover, it is deemed an appropriate way to eventually analyse theoretical approaches (Brinkmann and Kvale 2015).

Further, qualitative methods require multiple data sources (Gioia et al. 2013). Thus, for triangulation, we used archival digital data observation research methodology (Ventresca and Mohr 2017) as this has become quite popular in the field of management research in recent years (e.g. Cozzolino et al. 2021; Tob-Ogu et al. 2018). Such methodology allows scholars to deal with research questions that they could not have addressed in the past (Calantone and Vickery 2010); even more, it complements expert interviews well (Vogt et al. 2012). In this way, we were able to close our research design loop entirely.

3.2 Data Collection and Analysis

Semi-Structured Interviews. To answer RQ1 and RQ2, we used data collected in our expert interviews. As shown in Table 1, during the months of July and August (2022), we conducted 10 interviews with an even split between HealthTech start-up founders and leaders and other related practitioners. These interviews were recorded and transcribed.

We applied a semi-structured interview methodology as we wanted to receive a detailed response from our experts (Bogner and Menz 2009), and these provided a decent level of adequate information (Harrell and Bradley 2009). Our goal was to learn about common practices in the field while gaining new knowledge, if possible, by using open-ended questions (Labuschagne 2003).

Table 1 Experts interviewed

	Position	Organization	Interview date
E1	Senior radiologist	A public hospital	13/07/2022
E2	Founding partner & CIO	HealthTech-focused venture capital fund	14/07/2022
E3	Former HealthTech investor and current head of community	HealthTech bottom-up community	14/07/2022
E4	Head of Innovation Center	A public hospital	17/07/2022
E5	Director of Start-ups at Innovation Group	A public hospital	27/07/2022
E6	Co-Founder & CTO	HealthTech start-up	13/07/2022
E7	Founder & CEO	HealthTech start-up	14/07/2022
E8	CTO	HealthTech start-up	18/07/2022
E9	Co-Founder & CEO	HealthTech start-up	26/07/2022
E10	Co-Founder & CTO	HealthTech start-up	02/08/2022

For the interview analysis, we used a thematic analysis methodology (Aronson 1995) as it offers much research flexibility and enables researchers to find patterns within and between data correlating to the interviewees' experiences, beliefs, views, and practices (Braun and Clarke 2006). To establish reliability, two experienced researchers coded the 10 interviews separately with 93.92% agreement. The calculated Cohen's Kappa was 0.64, which is quite acceptable and significant (Banerjee et al. 1999).

Finally, to report our findings, we used extensive direct quotes and presented the results from actual data, which directly related to what the participants said (Yardley 2000).

Archival Data. To answer RQ3 and to complement RQ1 and RQ2 (Vogt et al. 2012), we used digital archival research (Ventresca and Mohr 2017). We browsed companies' websites and third parties' digital data websites, e.g. Start-up Nation Central Finder and Crunchbase, as such related and relevant data collection is acceptable for our study (Marra et al. 2015).

To analyse our gathered archival data, we built on Garbuio and Lin's (2019) methodology combined with Remane et al. (2016); we elaborate on this in the Discussion section. This combination is similar to our earlier work (Berman et al. 2021).

4 Findings and Discussion

4.1 Challenges of the Healthcare Industry

BMs are a dynamic framework (Teece 2010) and therefore should echo new market conditions (Demil and Lecocq 2010), such as changing customers' preferences (Markides 2006) or new technological developments (Giesen et al. 2010). Nevertheless, firms also occasionally face internal challenges and/or developments such as newly developed and/or lack of required organizational DCs (Teece 2018). Overall, more often than not, businesses attempt to endure such challenges via the diffusion of digital technologies (Spieth et al. 2021) and modify and transform their BMs accordingly (Egfjord and Sund 2020; Schallmo et al. 2017). Thus, they design their complete digital strategy based on these factors (Schallmo et al. 2019).

External Challenges. Our data indicate that the healthcare industry is suffering from global external challenges. These challenges have been troubling governments and healthcare leaders for many years (Helfert 2009).

Shortage of Medical Staff and Related Specialists. As mentioned earlier, the Western world is on the cusp of experiencing a worrying shortage of medical workers (Zhang et al. 2020). In the US alone, by 2034, there will be a momentous deficit of roughly 40,000–120,000 physicians (Dall et al. 2021). It is acceptable to concentrate on physicians and specialists, who mainly deal with treating serious health conditions; nonetheless, the problem does not end there. Other healthcare-related professionals, such as optometrists (Young 2022) and nurses (Mitchell 2022), are in a severe state of deficit as well. The nursing profession should not be taken lightly whatsoever as shortage of such a salient workforce may endanger patients and reduce the quality of care (Tang et al. 2019); any shortage of complementary professionals, such as optometrists, would increase the pressure on ophthalmologists (Baker et al. 2016) and reduce people's quality of life. "The demand for healthcare constantly increases, and, unfortunately, the staff numbers remain constant. It's true especially for us in the radiology department. If, two decades ago, we used to decipher roughly 5 CT tests in one night, nowadays, we complete 60. Don't get me wrong; the staff numbers have slightly gone up, but not 12 times obviously… Thus, the burden inflicted on the current staff members is truly troublesome." (E1). "One of the biggest challenges of optometry is that people don't study this profession anymore. Therefore, there's a huge shortage of optometrists…not only in countries like China or India but also in West Europe. I'm talking about a mere situation that, if someone's glasses broke, they'll need to wait in some of the German cities for six months until they can go to an optometrist and get a prescription for new ones. So, at the shops of this optics chain we work with, there's no one really who can help you… I mean, they are available in many locations; it's just that they don't have the manpower. There's no way to train new optometrists…" (E8).

Concurring with the findings of (Taylor 2020), this snowball effect, where the demand for medical staff far exceeds the supply, happens for three main reasons:

(i) Training—It takes many years to train doctors, nurses, and other related professionals, and creating more schools and academic programs for that purpose may take even longer (Scheffler and Arnold 2019). (ii) Retaining—The formerly mentioned shortage of nurses, for instance, has made the available nurses dissatisfied with their situation and inability to care for their patients well, resulting in many of them leaving the profession (Aiken et al. 2017). "I would like to see more nurses… And that's an incentives question, a public resources question… If you pay nurses a better wage and you give them better conditions, then you'll get more nurses. If you do what we've done during the pandemic, they're going to find another profession. So, we're not going to create a virtual nurse." (E3). (iii) Recruiting—Heavy bureaucracies, standards, budgets, and other related problems have prevented healthcare providers from enlisting new physicians (Ahmed et al. 2020; Taylor 2020). Needless to say, COVID-19 has made this entire situation even worse (Rosen et al. 2020).

Other than dealing with large numbers of patients at each shift, in addition, much of today's work for physicians is administrative (Woolhandler and Himmelstein 2014). This is inefficient on one hand and very costly on the other. Moreover, it creates additional work for a medical staff that, as mentioned, is already fully utilized. "Nowadays, the doctors roughly spend a quarter of their time with patients whereas half of their time is next to the computer… And they struggle with it. In the US, they were able to solve this by adding more occupations in healthcare, like physician assistant, which reduces such workload from the doctors and, thus, helps them focus more on the patients. The doctors in the US don't 'bang their heads' with the systems; they pass the information to others, who do so instead. That's one way that can help clear the doctors' minds and perhaps get them to do other things…" (E10).

System Overload. As explained, the shortage of workers has put the healthcare industry in a bad position. Further, the population increase has not been met with a complementary increase in hospital beds (MacIntyre et al. 2019). Moreover, global health budgets were cut on the understanding that spending money does not necessarily deliver corresponding results (Pecoraro et al. 2021). COVID-19 has merely exposed this problematic state of global healthcare systems (e.g. Davey 2022), and, even after it is long gone, these problems will likely remain (Moir and Barua 2022). Even more so, even if the supply of doctors was able to meet the demand, the healthcare challenges would be far from solved.

Life expectancy increase has been a very good development for humanity, and it seems we are able to outlive our ancestors on average (Jaleel et al. 2020; Wang and Li 2021). However, this has created a by-problem in which many of the people, though they live longer, spend a significant part of their lives in a problematic state of personal health (Jaleel et al. 2020). For example, roughly 50 million Europeans suffer from at least one chronic condition (Deloitte Centre for Health Solutions 2020b). Therefore, along with the deficit of medical staff, we clearly see an increase in the number of patients as well (Jaleel et al. 2020). "Overall, this system has operated relatively well, and, therefore, people live longer. Thus, people consume more health services. It's an inherent problem for healthcare… So, basically, we're talking about an increasing life expectancy and, as a result, an increasing population in most countries in the world. Some of that increase is due to more births whereas some is due to more immigration, and the longer we live, the diseases last longer as well… We're talking about mostly long-term sicknesses. Not a flu that'll pass within a week but diseases that stay with patients for many years…" (E4).

These two vectors have resulted in limited availability, especially for specialists, and uncomfortable office hours (Heath 2022). Overall, we see an increasing wait time for doctors' appointments and when visiting clinics or medical centres (Mills 2017). That has resulted in disgruntled patients (Heath 2018), who end up not showing up for their appointments or alternatively leave the clinic before and without seeing a doctor (Shaw et al. 2018). "The availability of doctors has reached a point of irrelevancy. If I have a problem now and I need to wait six months to inspect my situation… It's just not worth it… And it's gotten worse. I see that trend happening for five to six years now, and, in the past couple of years, also the availability of the medical institutions has worsened… If you need to go through an ultrasound test or anything of sort, in the past, they would schedule an appointment for the next day, and now, you usually have to wait for roughly three months… And that too is becoming irrelevant." (E10).

Therefore, in recent years, we have seen heavy movement of financially capable patients towards private healthcare services, where such issues are less likely to occur (Campbell 2022). "Private insurance allows us to get an appointment with a chosen doctor, even a surgeon, and at a chosen location or site… (The) American health system (is) based on 'if you have the money, you get the service.'" (E5). "In Israel, where healthcare is public, it drives the growth of private medicine, and I'm not sure that's really the plan…" (E10). Such a solution does not fit all cases, especially less privileged societies and communities, and that increases societal inequality (Dickman et al. 2017).

Internal Challenges. The IT capability (A. S. Bharadwaj 2000) level of healthcare providers has gone up in recent years (Agarwal et al. 2010), though it remains quite average. For instance, DT projects must be led by clever IT personnel (Dremel et al. 2017); unfortunately, in healthcare, this is insufficient because their capacity is naturally limited. Moreover, the lack of IT and cybersecurity specialists in healthcare has intensified the situation (McKeon 2022a). "Hospitals implement roughly 1–2 technological solutions annually. So, who gets promoted instead of being stuck in line at the IT department? This challenge might bring us to a consolidation of a sort with solutions becoming much more substantial." (E2). As a result, providers' levels of digital capability are also low. Our data indicate three reasons for this: interoperability, data privacy, and technology trust.

Interoperability. Interoperability is defined as the ability of two or more systems to interact and operate jointly (da Silva Serapião Leal et al. 2019). This concept relies on connectivity, in which many systems and products in our daily lives or various industries are connected through IoT or other related digital technologies, e.g. cloud computing (Mumtaz et al. 2017). In healthcare, we see the rise of the Internet of Medical Things (IoMT), which combines the concept of IoT and traditional medical devices and is the basis for state-of-the-art HealthTech solutions such as telemedicine (Jaleel et al. 2020).

However, the problem arises when trying to achieve interoperability in practice. Because various devices from various ventures would not connect, providers usually source all medical devices from one technological merchant, which results in an undesirable dependency and the creation of data silos (Jaleel et al. 2020). While many related challenges have been addressed with technological developments such as HealthGo by the merchants themselves (Jaleel et al. 2020), the data silo challenge remains. "We collect tons of digital data, but each is collected using a separate database, and that depends on the specific system that's being used. For instance, the follow-up notes are saved on Electronic Health Record (EHR) whereas the images are saved on the Picture Archiving and Communication System (PACS), which is completely different. These silos are very hard to consolidate eventually… And you need this consolidation for managerial and research needs… For instance, if I as a researcher in the hospital want to collect data and create a sort of cohort that has imagery data, clinical data, laboratory data, etc., that's something which is very difficult to achieve even these days. It demands an ad-hoc work, i.e. get a data engineer to sit down, maybe even a data scientist, depending on what needs to be achieved, and basically reinvent the wheel." (E1). "There isn't enough connectivity. That's something that must be addressed. I think the connectivity between players in the healthcare landscape is suboptimal particularly in the US, and the incentives aren't for the exchange of information but rather the 'siloing' of information because there's power in the ownership of data." (E3).

In the past few years, lots of data is created in healthcare, which is coming from lots of connected devices, such as wearables (Hulsen 2020). However, so far, bridging all these sources has been quite challenging (Shen et al. 2019). Data transference and sharing have been used in healthcare to improve care and especially for better research purposes (Azarm-Daigle et al. 2015). Thus, creating a digital ecosystem where providers, research centers, labs, and so on are united in sharing information is extremely valuable (Pine 2019). Part of the challenge in achieving proper interoperability is the fact that healthcare as a profession involves many intricacies (Grol and Wensing 2020) but even more so extreme regulations inflicted on providers regarding data privacy (Sajid and Abbas 2016). "One of the biggest challenges is interoperability. Transferring data from one body to another… To get the systems to 'talk' to each other. Most of the time, it's on purpose, and the regulator had to break it open really… (In the past) these guys would have 'locked you up' in their systems… You had to pay them lots of money or do it by yourself." (E2).

Data Privacy. Organizations have accumulated vast amounts of data in the past decade (Kitsios and Kamariotou 2021). Such data must be protected to maintain the privacy of multiple populations and millions of consumers (Jain et al. 2016). It is suggested that consumers care enough about their privacy to support setting regulations for accumulators, which are usually business organizations (Acquisti et al. 2020). This is even more so in healthcare, where the data are as private as it can be (Fox 2020; Philips 2021). "Medical data is private obviously, sensitive, some even more sensitive like genetics, HIV, and other similar things… This challenge manufactures other challenges and difficulties because you really need to share this data for managerial and research needs… Sometimes, you need to share this data with academic institutions, other hospitals… There's a very big ecosystem of technological developments around this issue." (E1).

Although its reliance on legacy systems and medical devices offered quite a challenge in this realm (McKeon 2022b), in the past, this issue was less problematic than it is now. For example, in the US, most of the health records were placed in hard copies. Nowadays, these records have been digitized and became EHRs (Kruse et al. 2017). Within the EHR concept, one may find, beyond the technical demographic data, the entire health history of the patients as well (CMS 2021). "Hospitals have been computerized with EHRs in the past decade due to President Obama's actions, and that has paved the way for more sophisticated technologies… Meaning, hospitals started accumulating lots of data and now seek ways to use it properly. We need to remember that, only 15 years ago, hospitals in the US were totally manual… It sounds hallucinatory, but it's real…" (E2).

Although significant developments as EHRs contribute to improved care, better decision making, and high-quality medical research (Cowie et al. 2017), from a cybersecurity point of view, this has created a privacy danger (Shahnaz et al. 2019). That danger in return led to the formation of strict regulation (Blumenthal and Tavenner 2010; NHS 2022) (Blumenthal and Tavenner 2010; NHS Digital 2022). Unfortunately, such regulation is a critical barrier for data sharing in healthcare (Zheng et al. 2018).

Technology Trust. Digital implementation is an integral part of holistic digitalization (Schallmo et al. 2022), because it is essential for executing the digital strategy and supporting the DTBM (Schallmo and Williams 2021). Implementing sophisticated digital technologies requires multiple efforts across the entire organization (Tabrizi et al. 2019). That is not an easy task, and many DT projects fail (Brock and von Wangenheim 2019). Employees are considered an essential part in any area of the business, which makes them acute for implementation (Schallmo et al. 2019) and a salient success factor (Lapointe and Rivard 2007).

There has been much debate by information systems scholars about technology acceptance (Marangunić and Granić, 2015), which is defined as the agreeableness of users to voluntarily or deliberately use a certain technology (Dillon and Morris 1996). Specifically, the concept of technology acceptance has stirred a large scholarly debate in healthcare (Pai and Huang 2011), because many of the medical staff are reluctant to give up their autonomy on one hand (Safi et al. 2018; Walter and Lopez 2008), and on the other build their trust in new technologies very slowly (Baudier et al. 2021). "There're few levels of trust. The first level is the ability to actually believe assisting instruments and technologies. Even if you are an early adopter, you need to see the technology in some situations that you test it in and then realize it actually works… Especially, if this isn't the technology you were taught to use back in medical school or your internship… Contrarily, you were taught by your mentor/teacher/idol to use something, for instance ECG, that's ultimately become the standard of care… And now, you're asked to be the first one to use something new… Then, this technology enters a testing process." (E7).

4.2 *Value-Creation Opportunities in Healthcare Enabled by Digital Technologies*

Workload Reduction. Moving the industry to healthcare 5.0 is a process that has recently started to materialize. We have already started to hear about the use of robotics in the industry, e.g. they assist surgeons in challenging operations (Javaid et al. 2020) and move patients around the wards (Giansanti 2022). Naturally, such a development is expected to bring about many intriguing opportunities (Riek 2017); thus, we expect more examples of it. Nonetheless, it still seems slow in the making, and digital doctors or digital physicians, i.e. robots that may replace a human doctor, though perhaps not so farfetched, remains quite far from happening (Shuaib et al. 2020). Moreover, a robot may never be able to provide the delicate human touch that is essential in medicine. "Nothing can replace the human touch… We deal with patients in situations and realities that are critical and crucial. In medical school, the soon-to-be doctors go through a workshop that deals with how you inform a patient about the worst things he or she can imagine…. One of the biggest challenges during COVID-19 was the required physical separation between staff and patients. This is something that can't be replace with technology… You hear about human and machine interactions in Japan and Korea, and we all think it's quite bizarre… I think that the Western world will keep seeing this as something really weird in the next hundreds of years… Seriously. I just don't see how the technology bridges such a challenge." (E5).

Nonetheless, the use of other digital technologies, as formerly mentioned, has helped and would help even more in the future to reduce the workload of the medical staff. For instance, it may take care of their administrative tasks autonomously and free them more to engage with patients. "The technology will, though, free the medical staff and help them perform a human function in a much more significant way. The other parameters and functions would be dealt with in a more systemic way." (E5).

Telemedicine. As previously explained, telemedicine is a concept that has a twofold value. The first, as discussed, is for the patients. However, telemedicine offers powerful value for the providers as well. Telemedicine is suggested to cut providers' expenditures and to reduce the medical staff's time (Deloitte Centre for Health Solutions 2015). In a recent survey, specialists, who suffer the most from overload, shared a very high interest in broadening and enlarging this concept (Deloitte Centre for Health Solutions 2020b). However, it is also reported that, since the WHO's announcement of the near end of the COVID-19 pandemic (Mishra 2022), and even before that, the application of telemedicine has gone down, and many people are back looking for physical appointments (Drenik 2022). "COVID-19 has influenced greatly the implementation of new technologies… Telemedicine, teleconsulting, seeing doctors remotely. Prior to the pandemic, it was at about 1–2% remote meetings with doctors in the US whereas, at its peak, these leaped to 80%. Today, it stands at about 40%… It may have dropped, but certainly we're not at the point we used to be not too long ago." (E2).

One thing that needs to be emphasized is the fact that the providers rushed into telemedicine during COVID-19 and created interim solutions they will not likely use in the long term (BDO United States 2021). "I started working for the hospital just when the first quarantine was initiated. Beforehand, the hospital had a roadmap that scheduled seeing a doctor remotely in roughly two to three years… And that'll only happen after they'll purchase a special system for that. Then came COVID-19, and in two weeks' time, such a system was ready and operating. They couldn't care less whether it was working well or working at all… Seriously… Is it connected really? Is it secured enough? Who cares?! Ha! It was quite remarkable…" (E4).

Clinical Decision Support. A clinical decision support system (CDSS) is a mechanism by which medical decisions are augmented and improved (Sutton et al. 2020). In recent years, such tools have been enhanced by digital technologies, e.g. the formerly mentioned AI's assistance to radiologists in deciphering imagery (Kulkov 2021). The need to continue developing more of such systems has increased lately as these tools could potentially significantly improve the outcomes for patients (AHRQ 2019).

With the increased workload of doctors over the years, it is essential that they receive proper support, and data and technology may enhance their ability to make the right calls. Moreover, such systems could significantly reduce costly and deadly mistakes while improving the workflow. Although doctors still seem a bit skeptical about the real capability of these systems (Petkus et al. 2020), the potential for them to become gamechangers is relatively high (Deloitte Centre for Health Solutions 2015). "Our system is not a decision-making system but a decision support system… The doctor is the bottom line and says yes or no… Let's treat it this way or that way. Naturally, there's reluctance to let go—and, by the way, rightfully so in many cases…" (E6).

Empowering Patients. As mentioned before, in recent years, patients started taking a much more involved role in their health management (Leone et al. 2021). Digital technologies have enabled the use of health-tracking apps, self-monitoring wearables, and information portals where people can get knowledge about almost any health-related question they have. For instance, within the websites of Israeli Health Maintenance Organizations (HMOs) there is substantial information about conditions, potential treatments, diagnostics, and so on.

Moreover, providers are paying extra attention to improving their customers' experience. New clinics and hospital wings are transformed via various digital technologies, e.g. robotics, AI, and many more (i24NEWS 2022). The same can be said about virtual engagement; providers are connected to patients via apps and other related means, and patients can receive digital prescriptions, schedule and cancel appointments, get reminders and notifications, and so on (Lal 2022). "… my HMO is sending the day before your doctor's appointment a reminding notification with the option to easily cancel it… It makes their system much more effective in a big way for sure. In many cases, people don't show up because they forgot all about it. So, if I can cancel my appointment with one click and another patient could go instead… It's not super revolutionary really… Especially not in a medical way… But the operational impact is quite big." (E6).

Improving Digital Capabilities. To achieve digital maturity, healthcare providers must improve their digital capabilities (Williams et al. 2022). Digital technologies can assist with achieving such an outcome.

Data Management. In a survey conducted by Philips (2021), many healthcare leaders complained about mismanagement of data and lack of interoperability. Hence, healthcare providers' focal data strategy (DalleMule and Davenport 2017) should be the ability to share data smoothly to, among other previously mentioned benefits, compile transparent, complete information about all patients (Philips 2021). Moreover, simple tasks like collecting the data are time consuming for the medical staff. This appears to be twice the challenge in virtual settings, such as telemedicine (Schulman 2022).

Data Protection and Security. It is quite challenging for healthcare providers to protect their own and their patients' data independently (McKeon 2022b). Further, the connectivity of IoMT (Schulman 2022), and the extensive use of legacy systems (McKeon 2022b) pose threats for breaches. Nowadays, novel digital technologies are being explored by both researchers and practitioners to offer a robust mechanism for data protection—for example, blockchain (Massaro 2023) and edge computing (Li et al. 2019).

Technology Trust. We decided to look at the technology trust challenge as an implementation and adoption challenge (X. Wang et al. 2021) rather than a value-creation opportunity. Although digital technological implementation is an integral part of the holistic digitalization theory (Schallmo et al. 2022), it is still not relevant to our RQ2.

4.3 Value-Based Healthcare Provided by Israeli Digital HealthTech Start-Ups

The HealthTech industry is a young and growing DEE (Moro Visconti 2021). Especially in a country like Israel, where entrepreneurship and innovation are well fostered (Hashai 2015), it is mostly composed of digital start-ups that mainly focus on the patients and ways to deliver better value to them (Towart 2021). In other words, these start-ups are mainly focusing on delivering VBHC. One may also find HealthTech start-ups in a directly B2B context, e.g. assisting providers with achieving better operational and financial results (Garbuio and Lin 2019) and becoming more cost-effective (Oderanti et al. 2021). Predominantly, these start-ups have been a growing group that supports BMI in various international markets (Oderanti et al. 2021).

Further, to achieve digital maturity, i.e. become an organization with a high level of digital capabilities (Williams et al. 2022), it is imperative for healthcare providers to create strategic partnerships and cooperate with digital start-ups (Philips 2021). "Naturally, you see many collaborations between technological companies and hospitals… We're seeing mostly medical device companies—TytoCare is an example for collaboration between such a company—but with HMOs… In the area of making data accessible for research, you can find also collaborations between hospitals and technological companies. I know personally what happens in Sheba Hospital, but I also know they're not the only ones…" (E10).

Telemedicine as a Rising C2B Model in Healthcare. Digital start-ups like the formerly mentioned Israel's TytoCare (enables physicians to generally check their patients remotely, e.g. check their ear canals, listen to their lungs, monitor their heartrate, and all other common exams doctors have been performing for years to understand their patients' condition) empowered the providers to offer new VPs to their patients (Baudier et al. 2021). Similar digital start-ups, especially in the area of telemedicine, have enabled a deep shift in the industry's BMs that, to date, have mainly been B2B or B2B2C models. Thus, such start-ups have been promoting DTBM.

In today's digital economy, customers have become very much involved in the value-creation process and, in fact, became co-creators (Ziaie et al. 2021). Building on the previously mentioned patients' involvement increase, they moved to a hybrid model incorporating many C2B components. A C2B model is defined as a model where consumers take a major part in the value chain to deliver some of the value themselves (Aspara et al. 2021). For instance, the Israeli navigation platform WAZE (acquired by Google in 2013) gains significant value from its users whenever they turn on their app in a crowdsourcing way, e.g. understanding when the traffic is soft or heavy or any other related update drivers and passengers willingly provide with a click of a button (Amin-Naseri et al. 2018). In such an example, the customer provides work and effort on one hand and receive useful data and information on the other (Aspara et al. 2021).

For more examples in healthcare, we look at Israeli companies like Healthy.io (which enables patients to perform their own urine diagnostics at home) or Nuvo (which enables pregnant women to monitor their own situation at home). Naturally, such digital start-ups provide VP of accessibility and time saving for the patients. However, for the providers, they again assist with cutting operational costs and reducing the inflicted stress and burden on the medical staff (Sun et al. 2020), who mostly handles cases where physical engagement with the patients is a must going forward.

Some customers take on a very active role in helping organizations with manufacturing digital solutions because they feel they know best what the optimal value creation is (Plekhanov et al. 2022; Sjödin et al. 2020). Therefore, in the above examples, the patients support the providers with three sorts of input: (i) the goods, as the customers test, monitor, and sometimes even treat themselves, (ii) data and information, which flow via digital technologies, e.g. wearables, back to the providers, and (iii) the effort, as the patients spend time and work just as formerly mentioned (Aspara et al. 2021).

Israeli HealthTech Landscape. Scholars are focusing their research on DT in the context of B2B and B2C (Kraus et al. 2022). Therefore, Fig. 1 represents the Israeli HealthTech landscape based on their value-creation and value-capture components. Like Gehde et al. (2022), we too drew our start-up categories from digital data. "The first group is those who develop a product that is made to directly assist patients so they can handle their condition and situation… The second group is those products that help the organizations with achieving faster, efficient, and precise diagnostics. It's a very big group in which you can include all start-ups who deal with deciphering imagery, e.g. x-rays, CT, MRI, etc. In this specific case, we're talking about lots of visual, but in other areas, we also see stuff like NLP, such as reading medical files and coming up with conclusions… We see recordings and using human voice… Almost any human–machine interaction format, such as visual, vocal, even text… Today helps diagnose… The third group is prediction tools that attempt to predict the future based on common available data… If the healthcare organization can predict well, then it can be better managed on one hand and perhaps prevent sickness before it becomes a problem on the other… The last group is management support systems. That's what I call them. These are tools that help big health organizations manage themselves much more efficiently, better, and more accurately… Saves lots of time for the patients and lots of time and manpower for the provider." (E4).

As can be seen, most of the start-ups provide a two-fold value for both patients and providers. This is a salient development in the global efforts of providers to deliver VBHC.

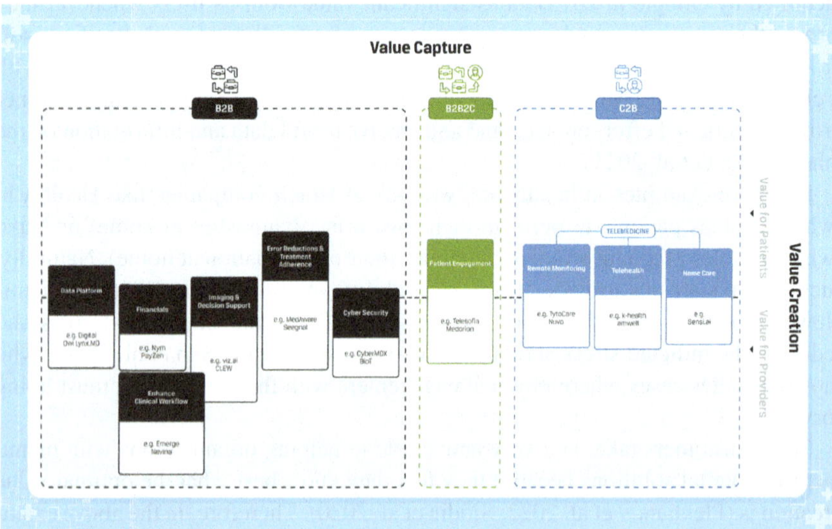

Fig. 1 Israel's HealthTech landscape

5 Conclusion

In recent years, digital technologies have challenged BMs in multiple industries (Loebbecke and Picot 2015), enabling the revisions and improvements of products, services, and processes in the BMs (Schallmo et al. 2017). These very important enablers have advanced substantially and thus made some of the old theories outdated (Steininger 2022). Therefore, a holistic look at digitalization across countries and industries is needed (Schallmo et al. 2022). That is what we achieved in this case study upon investigating DTBM and the way it is achieved in the Israeli HealthTech setting (Fig. 2).

Beyond that, our study made more contributions. First, we contributed to the literature on DT per recent call ups (e.g. Tijan et al. 2021) and connected many of the BMI research streams together (Schneckenberg et al. 2022). Further, we contributed to the emerging literature on the new C2B model by providing empirical evidence (Aspara et al. 2021). Additionally, we contributed to the DEE literature with empirical evidence from Israeli HealthTech (Sussan and Acs 2017). Last, specifically in healthcare, we provided empirical evidence for VBHC (Kokshagina 2021).

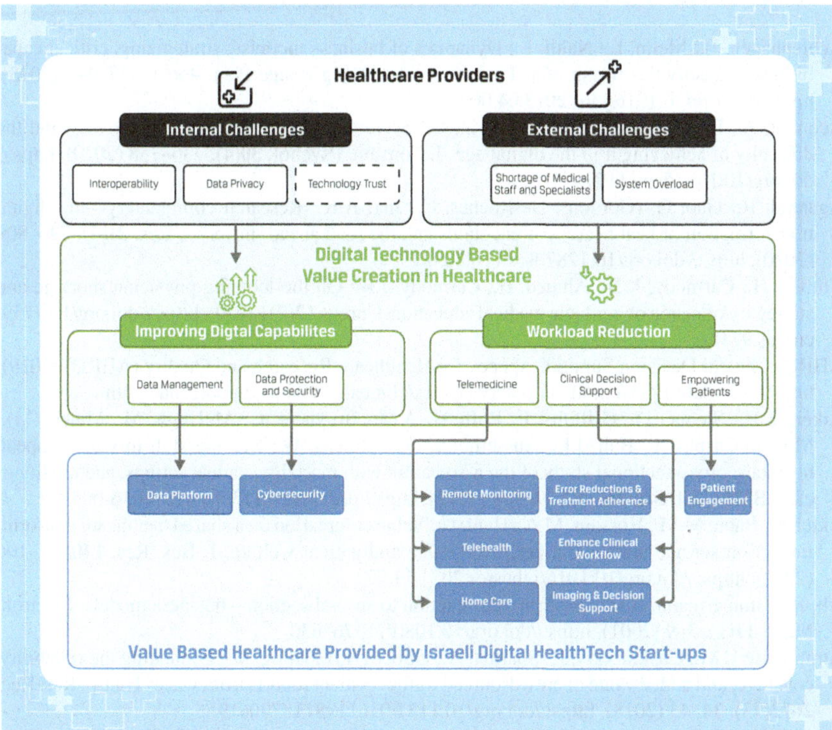

Fig. 2 Digital transformation of business models in the Israeli HealthTech scene

Our research is not without its limitations as it is based on an Israeli context and evidence. Although we emphasized why Israel is a fertile ground to conduct such research, study must still be broadened to a global perspective, i.e. to other significant HealthTech scenes, such as those in the US or the UK.

An avenue for future research may be dealing with the technological trust challenge we have mentioned in this paper, especially at the individual level (Trenerry et al. 2021). As digital implementation is an integral part of the holistic digitalization approach (Schallmo et al. 2022), it is crucial to research how its challenges vary across industries as well.

Last, we dealt with multiple issues in this paper, including how value-creation opportunities can be achieved using digital technologies in healthcare. Healthcare providers may find this research useful to understand what kind of value creators are available for them and which fitting challenges they solve. Vice versa, digital entrepreneurs may attempt to solve the mentioned challenges and create value in the process for such a salient industry.

References

Achtenhagen, L., Melin, L., Naldi, L.: Dynamics of business models—strategizing, critical capabilities and activities for sustained value creation. Long Range Plan. **46**(6), 427–442 (2013). https://doi.org/10.1016/j.lrp.2013.04.002

Acquisti, A., Brandimarte, L., Loewenstein, G.: Secrets and likes: the drive for privacy and the difficulty of achieving it in the digital age. J. Consum. Psychol. **30**(4), 736–758 (2020). https://doi.org/10.1002/jcpy.1191

Agarwal, R., Gao, G. (Gordon), DesRoches, C., Jha, A.K.: Research commentary—the digital transformation of healthcare: current status and the road ahead. Inf. Syst. Res. **21**(4), 796–809 (2010). https://doi.org/10.1287/isre.1100.0327

Ahmed, H., Carmody, J. B., Ahmed, H., Carmody, J.B.: On the looming physician shortage and strategic expansion of graduate medical education. Cureus **12**(7) (2020). https://doi.org/10.7759/cureus.9216

AHRQ: Clinical Decision Support. Agency for Healthcare Research and Quality (AHRQ) (2019). https://www.ahrq.gov/cpi/about/otherwebsites/clinical-decision-support/index.html

Aiken, L.H., Sloane, D., Griffiths, P., Rafferty, A.M., Bruyneel, L., McHugh, M., Maier, C.B., Moreno-Casbas, T., Ball, J.E., Ausserhofer, D., Sermeus, W.: Nursing skill mix in European hospitals: cross-sectional study of the association with mortality, patient ratings, and quality of care. BMJ Qual. Saf. **26**(7), 559–568 (2017). https://doi.org/10.1136/bmjqs-2016-005567

Akter, S., Babu, M.M., Hossain, M.A., Hani, U.: Value co-creation on a shared healthcare platform: impact on service innovation, perceived value and patient welfare. J. Bus. Res. **140**, 95–106 (2022). https://doi.org/10.1016/j.jbusres.2021.11.077

Alt, R., Zimmermann, H.-D.: Preface: introduction to special section—business models. Electron. Mark. **11**(1), 3–9 (2001). https://doi.org/10.1080/713765630

Amin-Naseri, M., Chakraborty, P., Sharma, A., Gilbert, S.B., Hong, M.: Evaluating the reliability, coverage, and added value of crowdsourced traffic incident reports from waze. Transp. Res. Rec. **2672**(43), 34–43 (2018). https://doi.org/10.1177/0361198118790619

Amit, R., Zott, C.: Creating value through business model innovation. MIT Sloan Manag. Rev. (2012). https://sloanreview.mit.edu/article/creating-value-through-business-model-innovation/

Amit, R., Zott, C.: Business Model Innovation Strategy: Transformational Concepts and Tools for Entrepreneurial Leaders. Wiley (2020)

Anthony, S.D., Trotter, A., Schwartz, E.I.: The top 20 business transformations of the last decade. Harv. Bus. Rev. (2019). https://hbr.org/2019/09/the-top-20-business-transformations-of-the-last-decade

Anwar, M.: Business model innovation and smes performance—does competitive advantage mediate? Int. J. Innov. Manag. **22**(07), 1850057 (2018). https://doi.org/10.1142/S1363919618500573

Aronson, J.: A pragmatic view of thematic analysis. Qual. Report **2**(1), 1–3 (1995). https://doi.org/10.46743/2160-3715/1995.2069

Aspara, J., Grant, D.B., Holmlund, M.: Consumer involvement in supply networks: a cubic typology of C2B2C and C2B2B business models. Ind. Mark. Manag. **93**, 356–369 (2021). https://doi.org/10.1016/j.indmarman.2020.09.004

Autio, E., Nambisan, S., Thomas, L.D.W., Wright, M.: Digital affordances, spatial affordances, and the genesis of entrepreneurial ecosystems. Strateg. Entrep. J. **12**(1), 72–95 (2018). https://doi.org/10.1002/sej.1266

Azarm-Daigle, M., Kuziemsky, C., Peyton, L.: A review of cross organizational healthcare data sharing. Procedia Comput. Sci. **63**, 425–432 (2015). https://doi.org/10.1016/j.procs.2015.08.363

Babenko, V., Zomchak, L., Nehrey, M., Salem, A.-B. M., Nakisko, O.: Agritech startup ecosystem in Ukraine: ideas and realization. In: Magdi, D.A., Helmy, Y.K., Mamdouh, M., Joshi, A. (eds.) Digital Transformation Technology, pp. 311–322. Springer (2022). https://doi.org/10.1007/978-981-16-2275-5_19

Baden-Fuller, C., Haefliger, S.: Business models and technological innovation. Long Range Plan. **46**(6), 419–426 (2013). https://doi.org/10.1016/j.lrp.2013.08.023

Baker, H., Ratnarajan, G., Harper, R.A., Edgar, D.F., Lawrenson, J.G.: Effectiveness of UK optometric enhanced eye care services: a realist review of the literature. Ophthalmic Physiol. Opt. **36**(5), 545–557 (2016). https://doi.org/10.1111/opo.12312

Banerjee, M., Capozzoli, M., McSweeney, L., Sinha, D.: Beyond kappa: a review of interrater agreement measures. Can. J. Stat. **27**(1), 3–23 (1999). https://doi.org/10.2307/3315487

Barreto, I.: Dynamic capabilities: a review of past research and an agenda for the future. J. Manag. **36**(1), 256–280 (2010). https://doi.org/10.1177/0149206309350776

Baudier, P., Kondrateva, G., Ammi, C., Chang, V., Schiavone, F.: Patients' perceptions of teleconsultation during COVID-19: a cross-national study. Technol. Forecast. Soc. Chang. **163**, 120510 (2021). https://doi.org/10.1016/j.techfore.2020.120510

BDO United States: 2021 healthcare digital transformation survey. BDO (2021). https://www.bdo.com/insights/industries/healthcare/2021-healthcare-digital-transformation-survey

Beaulieu, M., Lehoux, P.: The emergence of health technology firms through their sensegiving activities and competitive actions. Int. J. Innov. Manag. **21**(06), 1750043 (2017). https://doi.org/10.1142/S1363919617500438

Berman, S.J.: Digital transformation: opportunities to create new business models. Strateg. & Leadersh. **40**(2), 16–24 (2012). https://doi.org/10.1108/10878571211209314

Berman, T., Schallmo, D.: Digital transformation of business models in the Israeli agtech landscape. In: ISPIM Conference Proceedings, pp. 1–18 (2021). https://www.proquest.com/docview/2561108040/abstract/9353613864574280PQ/1

Berman, T., Schallmo, D., Williams, C.A.: Business model transformation through artificial intelligence in the Israeli InsurTech. In: ISPIM Conference Proceedings, pp. 1–42 (2021). https://www.proquest.com/docview/2617200297/abstract/F0AD372048994B1DPQ/1

Bharadwaj, A.S.: A resource-based perspective on information technology capability and firm performance: an empirical investigation. MIS Q. **24**(1), 169–196 (2000). https://doi.org/10.2307/3250983

Bharadwaj, A., El Sawy, O.A., Pavlou, P.A., Venkatraman, N.: Digital business strategy: toward a next generation of insights. MIS Q. **37**(2), 471–482 (2013)

Blumenthal, D., Tavenner, M.: The "meaningful use" regulation for electronic health records. N. Engl. J. Med. **363**(6), 501–504 (2010). https://doi.org/10.1056/NEJMp1006114

Bogner, A., Menz, W.: The theory-generating expert interview: epistemological interest, forms of knowledge, interaction. In: Bogner, A., Littig, B., Menz, W. (eds.) Interviewing Experts, pp. 43–80. Palgrave Macmillan UK (2009). https://doi.org/10.1057/9780230244276_3

Bonnet, D., Westerman, G.: The new elements of digital transformation. MIT Sloan Manag. Rev. **62**(2) (2020). https://sloanreview.mit.edu/article/the-new-elements-of-digital-transformation/

Braun, V., Clarke, V.: Using thematic analysis in psychology. Qual. Res. Psychol. **3**(2), 77–101 (2006). https://doi.org/10.1191/1478088706qp063oa

Brinkmann, S., Kvale, S.: InterViews: Learning the Craft of Qualitative Research Interviewing. SAGE Publications (2015). https://uk.sagepub.com/en-gb/eur/interviews/book239402

Brock, J.K.-U., von Wangenheim, F.: Demystifying AI: what digital transformation leaders can teach you about realistic artificial intelligence. Calif. Manag. Rev. **61**(4), 110–134 (2019). https://doi.org/10.1177/1536504219865226

Calantone, R.J., Vickery, S.K.: Introduction to the special topic forum: using archival and secondary data sources in supply chain management research. J. Supply Chain Manag. **46**(4), 3–12 (2010)

Campbell, D.: Private healthcare boom adds to fears of two-tier system in UK, 2 March 2022. The Guardian (2022). https://www.theguardian.com/society/2022/mar/02/private-healthcare-boom-two-tier-system-uk

Caputo, A., Pizzi, S., Pellegrini, M.M., Dabić, M.: Digitalization and business models: where are we going? A science map of the field. J. Bus. Res. **123**, 489–501 (2021). https://doi.org/10.1016/j.jbusres.2020.09.053

Casadesus-Masanell, R., Ricart, J.E.: From strategy to business models and onto tactics. Long Range Plan. **43**(2), 195–215 (2010). https://doi.org/10.1016/j.lrp.2010.01.004

Casadesus-Masanell, R., Zhu, F.: Business model innovation and competitive imitation: the case of sponsor-based business models. Strateg. Manag. J. **34**(4), 464–482 (2013). https://doi.org/10.1002/smj.2022

Chandwani, R., De, R., Dwivedi, Y.K.: Telemedicine for low resource settings: exploring the generative mechanisms. Technol. Forecast. Soc. Chang. **127**, 177–187 (2018). https://doi.org/10.1016/j.techfore.2017.06.014

Chanias, S., Myers, M.D., Hess, T.: Digital transformation strategy making in pre-digital organizations: the case of a financial services provider. J. Strateg. Inf. Syst. **28**(1), 17–33 (2019). https://doi.org/10.1016/j.jsis.2018.11.003

Chaudhuri, A., Subramanian, N., Dora, M.: Circular economy and digital capabilities of SMEs for providing value to customers: combined resource-based view and ambidexterity perspective. J. Bus. Res. **142**, 32–44 (2022). https://doi.org/10.1016/j.jbusres.2021.12.039

Chesbrough, H.: Business model innovation: it's not just about technology anymore. Strateg. & Leadersh. **35**(6), 12–17 (2007). https://doi.org/10.1108/10878570710833714

CMS: Electronic Health Records|CMS. CMS.Gov (2021). https://www.cms.gov/medicare/e-health/ehealthrecords

Cowie, M.R., Blomster, J.I., Curtis, L.H., Duclaux, S., Ford, I., Fritz, F., Goldman, S., Janmohamed, S., Kreuzer, J., Leenay, M., Michel, A., Ong, S., Pell, J.P., Southworth, M.R., Stough, W.G., Thoenes, M., Zannad, F., Zalewski, A.: Electronic health records to facilitate clinical research. Clin. Res. Cardiol. **106**(1), 1–9 (2017). https://doi.org/10.1007/s00392-016-1025-6

Cox, J.C., Sadiraj, V., Schnier, K.E., Sweeney, J.F.: Incentivizing cost-effective reductions in hospital readmission rates. J. Econ. Behav. Organ. **131**, 24–35 (2016). https://doi.org/10.1016/j.jebo.2015.03.014

Cozzolino, A., Corbo, L., Aversa, P.: Digital platform-based ecosystems: the evolution of collaboration and competition between incumbent producers and entrant platforms. J. Bus. Res. **126**, 385–400 (2021). https://doi.org/10.1016/j.jbusres.2020.12.058

da Silva Serapião, G., Guédria, W., Panetto, H.: Interoperability assessment: a systematic literature review. Comput. Ind. **106**, 111–132 (2019). https://doi.org/10.1016/j.compind.2019.01.002

da Silva, M.V.G., Rocha, C.F., Pagnoncelli, V., de Lima, L.A.A.: Ecosystem of innovation in industry 4.0: the case of collaborations in startups in Brazil. Int. J. Innov. Educ. Res. **6**(12), Article 12 (2018). https://doi.org/10.31686/ijier.vol6.iss12.1248

Dąbrowska, J., Almpanopoulou, A., Brem, A., Chesbrough, H., Cucino, V., Di Minin, A., Giones, F., Hakala, H., Marullo, C., Mention, A.-L., Mortara, L., Nørskov, S., Nylund, P.A., Oddo, C.M., Radziwon, A., Ritala, P.: Digital transformation, for better or worse: a critical multi-level research agenda. R&D Manag. **52**(5), 930–954 (2022). https://doi.org/10.1111/radm.12531

Dahl, A.J., Milne, G.R., Peltier, J.W.: Digital health information seeking in an omni-channel environment: a shared decision-making and service-dominant logic perspective. J. Bus. Res. **125**, 840–850 (2021). https://doi.org/10.1016/j.jbusres.2019.02.025

Dahlgaard, J.J., Dahlgaard, S.M.P.: Integrating business excellence and innovation management: developing a culture for innovation, creativity and learning. Total Qual. Manag. **10**(4–5), 465–472 (1999). https://doi.org/10.1080/0954412997415

Dall, T., Reynolds, R., Chakrabarti, R., Chylak, D., Jones, K., Iacobucci, W.: The complexities of physician supply and demand: projections from 2019 to 2034 (2021). https://www.aamc.org/data-reports/workforce/data/complexities-physician-supply-and-demand-projections-2019-2034

DalleMule, L., Davenport, T.H.: What's your data strategy? Harv. Bus. Rev. **95**(3), 112–121 (2017)

Danaher, T.S., Gallan, A.S.: Service research in health care: positively impacting lives. J. Serv. Res. **19**(4), 433–437 (2016). https://doi.org/10.1177/1094670516666346

Davey, M.: Emergency overload: how covid exposed Australia's straining hospital system, 14 May 2022. The Guardian (2022). https://www.theguardian.com/australia-news/2022/may/15/emergency-overload-how-covid-exposed-australias-straining-hospital-system

Deloitte Centre for Health Solutions: Connected health|Deloitte UK. Deloitte Centre for Health Solutions (2015). https://www2.deloitte.com/uk/en/pages/life-sciences-and-healthcare/articles/connected-health.html

Deloitte Centre for Health Solutions: Is the hospital of the future here today? Deloitte Center for Health Solutions (2020a). https://www2.deloitte.com/za/en/pages/life-sciences-and-healthcare/articles/is-the-hospital-of-the-future-here-today.html

Deloitte Centre for Health Solutions: Shaping the future of European healthcare. Deloitte Centre for Health Solutions (2020b). https://www2.deloitte.com/uk/en/pages/life-sciences-and-healthcare/articles/european-digital-health.html

Demil, B., Lecocq, X.: Business model evolution: in search of dynamic consistency. Long Range Plan. **43**(2), 227–246 (2010). https://doi.org/10.1016/j.lrp.2010.02.004

Demil, B., Lecocq, X., Ricart, J.E., Zott, C.: Introduction to the SEJ Special Issue on Business Models: business models within the domain of strategic entrepreneurship. Strateg. Entrepr. J. **9**(1), 1–11 (2015). https://doi.org/10.1002/sej.1194

Dewett, T., Jones, G.R.: The role of information technology in the organization: a review, model, and assessment. J. Manag. **27**(3), 313–346 (2001). https://doi.org/10.1177/014920630102700306

Dickman, S.L., Himmelstein, D.U., Woolhandler, S.: Inequality and the health-care system in the USA. The Lancet **389**(10077), 1431–1441 (2017). https://doi.org/10.1016/S0140-6736(17)30398-7

Dillon, A., Morris, M.G.: User acceptance of information technology: theories and models. Annu. Rev. Inf. Sci. Technol.: (ARIST) **31**, 3–32 (1996)

Doz, Y.L., Kosonen, M.: Embedding strategic agility: a leadership agenda for accelerating business model renewal. Long Range Plan. **43**(2), 370–382 (2010). https://doi.org/10.1016/j.lrp.2009.07.006

Drago, C., Gatto, A., Ruggeri, M.: Telemedicine as technoinnovation to tackle COVID-19: a bibliometric analysis. Technovation **120**, 102417 (2023). https://doi.org/10.1016/j.technovation.2021.102417

Dremel, C., Herterich, M., Wulf, J., Waizmann, J.-C., Brenner, W.: How AUDI AG established big data analytics in its digital transformation. MIS Q. Exec. **16**(2) (2017). https://aisel.aisnet.org/misqe/vol16/iss2/3

Drenik, G.: The future of telehealth in a post-pandemic world. Forbes (2022). https://www.forbes.com/sites/garydrenik/2022/06/02/the-future-of-telehealth-in-a-post-pandemic-world/

Du, W. (Derek), Pan, S.L., Zhou, N., Ouyang, T.: From a marketplace of electronics to a digital entrepreneurial ecosystem (DEE): the emergence of a meta-organization in Zhongguancun, China. Inf. Syst. J. **28**(6), 1158–1175 (2018). https://doi.org/10.1111/isj.12176

Egfjord, K.F.-H., Sund, K.J.: Do you see what I see? How differing perceptions of the environment can hinder radical business model innovation. Technol. Forecast. Soc. Chang. **150**, 119787 (2020). https://doi.org/10.1016/j.techfore.2019.119787

Eisenhardt, K.M., Graebner, M.E.: Theory building from cases: opportunities and challenges. Acad. Manag. J. **50**(1), 25–32 (2007). https://doi.org/10.5465/amj.2007.24160888

Fitzgerald, M., Kruschwitz, N., Bonnet, D., Welch, M.: Embracing digital technology. MIT Sloan Manag. Rev. **55**(2) (2013). https://sloanreview.mit.edu/projects/embracing-digital-technology/

Foss, N.J., Saebi, T.: Fifteen years of research on business model innovation: how far have we come, and where should we go? J. Manag. **43**(1), 200–227 (2017). https://doi.org/10.1177/0149206316675927

Fox, G.: "To protect my health or to protect my health privacy?" A mixed-methods investigation of the privacy paradox. J. Am. Soc. Inf. Sci. **71**(9), 1015–1029 (2020). https://doi.org/10.1002/asi.24369

Garbuio, M., Lin, N.: Artificial intelligence as a growth engine for health care startups: emerging business models. Calif. Manag. Rev. **61**(2), 59–83 (2019). https://doi.org/10.1177/0008125618811931

Garcia-Perez, A., Cegarra-Navarro, J.G., Sallos, M.P., Martinez-Caro, E., Chinnaswamy, A.: Resilience in healthcare systems: cyber security and digital transformation. Technovation **121**, 102583 (2023). https://doi.org/10.1016/j.technovation.2022.102583

Gehde, K.M., Rausch, F., Leker, J.: Business model configurations in digital healthcare—a german case study about digital transformation. Int. J. Innov. Manag. **26**(03), 2240018 (2022). https://doi.org/10.1142/S1363919622400187

Giansanti, D.: Assistive technologies, robotics, automatic machines: perspectives of integration in the health domain. Healthcare **10**(6), Article 6 (2022). https://doi.org/10.3390/healthcare10061080

Giesen, E., Riddleberger, E., Christner, R., Bell, R.: When and how to innovate your business model. Strateg. & Leadersh. **38**(4), 17–26 (2010). https://doi.org/10.1108/10878571011059700

Gioia, D.A., Corley, K.G., Hamilton, A.L.: Seeking qualitative rigor in inductive research: notes on the gioia methodology. Organ. Res. Methods **16**(1), 15–31 (2013). https://doi.org/10.1177/1094428112452151

Go Jefferies, J., Bishop, S., Hibbert, S.: Customer boundary work to navigate institutional arrangements around service interactions: exploring the case of telehealth. J. Bus. Res. **105**, 420–433 (2019). https://doi.org/10.1016/j.jbusres.2019.03.052

Goldberg, U.: What's Next For The Startup Nation? A Blueprint For Sustainable Innovation. AuthorHouse (2012)

Grol, R., Wensing, M.: Implementation of change in healthcare. In: Improving Patient Care, pp. 1–20. John Wiley & Sons, Ltd. (2020). https://doi.org/10.1002/9781119488620.ch1

Hacklin, F., Björkdahl, J., Wallin, M.W.: Strategies for business model innovation: how firms reel in migrating value. Long Range Plan. **51**(1), 82–110 (2018). https://doi.org/10.1016/j.lrp.2017.06.009

Haggerty, E.: Healthcare and digital transformation. Netw. Secur. **2017**(8), 7–11 (2017). https://doi.org/10.1016/S1353-4858(17)30081-8

Hammer, M.: Deep change: how operational innovation can transform your company. Harv. Bus. Rev. **82**(4), 84–93 (2004)

Hanelt, A., Bohnsack, R., Marz, D., Antunes Marante, C.: A systematic review of the literature on digital transformation: insights and implications for strategy and organizational change. J. Manag. Stud. **58**(5), 1159–1197 (2021). https://doi.org/10.1111/joms.12639

Harrell, M.C., Bradley, M.A.: Data collection methods. Semi-structured interviews and focus groups. The Defense Technical Information Center (DTIC) (2009). https://apps.dtic.mil/sti/citations/ADA512853

Hashai, N.: Within-industry diversification and firm performance—an S-shaped hypothesis. Strateg. Manag. J. **36**(9), 1378–1400 (2015). https://doi.org/10.1002/smj.2290

Heath, S.: Long appointment wait time a detriment to high patient satisfaction, 23 March 2018. PatientEngagementHIT (2018). https://patientengagementhit.com/news/long-appointment-wait-time-a-detriment-to-high-patient-satisfaction

Heath, S.: Top challenges impacting patient access to healthcare, 22 February 2022. PatientEngagementHIT (2022). https://patientengagementhit.com/news/top-challenges-impacting-patient-access-to-healthcare

Helfert, M.: Challenges of business processes management in healthcare: experience in the Irish healthcare sector. Bus. Process. Manag. J. **15**(6), 937–952 (2009). https://doi.org/10.1108/14637150911003793

Hess, T., Matt, C., Benlian, A., Wiesböck, F.: Options for Formulating a Digital Transformation Strategy. MIS Q. Exec. **15/2**(131), Article 131 (2016)

Hu, P.J., Chau, P.Y.K., Sheng, O.R.L., Tam, K.Y.: Examining the technology acceptance model using physician acceptance of telemedicine technology. J. Manag. Inf. Syst. **16**(2), 91–112 (1999). https://doi.org/10.1080/07421222.1999.11518247

Hughes, J.: Learning across boundaries: educator and startup involvement in the educational technology innovation ecosystem. Contemp. Issues Technol. Teach. Educ. **19**(1), 62–96 (2019)

Hulsen, T.: Sharing is caring—data sharing initiatives in healthcare. Int. J. Environ. Res. Public Health **17**(9), Article 9 (2020). https://doi.org/10.3390/ijerph17093046

i24NEWS: Israeli scientists unveil "first" 3D print of heart with human tissue, vessels, 15 April 2019. I24news (2019). https://www.i24news.tv/en/news/israel/technology-science/1555327041-israeli-scientists-unveil-first-3d-print-of-heart-with-human-tissue-vessels

i24NEWS: Israel: World's largest emergency room opens in Tel Aviv, 3 August 2022. I24news (2022). https://www.i24news.tv/en/news/israel/technology-science/1659541996-israel-world-s-largest-emergency-room-opens-in-tel-aviv

Ivančić, L., Vukšić, V.B., Spremić, M.: Mastering the digital transformation process: business practices and lessons learned. Technol. Innov. Manag. Rev. **9**(2), 36–50 (2019)

Jain, P., Gyanchandani, M., Khare, N.: Big data privacy: a technological perspective and review. J. Big Data **3**(1), 25 (2016). https://doi.org/10.1186/s40537-016-0059-y

Jaleel, A., Mahmood, T., Hassan, M.A., Bano, G., Khurshid, S.K.: Towards medical data interoperability through collaboration of healthcare devices. IEEE Access **8**, 132302–132319 (2020). https://doi.org/10.1109/ACCESS.2020.3009783

Javaid, M., Haleem, A., Vaish, A., Vaishya, R., Iyengar, K.P.: Robotics applications in COVID-19: a review. J. Ind. Integr. and Manag. **05**(04), 441–451 (2020). https://doi.org/10.1142/S2424862220300033

Kaplan, R.S., Porter, M.E.: The big idea: how to solve the cost crisis in health care. Harv. Bus. Rev. **89**, 46–52 (2011)

Kitsios, F., Kamariotou, M.: Artificial intelligence and business strategy towards digital transformation: a research agenda. Sustainability **13**(4), Article 4 (2021). https://doi.org/10.3390/su13042025

Kokshagina, D.O.: Managing shifts to value-based healthcare and value digitalization as a multilevel dynamic capability development process. Technol. Forecast. Soc. Chang. **172**, 121072 (2021). https://doi.org/10.1016/j.techfore.2021.121072

Kopalle, P.K., Kumar, V., Subramaniam, M.: How legacy firms can embrace the digital ecosystem via digital customer orientation. J. Acad. Mark. Sci. **48**(1), 114–131 (2020). https://doi.org/10.1007/s11747-019-00694-2

Korstjens, I., Moser, A.: Series: practical guidance to qualitative research. Part 2: context, research questions and designs. Eur. J. Gen. Pract. **23**(1), 274–279 (2017). https://doi.org/10.1080/13814788.2017.1375090

Kraus, S., Durst, S., Ferreira, J.J., Veiga, P., Kailer, N., Weinmann, A.: Digital transformation in business and management research: an overview of the current status quo. Int. J. Inf. Manag. **63**, 102466 (2022). https://doi.org/10.1016/j.ijinfomgt.2021.102466

Kraus, S., Schiavone, F., Pluzhnikova, A., Invernizzi, A.C.: Digital transformation in healthcare: analyzing the current state-of-research. J. Bus. Res. **123**, 557–567 (2021). https://doi.org/10.1016/j.jbusres.2020.10.030

Kruse, C.S., Smith, B., Vanderlinden, H., Nealand, A.: Security techniques for the electronic health records. J. Med. Syst. **41**(8), 127 (2017). https://doi.org/10.1007/s10916-017-0778-4

Kulkov, I.: Next-generation business models for artificial intelligence start-ups in the healthcare industry. Int. J. Entrep. Behav. & Res. ahead-of-print(ahead-of-print) (2021). https://doi.org/10.1108/IJEBR-04-2021-0304

Kulkov, I., Tsvetkova, A., Ivanova-Gongne, M.: Identifying institutional barriers when implementing new technologies in the healthcare industry. Eur. J. Innov. Manag. ahead-of-print(ahead-of-print) (2021). https://doi.org/10.1108/EJIM-02-2021-0093

Labuschagne, A.: Qualitative research—airy fairy or fundamental? Qual. Report **8**(1), 100–103 (2003). https://doi.org/10.46743/2160-3715/2003.1901

Lal, A.: Council post: healthcare digital transformation: connected care is mobile and omnichannel. Forbes (2022). https://www.forbes.com/sites/forbesbusinesscouncil/2022/03/22/healthcare-digital-transformation-connected-care-is-mobile-and-omnichannel/

Lapointe, L., Rivard, S.: A triple take on information system implementation. Organ. Sci. **18**(1), 89–107 (2007). https://doi.org/10.1287/orsc.1060.0225

Laurenza, E., Quintano, M., Schiavone, F., Vrontis, D.: The effect of digital technologies adoption in healthcare industry: a case based analysis. Bus. Process. Manag. J. **24**(5), 1124–1144 (2018). https://doi.org/10.1108/BPMJ-04-2017-0084

Lee, S.M., Lee, D.: Opportunities and challenges for contactless healthcare services in the post-COVID-19 Era. Technol. Forecast. Soc. Chang. **167**, 120712 (2021). https://doi.org/10.1016/j.techfore.2021.120712

Lentz, R.: What if you only paid doctors when you were healthy? June 13 2015 (2015) https://www.seagateworld.com/2015/06/western-medicine-get-paid-when-you-get-sick/

Leone, D., Schiavone, F., Appio, F.P., Chiao, B.: How does artificial intelligence enable and enhance value co-creation in industrial markets? An exploratory case study in the healthcare ecosystem. J. Bus. Res. **129**, 849–859 (2021). https://doi.org/10.1016/j.jbusres.2020.11.008

Levallet, N., Chan, Y.: Role of digital capabilities in unleashing the power of managerial improvisation. MIS Q. Exec. **17**(1) (2018). https://aisel.aisnet.org/misqe/vol17/iss1/3

Li, X., Huang, X., Li, C., Yu, R., Shu, L.: EdgeCare: leveraging edge computing for collaborative data management in mobile healthcare systems. IEEE Access **7**, 22011–22025 (2019). https://doi.org/10.1109/ACCESS.2019.2898265

Lingens, B., Miehé, L., Gassmann, O.: The ecosystem blueprint: how firms shape the design of an ecosystem according to the surrounding conditions. Long Range Plan. **54**(2), 102043 (2021). https://doi.org/10.1016/j.lrp.2020.102043

Llopis-Albert, C., Rubio, F., Valero, F.: Impact of digital transformation on the automotive industry. Technol. Forecast. Soc. Chang. **162**, 120343 (2021). https://doi.org/10.1016/j.techfore.2020.120343

Loebbecke, C., Picot, A.: Reflections on societal and business model transformation arising from digitization and big data analytics: a research agenda. J. Strateg. Inf. Syst. **24**(3), 149–157 (2015). https://doi.org/10.1016/j.jsis.2015.08.002

Lovis, C., Gamzu, R.: Big Data in Israeli healthcare: hopes and challenges report of an international workshop. Isr. J. Health Policy Res. **4**(1), 61 (2015). https://doi.org/10.1186/s13584-015-0057-0

Lyytinen, K., Yoo, Y., Boland, R.J., Jr.: Digital product innovation within four classes of innovation networks. Inf. Syst. J. **26**(1), 47–75 (2016). https://doi.org/10.1111/isj.12093

MacIntyre, C.R., Costantino, V., Kunasekaran, M.P.: Health system capacity in Sydney, Australia in the event of a biological attack with smallpox. PLoS ONE **14**(6), e0217704 (2019). https://doi.org/10.1371/journal.pone.0217704

Magistretti, S., Dell'Era, C., Messeni Petruzzelli, A.: How intelligent is Watson? Enabling digital transformation through artificial intelligence. Bus. Horiz. **62**(6), 819–829 (2019). https://doi.org/10.1016/j.bushor.2019.08.004

Marangunić, N., Granić, A.: Technology acceptance model: a literature review from 1986 to 2013. Univ. Access Inf. Soc. **14**(1), 81–95 (2015). https://doi.org/10.1007/s10209-014-0348-1

Markides, C.: Disruptive innovation: in need of better theory*. J. Prod. Innov. Manag. **23**(1), 19–25 (2006). https://doi.org/10.1111/j.1540-5885.2005.00177.x

Marques, I.C.P., Ferreira, J.J.M.: Digital transformation in the area of health: systematic review of 45 years of evolution. Heal. Technol. **10**(3), 575–586 (2020). https://doi.org/10.1007/s12553-019-00402-8

Marra, A., Antonelli, P., Dell'Anna, L., Pozzi, C.: A network analysis using metadata to investigate innovation in clean-tech—implications for energy policy. Energy Policy **86**, 17–26 (2015). https://doi.org/10.1016/j.enpol.2015.06.025

Massa, L., Tucci, C.L., Afuah, A.: A critical assessment of business model research. Acad. Manag. Ann. **11**(1), 73–104 (2017). https://doi.org/10.5465/annals.2014.0072

Massaro, M.: Digital transformation in the healthcare sector through blockchain technology. Insights from academic research and business developments. Technovation **120**, 102386 (2023). https://doi.org/10.1016/j.technovation.2021.102386

Mathews, S.C., McShea, M.J., Hanley, C.L., Ravitz, A., Labrique, A.B., Cohen, A.B.: Digital health: a path to validation. NPJ Digit. Med. **2**(1), Article 1 (2019). https://doi.org/10.1038/s41746-019-0111-3

Matt, C., Hess, T., Benlian, A.: Digital transformation strategies. Bus. Inf. Syst. Eng. **57**(5), 339–343 (2015). https://doi.org/10.1007/s12599-015-0401-5

McKeon, J.: How Jefferson health is tackling the cybersecurity workforce shortage. HealthITSecurity, 25 March 2022 (2022a). https://healthitsecurity.com/features/how-jefferson-health-is-tackling-the-cybersecurity-workforce-shortage

McKeon, J.: What is holding healthcare back from digital transformation? HealthITSecurity, 27 April 2022 (2022b). https://healthitsecurity.com/features/what-is-holding-healthcare-back-from-digital-transformation

Mende, M.: The innovation imperative in healthcare: an interview and commentary. AMS Rev. **9**(1), 121–131 (2019). https://doi.org/10.1007/s13162-019-00140-0

Mills, D.: Doctor appointments: longer wait times, 12 April 2017. Healthline (2017). https://www.healthline.com/health-news/why-you-have-to-wait-longer-to-get-a-doctors-appointment

Mishra, M.: End of COVID pandemic is "in sight"—WHO chief, 14 September 2022. Reuters (2022). https://www.reuters.com/business/healthcare-pharmaceuticals/who-chief-says-end-sight-covid-19-pandemic-2022-09-14/

Mitchell, G.: NHS facing 38,000 nurse shortage even if government hits recruitment target, 20 July 2022. Nursing Times (2022). https://www.nursingtimes.net/news/workforce/nhs-facing-38000-nurse-shortage-even-if-government-hits-recruitment-target-20-07-2022/

Moir, M., Barua, B.: Comparing performance of universal health care countries, 2022. Fraser Institute (2022). https://bit.ly/3PWqEZ5

Moro Visconti, R.: The Valuation of E-Health and Telemedicine Startups (SSRN Scholarly Paper No. 4132488) (2021). https://doi.org/10.2139/ssrn.4132488

Morris, M., Schindehutte, M., Allen, J.: The entrepreneur's business model: toward a unified perspective. J. Bus. Res. **58**(6), 726–735 (2005). https://doi.org/10.1016/j.jbusres.2003.11.001

Mumtaz, S., Alsohaily, A., Pang, Z., Rayes, A., Tsang, K.F., Rodriguez, J.: Massive internet of things for industrial applications: addressing wireless IIoT connectivity challenges and ecosystem fragmentation. IEEE Ind. Electron. Mag. **11**(1), 28–33 (2017). https://doi.org/10.1109/MIE.2016.2618724

Nambisan, S., Lyytinen, K., Majchrzak, A., Song, M.: Digital innovation management: reinventing innovation management research in a digital world. MIS Q. **41**(1), 223–238 (2017)

Nambisan, S., Wright, M., Feldman, M.: The digital transformation of innovation and entrepreneurship: progress, challenges and key themes. Res. Policy **48**(8), 103773 (2019). https://doi.org/10.1016/j.respol.2019.03.018

NHS: Protecting patient data. NHS Digital (2022). https://digital.nhs.uk/services/national-data-opt-out/understanding-the-national-data-opt-out/protecting-patient-data

Niemelä, R., Pikkarainen, M., Ervasti, M., Reponen, J.: The change of pediatric surgery practice due to the emergence of connected health technologies. Technol. Forecast. Soc. Chang. **146**, 352–365 (2019). https://doi.org/10.1016/j.techfore.2019.06.001

Oderanti, F.O., Li, F., Cubric, M., Shi, X.: Business models for sustainable commercialisation of digital healthcare (eHealth) innovations for an increasingly ageing population. Technol. Forecast. Soc. Chang. **171**, 120969 (2021). https://doi.org/10.1016/j.techfore.2021.120969

Ojaghi, H., Mohammadi, M., Yazdani, H.R.: A synthesized framework for the formation of startups' innovation ecosystem: a systematic literature review. J. Sci. Technol. Policy Manag. **10**(5), 1063–1097 (2019). https://doi.org/10.1108/JSTPM-07-2018-0071

Orbach, M., Ravet, H.: Top Israeli Startups 2020: Most Promising MedTech Companies, 28 April 2020. CTECH (2020). www.calcalistech.com, https://www.calcalistech.com/ctech/articles/0,7340,L-3812513,00.html

Osterwalder, A., Pigneur, Y., Bernarda, G., Smith, A.: Value Proposition Design: How to Create Products and Services Customers Want. Wiley (2015)

Pai, F.-Y., Huang, K.-I.: Applying the technology acceptance model to the introduction of healthcare information systems. Technol. Forecast. Soc. Chang. **78**(4), 650–660 (2011). https://doi.org/10.1016/j.techfore.2010.11.007

Palmié, M., Boehm, J., Friedrich, J., Parida, V., Wincent, J., Kahlert, J., Gassmann, O., Sjödin, D.: Startups versus incumbents in 'green' industry transformations: a comparative study of business model archetypes in the electrical power sector. Ind. Mark. Manag. **96**, 35–49 (2021). https://doi.org/10.1016/j.indmarman.2021.04.003

Palmié, M., Wincent, J., Parida, V., Caglar, U.: The evolution of the financial technology ecosystem: an introduction and agenda for future research on disruptive innovations in ecosystems. Technol. Forecast. Soc. Chang. **151**, 119779 (2020). https://doi.org/10.1016/j.techfore.2019.119779

Pecoraro, F., Luzi, D., Clemente, F.: The efficiency in the ordinary hospital bed management: a comparative analysis in four European countries before the COVID-19 outbreak. PLoS ONE **16**(3), e0248867 (2021). https://doi.org/10.1371/journal.pone.0248867

Peters, C., Blohm, I., Leimeister, J.M.: Anatomy of successful business models for complex services: insights from the telemedicine field. J. Manag. Inf. Syst. **32**(3), 75–104 (2015). https://doi.org/10.1080/07421222.2015.1095034

Petkus, H., Hoogewerf, J., Wyatt, J.C.: What do senior physicians think about AI and clinical decision support systems: quantitative and qualitative analysis of data from specialty societies. Clin. Med. **20**(3), 324–328 (2020). https://doi.org/10.7861/clinmed.2019-0317

Philips: Seven key success factors for digital transformation in healthcare. Philips (2021). https://www.philips.com/a-w/about/news/archive/features/2022/20220413-seven-key-success-factors-for-digital-transformation-in-healthcare.html

Pine, K.H.: The qualculative dimension of healthcare data interoperability. Health Inf. J. **25**(3), 536–548 (2019). https://doi.org/10.1177/1460458219833095

Plekhanov, D., Franke, H., Netland, T.H.: Digital transformation: a review and research agenda. Eur. Manag. J. (2022). https://doi.org/10.1016/j.emj.2022.09.007

Porter, M.E., Lee, T.H.: The strategy that will fix health care. Harv. Bus. Rev. **91**(10), 50–70 (2013)

Rachinger, M., Rauter, R., Müller, C., Vorraber, W., Schirgi, E.: Digitalization and its influence on business model innovation. J. Manuf. Technol. Manag. **30**(8), 1143–1160 (2018). https://doi.org/10.1108/JMTM-01-2018-0020

Randhawa, K., West, J., Skellern, K., Josserand, E.: Evolving a value chain to an open innovation ecosystem: cognitive engagement of stakeholders in customizing medical implants. Calif. Manag. Rev. **63**(2), 101–134 (2021). https://doi.org/10.1177/0008125620974435

Remane, G., Nickerson, R., Hanelt, A., Tesch, J., Kolbe, L.: A taxonomy of carsharing business models. In: ICIS 2016 Proceedings, 11 December 2016 (2016). https://aisel.aisnet.org/icis2016/Crowdsourcing/Presentations/18

Reynaud, C., Miccoli, S.: Depopulation and the aging population: the relationship in Italian municipalities. Sustainability **10**(4), Article 4 (2018). https://doi.org/10.3390/su10041004

Riek, L.D.: Healthcare robotics. Commun. ACM **60**(11), 68–78 (2017). https://doi.org/10.1145/3127874

Ritter, T., Lettl, C.: The wider implications of business-model research. Long Range Plan. **51**(1), 1–8 (2018). https://doi.org/10.1016/j.lrp.2017.07.005

Ritter, T., Pedersen, C.L.: Digitization capability and the digitalization of business models in business-to-business firms: past, present, and future. Ind. Mark. Manag. **86**, 180–190 (2020). https://doi.org/10.1016/j.indmarman.2019.11.019

Rizwan, P., Babu, M.R., Balamurugan, B., Suresh, K.: Real-time big data computing for internet of things and cyber physical system aided medical devices for better healthcare. Majan Int. Conf. (MIC) **2018**, 1–8 (2018). https://doi.org/10.1109/MINTC.2018.8363160

Rong, K., Patton, D., Chen, W.: Business models dynamics and business ecosystems in the emerging 3D printing industry. Technol. Forecast. Soc. Chang. **134**, 234–245 (2018). https://doi.org/10.1016/j.techfore.2018.06.015

Rosen, B., Preisman, M., Hunter, J., Maunder, R.: Applying psychotherapeutic principles to bolster resilience among health care workers during the COVID-19 pandemic. Am. J. Psychother. **73**(4), 144–148 (2020). https://doi.org/10.1176/appi.psychotherapy.20200020

Safi, S., Thiessen, T., Schmailzl, K.J.: Acceptance and resistance of new digital technologies in medicine: qualitative study. JMIR Research Protocols **7**(12), e11072 (2018). https://doi.org/10.2196/11072

Sajid, A., Abbas, H.: Data privacy in cloud-assisted healthcare systems: state of the art and future challenges. J. Med. Syst. **40**(6), 155 (2016). https://doi.org/10.1007/s10916-016-0509-2

Schallmo, D., Williams, C. A.: An integrated approach to digital implementation: TOSC-model and DPSEC-circle. In: Schallmo, D., Tidd, J. (eds.) Digitalization: Approaches, Case Studies, and Tools for Strategy, Transformation and Implementation, pp. 371–380. Springer International Publishing (2021). https://doi.org/10.1007/978-3-030-69380-0_21

Schallmo, D., Williams, C.A., Boardman, L.: Digital transformation of business models—best practice, enablers, and roadmap. Int. J. Innov. Manag. **21**(08), 1740014 (2017). https://doi.org/10.1142/S136391961740014X

Schallmo, D., Williams, C.A., Lohse, J.: Digital strategy—integrated approach and generic options. Int. J. Innov. Manag. **23**(08), 1940005 (2019). https://doi.org/10.1142/S136391961940005X

Schallmo, D., Williams, C.A., Tidd, J.: The art of holistic digitalisation: a meta-view on strategy, transformation, implementation, and maturity. Int. J. Innov. Manag. **26**(03), 2240007 (2022). https://doi.org/10.1142/S1363919622400072

Scheffler, R.M., Arnold, D.R.: Projecting shortages and surpluses of doctors and nurses in the OECD: what looms ahead. Health Econ. Policy Law **14**(2), 274–290 (2019). https://doi.org/10.1017/S174413311700055X

Schneckenberg, D., Matzler, K., Spieth, P.: Theorizing business model innovation: an organizing framework of research dimensions and future perspectives. R&D Manag. **52**(3), 593–609 (2022). https://doi.org/10.1111/radm.12506

Schneider, S.: How to approach business model innovation: the role of opportunities in times of (no) exogenous change. R&D Manag. **49**(4), 399–420 (2019). https://doi.org/10.1111/radm.12302

Schneider, S., Spieth, P.: Business model innovation: towards an integrated future research agenda. Int. J. Innov. Manag. **17**(01), 1340001 (2013). https://doi.org/10.1142/S136391961340001X

Schroeder, S.A., Frist, W., National Commission on Physician Payment Reform: Phasing out fee-for-service payment. N. Engl. J. Med. **368**(21), 2029–2032 (2013). https://doi.org/10.1056/NEJMsb1302322

Schulman, H.: Digital transformation in healthcare: benefits vs. challenges (2022). https://www.lightico.com/, https://www.lightico.com/blog/digital-transformation-in-healthcare-benefits-vs-challenges/

Sermontyte-Baniule, R., Pundziene, A., Giménez, V., Narbón-Perpiñá, I.: Role of cultural dimensions and dynamic capabilities in the value-based performance of digital healthcare services. Technol. Forecast. Soc. Chang. **176**, 121490 (2022). https://doi.org/10.1016/j.techfore.2022.121490

Shahnaz, A., Qamar, U., Khalid, A.: Using blockchain for electronic health records. IEEE Access **7**, 147782–147795 (2019). https://doi.org/10.1109/ACCESS.2019.2946373

Shaw, T., Metras, J., Ting, Z.A.L., Courtney, E., Li, S.-T., Ngeow, J.: Impact of appointment waiting time on attendance rates at a clinical cancer genetics service. J. Genet. Couns. **27**(6), 1473–1481 (2018). https://doi.org/10.1007/s10897-018-0259-z

Shen, B., Guo, J., Yang, Y.: MedChain: efficient healthcare data sharing via blockchain. Appl. Sci. **9**(6), Article 6 (2019). https://doi.org/10.3390/app9061207

Shuaib, A., Arian, H., Shuaib, A.: The increasing role of artificial intelligence in health care: will robots replace doctors in the future? Int. J. Gen. Med. **13**, 891–896 (2020). https://doi.org/10.2147/IJGM.S268093

Sjödin, D., Parida, V., Jovanovic, M., Visnjic, I.: Value creation and value capture alignment in business model innovation: a process view on outcome-based business models. J. Prod. Innov. Manag. **37**(2), 158–183 (2020). https://doi.org/10.1111/jpim.12516

Spadoni, R., Nanetti, M., Bondanese, A., Rivaroli, S.: Innovative solutions for the wine sector: the role of startups. Wine Econ. Policy **8**(2), 165–170 (2019). https://doi.org/10.1016/j.wep.2019.08.001

Spieth, P., Röth, T., Clauss, T., Klos, C.: Technological frames in the digital age: theory, measurement instrument, and future research areas. J. Manag. Stud. **58**(7), 1962–1993 (2021). https://doi.org/10.1111/joms.12720

Spieth, P., Schneckenberg, D., Ricart, J.E.: Business model innovation—state of the art and future challenges for the field. R&D Manag. **44**(3), 237–247 (2014). https://doi.org/10.1111/radm.12071

Squires, D., Anderson, C.: U.S. health care from a global perspective, 8 October 2015. The Commonwealth Fund (2015). https://doi.org/10.26099/77tf-5060

Srinivasan, R., Swink, M.: An investigation of visibility and flexibility as complements to supply chain analytics: an organizational information processing theory perspective. Prod. Oper. Manag. **27**(10), 1849–1867 (2018). https://doi.org/10.1111/poms.12746

Start-Up Nation Central: With $1.9B in funding in 2021, Israel's digital health companies smash investment records. Start-Up Nation Central (2022). https://startupnationcentral.org/news/with-1-9b-in-funding-in-2021-israels-digital-health-companies-smash-investment-records/

Steininger, D.: Interview with Frank Petry on "digital entrepreneurship: opportunities, challenges, and impacts." Bus. Inf. Syst. Eng. **64**(1), 111–114 (2022). https://doi.org/10.1007/s12599-021-00738-4

Sun, S., Lu, S.F., Rui, H.: Does telemedicine reduce emergency room congestion? Evidence from New York State. Inf. Syst. Res. **31**(3), 972–986 (2020). https://doi.org/10.1287/isre.2020.0926

Susanto, H., Fang Yie, L., Mohiddin, F., Rahman Setiawan, A.A., Haghi, P.K., Setiana, D.: Revealing social media phenomenon in time of COVID-19 pandemic for boosting start-up businesses through digital ecosystem. Appl. Syst. Innov. **4**(1), Article 1 (2021). https://doi.org/10.3390/asi4010006

Sussan, F., Acs, Z.: The digital entrepreneurial ecosystem. Small Bus. Econ. **49**(1), 55–73 (2017). https://doi.org/10.1007/s11187-017-9867-5

Sutton, R.T., Pincock, D., Baumgart, D. C., Sadowski, D.C., Fedorak, R.N., Kroeker, K.I.: An overview of clinical decision support systems: benefits, risks, and strategies for success. NPJ Digit. Med. **3**(1), Article 1 (2020). https://doi.org/10.1038/s41746-020-0221-y

Tabrizi, B., Lam, E., Girard, K., Irvin, V.: Digital transformation is not about technology. Harv. Bus. Rev. **13**, 1–6 (2019)

Tang, J.H.-C., Hudson, P., Smith, M., Maas, R.: Evidence-based practice guideline: nurse retention for nurse managers. J. Gerontol. Nurs. **45**(11), 11–19 (2019). https://doi.org/10.3928/00989134-20191011-03

Taylor, M.: Why is there a shortage of doctors in the UK? Bull. R. Coll. Surg. Engl. **102**(3), 78–81 (2020). https://doi.org/10.1308/rcsbull.2020.78

Teece, D.J.: Explicating dynamic capabilities: the nature and microfoundations of (sustainable) enterprise performance. Strateg. Manag. J. **28**(13), 1319–1350 (2007). https://doi.org/10.1002/smj.640

Teece, D.J.: Business models, business strategy and innovation. Long Range Plan. **43**(2), 172–194 (2010). https://doi.org/10.1016/j.lrp.2009.07.003

Teece, D.J.: The foundations of enterprise performance: dynamic and ordinary capabilities in an (economic) theory of firms. Acad. Manag. Perspect. **28**(4), 328–352 (2014). https://doi.org/10.5465/amp.2013.0116

Teece, D.J.: Business models and dynamic capabilities. Long Range Plan. **51**(1), 40–49 (2018). https://doi.org/10.1016/j.lrp.2017.06.007

Teece, D.J., Linden, G.: Business models, value capture, and the digital enterprise. J. Organ. Des. **6**(1), 8 (2017). https://doi.org/10.1186/s41469-017-0018-x

Tijan, E., Jović, M., Aksentijević, S., Pucihar, A.: Digital transformation in the maritime transport sector. Technol. Forecast. Soc. Chang. **170**, 120879 (2021). https://doi.org/10.1016/j.techfore.2021.120879

Tob-Ogu, A., Kumar, N., Cullen, J.: ICT adoption in road freight transport in Nigeria—a case study of the petroleum downstream sector. Technol. Forecast. Soc. Chang. **131**, 240–252 (2018). https://doi.org/10.1016/j.techfore.2017.09.021

Tortorella, G.L., Fogliatto, F.S., Saurin, T.A., Tonetto, L.M., McFarlane, D.: Contributions of healthcare 4.0 digital applications to the resilience of healthcare organizations during the COVID-19 outbreak. Technovation **111**, 102379 (2022). https://doi.org/10.1016/j.technovation.2021.102379

Tortorella, G.L., Saurin, T.A., Fogliatto, F.S., Rosa, V.M., Tonetto, L.M., Magrabi, F.: Impacts of Healthcare 4.0 digital technologies on the resilience of hospitals. Technol. Forecast. Soc. Chang. **166**, 120666 (2021). https://doi.org/10.1016/j.techfore.2021.120666

Towart, L.: How coronavirus accelerated Israel's buzzing health-tech startup scene, 4 October 2021. Forbes Israel (2021). https://forbes.co.il/e/israel-health-tech/

Treacy, M., Wiersema, F.: Customer intimacy and other value disciplines. Harv. Bus. Rev. **71**(1), 84–93 (1993)

Trenerry, B., Chng, S., Wang, Y., Suhaila, Z.S., Lim, S.S., Lu, H.Y., Oh, P.H.: Preparing workplaces for digital transformation: an integrative review and framework of multi-level factors. Front. Psychol. **12** (2021). https://www.frontiersin.org/articles/10.3389/fpsyg.2021.620766

Tsou, H.-T., Chen, J.-S.: How does digital technology usage benefit firm performance? Digital transformation strategy and organisational innovation as mediators. Technol. Anal. & Strateg. Manag. 1–14 (2021). https://doi.org/10.1080/09537325.2021.1991575

van Velthoven, M.H., Cordon, C., Challagalla, G.: Digitization of healthcare organizations: the digital health landscape and information theory. Int. J. Med. Inf. **124**, 49–57 (2019). https://doi.org/10.1016/j.ijmedinf.2019.01.007

Veit, D., Clemons, E., Benlian, A., Buxmann, P., Hess, T., Kundisch, D., Leimeister, J.M., Loos, P., Spann, M.: Business models. Bus. Inf. Syst. Eng. **6**(1), 45–53 (2014). https://doi.org/10.1007/s12599-013-0308-y

Ventresca, M.J., Mohr, J.W.: Archival research methods. In: The Blackwell Companion to Organizations, pp. 805–828. John Wiley & Sons, Ltd. (2017). https://doi.org/10.1002/9781405164061.ch35

Verhoef, P.C., Broekhuizen, T., Bart, Y., Bhattacharya, A., Qi Dong, J., Fabian, N., Haenlein, M.: Digital transformation: a multidisciplinary reflection and research agenda. J. Bus. Res. **122**, 889–901 (2021). https://doi.org/10.1016/j.jbusres.2019.09.022

Vesselkov, A., Hämmäinen, H., Töyli, J.: Technology and value network evolution in telehealth. Technol. Forecast. Soc. Chang. **134**, 207–222 (2018). https://doi.org/10.1016/j.techfore.2018.06.011

Vial, G.: Understanding digital transformation: a review and a research agenda. J. Strateg. Inf. Syst. **28**(2), 118–144 (2019). https://doi.org/10.1016/j.jsis.2019.01.003

Vogt, W.P., Gardner, D.C., Haeffele, L.M.: When to Use What Research Design. Guilford Press (2012)

von Briel, F., Recker, J., Davidsson, P.: Not all digital venture ideas are created equal: Implications for venture creation processes. J. Strateg. Inf. Syst. **27**(4), 278–295 (2018). https://doi.org/10.1016/j.jsis.2018.06.002

Walter, Z., Lopez, M.S.: Physician acceptance of information technologies: role of perceived threat to professional autonomy. Decis. Support. Syst. **46**(1), 206–215 (2008). https://doi.org/10.1016/j.dss.2008.06.004

Wang, Q., Li, L.: The effects of population aging, life expectancy, unemployment rate, population density, per capita GDP, urbanization on per capita carbon emissions. Sustain. Prod. Consum. **28**, 760–774 (2021). https://doi.org/10.1016/j.spc.2021.06.029

Wang, X., Wong, Y.D., Chen, T., Yuen, K.F.: Adoption of shopper-facing technologies under social distancing: a conceptualisation and an interplay between task-technology fit and technology trust. Comput. Hum. Behav. **124**, 106900 (2021). https://doi.org/10.1016/j.chb.2021.106900

Warner, K.S.R., Wäger, M.: Building dynamic capabilities for digital transformation: an ongoing process of strategic renewal. Long Range Plan. **52**(3), 326–349 (2019). https://doi.org/10.1016/j.lrp.2018.12.001

Weill, P., Woerner, S.L.: Optimizing your digital business model. MIT Sloan Manag. Rev. **43**(1), 123–131 (2013)

Westerman, G., Bonnet, D.: Revamping your business through digital transformation. MIT Sloan Manag. Rev. **56**(3), 10–13 (2015)

Westerman, G., Bonnet, D., McAfee, A.: The nine elements of digital transformation. MIT Sloan Manag. Rev. **55**(3), 1–6 (2014)

WHO Global Observatory for eHealth: Telemedicine: Opportunities and developments in Member States: report on the second global survey on eHealth. World Health Organization (2010). https://apps.who.int/iris/handle/10665/44497

Williams, C.A., Schallmo, D., Scornavacca, E.: How applicable are digital maturity models to SMES? A conceptual framework and empirical validation approach. Int. J. Innov. Manag. **26**(03), 2240010 (2022). https://doi.org/10.1142/S1363919622400102

Williamson, P.J., De Meyer, A.: Ecosystem advantage: how to successfully harness the power of partners. Calif. Manage. Rev. **55**(1), 24–46 (2012). https://doi.org/10.1525/cmr.2012.55.1.24

Wirtz, B.W., Pistoia, A., Ullrich, S., Göttel, V.: Business models: origin, development and future research perspectives. Long Range Plan. **49**(1), 36–54 (2016). https://doi.org/10.1016/j.lrp.2015.04.001

Woolhandler, S., Himmelstein, D.U.: Administrative work consumes one-sixth of U.S. physicians' working hours and lowers their career satisfaction. Int. J. Health Serv.: Plan. Adm. Eval. **44**(4), 635–642 (2014). https://doi.org/10.2190/HS.44.4.a

Yardley, L.: Dilemmas in qualitative health research. Psychol. Health **15**(2), 215–228 (2000). https://doi.org/10.1080/08870440008400302

Yin, R.K.: Case Study Research and Applications: Design and Methods, 6th edn. SAGE Publications, Inc. (2017)

Yoo, Y., Boland, R.J., Lyytinen, K., Majchrzak, A.: Organizing for innovation in the digitized world. Organ. Sci. **23**(5), 1398–1408 (2012). https://doi.org/10.1287/orsc.1120.0771

Yoo, Y., Henfridsson, O., Lyytinen, K.: Research commentary—the new organizing logic of digital innovation: an agenda for information systems research. Inf. Syst. Res. **21**(4), 724–735 (2010). https://doi.org/10.1287/isre.1100.0322

Young, K.: A growing domiciliary demand. Optometry Today (2022). https://www.aop.org.uk/ot/industry/equipment-and-suppliers/2022/02/03/a-growing-domiciliary-demand

Zhang, X., Lin, D., Pforsich, H., Lin, V.W.: Physician workforce in the United States of America: forecasting nationwide shortages. Hum. Resour. Health **18**(1), 8 (2020). https://doi.org/10.1186/s12960-020-0448-3

Zheng, X., Mukkamala, R.R., Vatrapu, R., Ordieres-Mere, J.: Blockchain-based personal health data sharing system using cloud storage. In: 2018 IEEE 20th International Conference on E-Health Networking, Applications and Services (Healthcom), pp. 1–6 (2018). https://doi.org/10.1109/HealthCom.2018.8531125

Ziaie, A., ShamiZanjani, M., Manian, A.: Systematic review of digital value propositions in the retail sector: new approach for digital experience study. Electron. Commer. Res. Appl. **47**, 101053 (2021). https://doi.org/10.1016/j.elerap.2021.101053

Zott, C., Amit, R.: The fit between product market strategy and business model: implications for firm performance. Strateg. Manag. J. **29**(1), 1–26 (2008). https://doi.org/10.1002/smj.642

Zott, C., Amit, R., Massa, L.: The business model: recent developments and future research. J. Manag. **37**(4), 1019–1042 (2011). https://doi.org/10.1177/0149206311406265

Tal Berman is a DPhil candidate at Johannesburg Business School. He holds an MBA majoring in strategy and entrepreneurship. His research lies where entrepreneurship intersects with strategic management and information systems. His main research interests are digital entrepreneurship and digital transformation. Moreover, he is a research associate at the Institute for Entrepreneurship at Neu-Ulm University of Applied Sciences and a lecturer at various Israeli academic institutions.

Daniel Schallmo is Professor for Digital Transformation and Entrepreneurship at Neu-Ulm University of Applied Sciences. His work and research focuses on the context of digitalisation: measuring digital maturity, developing digital strategies, the digital transformation of business models and implementing digital initiatives. This includes, for example, leadership in the digital age, technologies and the design of organisations.

Christopher A. Williams is a researcher and consultant in innovation management and entrepreneurship. He holds a BA in Communication, an MBA in General Management, an MA in Learning, Technology and Education, and a Ph.D. in Social Sciences, Economics & Business. His research focuses on strategic management, human resources management, corporate communication, and learning and instruction.

Digital Business Models and Financial Performance: On the Importance of Business Renewal

Minna Saunila, Juhani Ukko, Tero Rantala, Mira Holopainen, and Mina Nasiri

Abstract This study focuses on the mediating role of business renewal in the relationship between digital business models and financial performance. An enhanced understanding of the direct and indirect influences of digital business models and business renewal will aid the construction of a more comprehensive picture of managing business models in digital transformation. The results are based on a survey of 275 Finnish SMEs. The results confirm the mediating effect of business renewal between digital business models and financial performance. This means that changes in the digital business model cannot, on their own, cause any changes in financial performance; however, through business renewal, changes in the digital business model can impact financial performance.

Keywords Digital business model · Business renewal · Financial performance · Digitalization · Digital transformation · Performance · SME

1 Introduction

As a result of the ongoing digital transformation, the business environments of companies are changing at a rapid pace. This in turn affects companies' business models. Companies are having to adopt partially or completely digital business models that challenge their traditional business models (Palmié et al. 2022; Sedera et al. 2022; Sjödin et al. 2020). According to Kohtamäki et al. (2019), digitalization

M. Saunila (✉) · J. Ukko · T. Rantala · M. Holopainen · M. Nasiri
LUT University, Mukkulankatu 19, 15210 Lahti, Finland
e-mail: minna.saunila@lut.fi

J. Ukko
e-mail: juhani.ukko@lut.fi

T. Rantala
e-mail: tero.rantala@lut.fi

M. Holopainen
e-mail: mira.holopainen@lut.fi

© The Author(s), under exclusive license to Springer Nature Switzerland AG 2024
D. Schallmo et al. (eds.), *Digital Disruption and Transformation*, Springer Proceedings in Business and Economics, https://doi.org/10.1007/978-3-031-47888-8_4

increases servitization in traditional manufacturing firms, providing opportunities regarding, for example, new platforms, intelligent products, and business models. Previous studies in the field of servitization also discuss how companies' business models change because of the transition towards the digital business model (Gebauer et al. 2020; Sjödin et al. 2020). While shifting towards the digital business model, instead of traditional, transaction-based products and services, companies deliver comprehensive, intelligent solutions that provide possibilities for real-time tracking and control of delivered solutions (Rabetino et al. 2021; Baines et al. 2020; Gebauer et al. 2020; Porter and Heppelmann 2015). Among servitization scholars, the increase in digitalization is considered an enabler and driver of the business model and value creation (Kohtamäki et al. 2019; Parida et al. 2019). In addition to the added value of providing an improved service to customers, the marketing, sales, and distribution of products and services are increasingly taking place on digital platforms and, in some cases, also as part of larger digital ecosystems. In addition to leveraging customer-centric digital applications, the focus of other stakeholders within digital business models is changing rapidly. For example, it is now possible for companies to track their suppliers in real time and reciprocally.

While the transition to the digital business model offers significant new opportunities for companies, it also affects their traditional business and requires a wide range of new skills and competencies (Palmié et al. 2022). For example, the study of Huikkola et al. (2022) demonstrated that as manufacturing organizations alter their operations to become smart solution providers, they need to adjust their strategic capabilities by employing their dynamic capabilities. In addition to the development and acquisition of new capabilities, the transition to the digital business model may require investments in equipment, digital systems, and software. Thus, according to Kohtamäki et al. (2019), companies' implementation of digital servitization related to the business model adds complexity in organizations. Töytäri et al. (2018) adds that it is not obvious that digitalization (as part of the digital business model) automatically generates business benefits, but companies may achieve financial benefits by delivering added value to their customers via new types of solutions. Kohtamäki et al. (2020), citing Talaoui et al. (2018), further argues that even though companies are increasingly investing in digital solutions, such as remote diagnostics, analytics, and data visualization tools, there exists limited evidence of possible profit gains as a result of these investments. Prior research has also demonstrated that even though digital platforms provide companies opportunities and flexibility to make decisions about the sales of their services and products (Hoang et al. 2020), they may not always be beneficial from a business perspective (Hänninen and Smedlund 2021). For example, the competition on digital platforms can reduce the earnings and benefits of companies operating on those platforms as part of their digital business model (Hänninen and Smedlund 2021). As such, the implementation of the digital business model generates costs for companies in the form of various investments, and reciprocally, it should generate better performance to enable the company to operate profitably in the future. For this reason, it is important to understand how the digital business model affects the performance of companies (Abou-Foul et al. 2021).

2 Problem and Research Questions

Based on prior research, gaining profits from digital business models is a very complicated task (Linde et al. 2020; Sjödin et al. 2020). Profiting from digital business models requires curbing the commercialization of the digital business model to avoid falling into the trap of unreasonable customer requests and aggressive internal sales targets. This situation calls for business renewal to support the digital business model by providing agility (Foss and Saebi 2017) and innovating the business model continuously (Montealegre and Iyengar 2021). Business renewal refers to actions that highlight the importance of managing changes in organizations' internal and external operating environments (Deprez et al. 2018). It requires companies to stay up-to-date and understand the business opportunities of digital applications, the demands they place on companies, and how they interact with business performance. However, current literature offers few insights into how business renewal assists digital business models in delivering significant financial benefits, and significant gaps remain.

Despite the profusion of digital business model studies, there is a lack of research on the exact role of business renewal in benefiting from digital business models. This study seeks to close previously identified research gaps by examining the relationships between digital business models, business renewal, and financial performance in SMEs. Thus, the first objective is to provide evidence of the role of digital business models in enhancing financial performance within strategic renewal. The second objective is to extend the research in this stream by examining the role of business renewal in mediating the effects of the digital business model on financial performance. The phenomenon is explored through two research questions:

RQ1: How do digital business models affect companies' financial performance?

RQ2: What is the role of business renewal in mediating between a company's digital business model and its financial performance?

As an increasing proportion of companies utilize a digital business model and there is a growing need for a better understanding of their impact on business performance, the results of this study are relevant to a variety of societal stakeholders. Anyone who is somehow part of the digital transformation may find it interesting to understand more about the impact of digital business models on the performance of companies in different contexts. In addition, in spite of the limited attention it has received thus far, corporate business renewal is involved in the development and maintenance of digital business models, which is why the results of this study reveal the interplay between the digital business model, business renewal, and financial performance. An enhanced understanding of the direct and indirect influences of digital business models and business renewal will assist in forming a solid picture of the management of strategic renewal.

The rest of the study is structured as follows. First, the theoretical underpinnings of the study are presented, after which the hypotheses about the phenomenon are constructed. Following the theoretical background of the study, the research model and methodology of the study are presented. Then the results of the study are presented and discussed, after which the paper concludes with a presentation of the theoretical and managerial implications of the findings. The conclusion also provides avenues for future studies.

3 Theoretical Background and Research Model

3.1 Theoretical Underpinnings and Key Constructs

Business models can be explained as a pathway for deeply understanding business opportunities through description of value creation and value capture (Xu and Koivumäki 2019; Wirtz et al. 2016). When digital technologies serve as main actors in business opportunities, digital business models replace traditional business models, as competing in a digital environment is not possible with a traditional business model (Iansiti and Lakhani 2014; Pagani and Pardo 2017; Remane et al. 2017). Digital business models are needed because there are some differences in operating with digital products and services in comparison with traditional products. One of these differences is that reproduction of digital products and services has no marginal costs in practice, as the more users join, the more value is provided (Shapiro and Varian 1999). The other difference is that the value of digital products and services is measured by their usage, whereas in traditional products, the value is created and sold to the customers (Vargo and Lusch 2008). The next difference relates to the important role of digital platforms in digital business models—they create a balance within an ecosystem of many companies and parties (Iansiti and Levien 2004).

This type of investments in digital technologies are the main ingredients benefiting digital transformation (Venkitachalam and Bosua 2019). They offer companies new ways to reduce costs and increase revenue streams with new value propositions (Vaska et al. 2021). Thus, companies need a digital business model to identify the ways in which value is created, delivered, and captured by digital technologies (Li 2020; Verhoef et al. 2021; Weill and Woerner 2013), as well as to create guidelines for digital operations and digital business logic (Xu and Koivumäki 2019). However, in many cases, companies do not achieve the desired results, which would be reflected by an increase in customer value and improved financial performance (Tabrizi et al. 2019; Davenport and Westerman 2018). With regard to achieving the potential economic benefits, Tabrizi et al. (2019) and Matt et al. (2015) saw the digital transformation as a strategic business reform that incorporates the leverage of new digital technologies, creates new digital business models, and enables new ways to generate value. In addition, Fernández-Portillo et al. (2022) noticed that connecting digital technologies to companies' innovation strategies has a direct and positive effect on financial performance, thus mediating the desired results of the digital business. However, since digital business models can quickly fail, it is critical for most companies to strengthen their digital business model. Business renewal can mitigate this danger, supporting the digital business model by providing agility (Foss and Saebi 2017) and innovating the business model continuously (Teece 2010).

Business renewal is a bundle of activities characterized by flexibility, experiments, and innovation undertaken by companies to achieve success or alter their path dependence, which extends firms' survival in the long run (Montealegre and Iyengar 2021; Riviere et al. 2018). Digital technologies provide the possibility to cross geographical borders, thus increasing global competition, which should motivate companies to renew themselves to stay competitive (Amankwah-Amoah et al. 2021). Renewal is critical in digital business models and the provision of financial performance, as it enables companies to attain sustainable competitive advantages in the face of transformation (Al Humaidan and Sabatier 2017; Schmitt et al. 2016).

3.2 Hypotheses Development

In recent years, digital transformation and the resulting business model innovations have profoundly changed consumer expectations and behavior, as well as numerous markets, leading companies to rethink their business (Verhoef et al. 2021; Weill and Woerner 2013). In order to seek new ways of doing business, companies are seizing new digital business opportunities by investing in digital technologies and developing new digital products, services, processes, and business models to reinforce the value created for customers (Matarazzo et al. 2021; Vaska et al. 2021). For example, digital technologies have the potential to improve communication with customers, enable a better understanding of customer needs, provide a high level of involvement for customers, and deliver new value for customers through new offerings (Matarazzo et al. 2021; Vaska et al. 2021). Thus, the new digital environment has increased the need to reflect on business practices and create advanced digital business models to deliver added value from innovations (Teece 2010). In addition, the development of a new digital business model can provide digital business managers more control over their business and the ability to compete in the uncertain digital environment (Al-Debi et al. 2008).

As described, business models can be explained as a pathway for deeply understanding business opportunities through description of value creation and value capture (Xu and Koivumäki 2019; Wirtz et al. 2016). Digital technologies play a key role in the innovation and development of new business models, enabling new ways to create value through the expansion of offerings, new forms of commerce, and new forms of cross-border organization and relationship-marketing approaches (Li 2020). In the new digital world, business models help companies to explain and focus on how to achieve economic value through digital technology (Chesbrough and Rosenbloom 2002). They serve as a tool to outline the architecture of business revenue, cost, and profit, determining how a business generates value for customers and converts the value generated into profits (Teece 2010). In addition, it is worth noting that the business model for digital business should be reviewed at regular intervals to ensure its continued suitability in an uncertain digital environment (Weill and Woerner 2013; Al-Debi et al. 2008). Thus, to compete in the digital environment, companies must design their digital business model wisely and innovatively to ensure alignment with the business strategy and improve financial performance (Latifi et al. 2021; Al-Debi et al. 2008; Weill and Woerner 2013). As a digital business model is necessary to transform digital opportunities and new forms of commerce into revenue-generating activities, its impact on financial performance should be assessed (Li 2020). Based on the arguments presented above, the following hypothesis related to digital business models and financial performance is presented:

H1: Digital business models positively affect financial performance.

This study investigates the mediating influence of business renewal on the digital business model–financial performance relationship. As described earlier, there is an established link between the digital business model and financial performance. However, there is evidence that this connection may be indirect, as within digital business models, different technologies are used to generate new offerings that demand capabilities for data collection, exchange, and analysis (Schallmo et al. 2017). All these initiate novel processes, activities, and resources that require a reconsideration of how the firm generates value (Correani et al. 2020). Thus, the renewal of business processes and strategies is becoming an increasingly crucial factor for survival in the digital age (Coskun-Setirek and Tanrikulu 2021), which "includes not only the improvement of existing processes but a fundamental revisiting of the direction and portfolio of opportunities a firm is focused" (Muzyka et al. 1995). This is also supported by Witschel et al. (2019), who concluded that firms with strong dynamic capabilities are likely to successfully enact business model change in response to digitization. Dynamic capabilities refers to "the ability of an organization and its management to integrate, build, and reconfigure internal and external competences to address rapidly changing environments" (Teece 2007). Dynamic capabilities are akin to our definition of business renewal. We propose that business renewal performs a similar mediating role in the connection between digital business models and financial performance.

Our hypothesis reflects the position that digital business models require managing changes in the operating environment. The technologies involved in strategic change speed up the change, causing complexity and uncertainty in the operating environment (Matt et al. 2015; Warner and Wäger 2019). Although digital technologies initially elicit a change in the business model, they tend to also effect changes in organizational processes and culture (Warner and Wäger 2019), which means that business models in the context of digital transformation require balancing actions to adjust the digital business model to existing product processes (Rummel et al. 2021). Thus, the digital business model requires broader business renewal beyond mere changes to the existing business model. Furthermore, business renewal should enhance firms' financial performance, as firms need to renew their processes in light of digital transformation requirements in order to align the operation with the business strategy, as this is the pathway to competitiveness (Warner and Wäger 2019; Correani et al. 2020). By enhancing the potential to profit from the digitalization of the business model, the firm renews its business processes in response to needs elicited from the digital business model. Therefore, we propose that as a firm becomes more practiced in coping with the requirements of its digital business model, this will have a positive influence on financial performance. Following the former discussion, we hypothesize the relationship between the digital business model and financial performance to be indirect, realized via business renewal:

H2: Business renewal positively mediates the relationship between digital business models and financial performance.

3.2.1 Research Model

The research model (Fig. 1) is designed to contribute to the scant body of knowledge regarding the ways in which digital business models contribute to the financial performance of firms. Drawing on the conducted literature review, the digital business model is understood as the way value is created, delivered, and captured by digital technologies (Li 2020; Verhoef et al. 2021; Weill and Woerner 2013) by creating guidelines for digital operations and digital business logic (Xu and Koivumäki 2019). We propose in our research model that digital business models facilitate firms' financial performance. However, we test a model which interrogates whether the enhancement of financial performance is a result of the digital business model itself or rather the mediating influence of business renewal, which is central to financial performance. An enhanced understanding of the direct and indirect influences of digital business models and business renewal will aid the construction of a more comprehensive picture of managing business models in digital transformation.

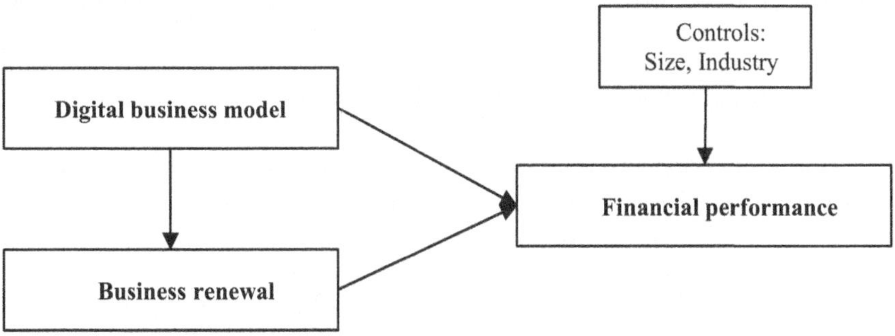

Fig. 1 Research model

4 Research Design

4.1 Sample and Data Collection

This study uses a survey approach to show the roles of digital business models and business renewal in financial performance. Data collected from randomly selected Finnish SMEs was utilized to test the proposed hypotheses built on the basis of the research model. SMEs have been selected for this study as they account for around 60% of value added and around 65% of employment in Finland.

About 5,800 out of 20,000 total Finnish SMEs were invited to participate in the study. The survey link was sent to the CEOs of these firms. After sending four reminders and deleting invalid responses, a total of 275 usable responses were received. About 70% of the responses were received from small companies (employing 10–49 persons and having a revenue of 2–10 million euros), while the rest of the responses were received from medium-sized companies (employing 50–249 persons and having a revenue of 10–50 million euros). About 43% of the responses were received from manufacturing companies, while 57% of the responses were received from service companies.

4.2 Measures

A survey was constructed to gather quantitative data on the digital business models, business renewal, and financial performance of SMEs. The survey was tested prior to sending it to the respondents. First, a literature review was conducted to familiarize the authors with the previous research and items previously used. Based on the review, the items were constructed by the authors. Then, researchers familiar with the topic were asked to review the items for progress, clarity, and completeness. The items were slightly modified during this process. Table 1 shows the final constructs, items, and their references.

Digital business models were measured by four items to which respondents could answer on a scale of 1–7 (1 = strongly agree; 7 = strongly disagree). They were asked to indicate whether they agreed that digitalization provides business opportunities, makes changes in forms of commerce, acts as an enabler for the extension of offerings, and acts as an enabler for relationship-marketing approaches. Business renewal was measured by four items that asked respondents to assess their firm in terms of business brand and image, sales, market share, and ability to innovate on a scale of 1–4 (1 = weak; 4 = excellent). Financial performance was measured by a single item that asked respondents to assess their firm's financial performance over the last three years (1 = weak; 4 = excellent). Two control variables—company size and industry—were used in the analysis. Company size (measured by number of employees) was coded into a dummy variable and split up into small and medium-sized firms. Likewise, industry

Table 1 Survey instrument

Construct	Items	Std. weight	α	CR	AVE
Digital business model (e.g., Li 2020; Verhoef et al. 2021; Weill and Woerner 2013)	Our company provides business opportunities with digitalization	0.693	0.799	0.873	0.633
	In our company, digitalization makes changes in the forms of commerce	0.615			
	In our company, we utilize digitalization as an enabler for extension of offerings (products and services)	0.886			
	In our company, we utilize digitalization as an enabler for relationship-marketing approaches	0.652			
Business renewal (e.g., Montealegre and Iyengar 2021; Riviere et al. 2018)	Business brand and image	0.464	0.713	0.827	0.548
	Company sales	0.810			
	Market share	0.786			
	Ability to innovate	0.457			

was coded into a dummy variable and split up into service industry or manufacturing industry.

Next the remedies to assess the reliability and construct validity are presented. The reliability of each construct was estimated with Cronbach's α values that were above the threshold of 0.70 (Nunnally and Bernstein 1978). Confirmatory factor analysis was used to check convergent validity. The standardized weights of all items were close to 0.50. Convergent validity was further examined by calculating composite reliability (CR) and average variance extracted (AVE) for the study variables. The CR values were over the 0.70 limit (Fornell and Larcker 1981), and the AVE values were over 0.50 (Fornell and Larcker 1981). Thus, convergent validity is supported. Discriminant validity was tested by comparing the square root of AVE and correlations between the two constructs. The square roots of both AVEs (0.706 for digital business strategy and 0.634 for business renewal) were larger than the correlations of the construct to all the other constructs (Table 2) (Fornell and Larcker 1981), which supports discriminant validity. Thus, the convergent and discriminant validity of the constructs were approved.

4.3 Bias

A test for non-response bias was executed to check the difference between first responses (the responses during the first week after the survey was sent) and later

Table 2 Correlation matrix

	Mean	Std. deviation	Digital business model	Business renewal	Financial performance
Digital business model	5.03	1.265	1.000		
Business renewal	2.79	0.519	0.212***	1.000	
Financial performance	2.82	0.881	0.129*	0.438***	1.000

Significance level *** P-value ≤ 0.001, ** 0.001 < P-value ≤ 0.01, * 0.01 < P-value ≤ 0.05

responses (the responses during the last week before the link was closed) (Armstrong and Overton 1977; Podsakoff et al. 2003). The results evidenced no statistically significant differences between the first responses and later responses, which means that non-response bias is not of much concern.

A test for common method bias was executed to check whether the single-respondent design biased the results. Following Podsakoff et al. (2003), exploratory factor analysis was performed for all the study items. No single factor emerged, and the main factor extracted 34.4% of the total variance (less than the threshold of 50%). This means that common method bias is not a severe problem in this study.

5 Findings

Different model-fit criteria, including root-mean-square error of approximation (RMSEA), normed fit index (NFI), relative fit index (RFI), incremental fit index (IFI), Tucker–Lewis Index (TLI), and comparative fit index (CFI), were used to assess the fitness of the model. According to Schumacker and Lomax (2016), an RMSEA between 0.05 and 0.08 indicates a close fit of the model, while values of TLI and NFI close to 0.9 indicate a good fit of the model. According to Bentler and Bonett (1980), a value greater than 0.9 for CFI and IFI confirms the good fit of the model. Table 3 shows the results of the model-fit criteria and makes a comparison between the default model (including all the effects, as well as direct and indirect relations) and the competing model (including only direct relations). As shown in Table 3, the values of the model-fit criteria for the default model are better than those of the competing model.

Regression analysis using IBM SPSS AMOS was used to test the model (Table 4). First, the effect of the control variables (size and industry) on the dependent variable (financial performance) was checked. Then the direct effect of the independent variable (digital business model) on the dependent variable (financial performance) was checked. Finally, the mediating effect, which includes both the direct effect of the independent variable (digital business model) on the mediating variable (business renewal) and the direct effect of the mediating variable (business renewal) on the dependent variable (financial performance), was checked. As shown in Table 4,

Table 3 The results of the model-fit criteria

Model	RMSEA	NFI	RFI	IFI	TLI	CFI
Default model	0.066	0.881	0.813	0.932	0.889	0.930
Competing model (only direct relations)	0.070	0.869	0.799	0.920	0.874	0.918

none of the control variables, including size (C.R. = −1.885, P-value = 0.059 > 0.05, non-significant) and industry (C.R. = 1.722, P-value = 0.085 > 0.05, non-significant), significantly affect financial performance. This means that changes in the size and type of industry cannot change the financial performance of companies in a given setting. Regarding the second step, as the results of the analyses indicate in Table 4, there is no significant direct relationship between the digital business model and financial performance (C.R. = 0.241, P-value = 0.810 > 0.05, non-significant). Thus, the first hypothesis (digital business models positively affect financial performance) is rejected. Regarding the final step, which tested the mediating effect, the significant effect of the digital business model on business renewal (C.R. = 2.857, P-value = 0.004 < 0.05, significant) and of business renewal on financial performance (C.R. = 5.829, P-value = 0.000 < 0.05, significant) confirm the mediating effect of business renewal between digital business model and financial performance. This means that changes in a digital business model cannot, on their own, elicit changes in financial performance; however, through business renewal, the digital business model can effect a change in financial performance. In other words, financial performance can improve via growth in business renewal when business renewal is paired with the digital business model. Thus, the second hypothesis (business renewal positively mediates the relationship between digital business models and financial performance) is accepted.

6 Discussion

This study has examined the relationships between digital business models, business renewal, and financial performance in SMEs. The results are discussed below.

First, referring to H1, the results showed that digital business models do not have a direct effect on financial performance. This study was justified by the notion that digital transformation has changed the business environment, which has led to business model innovations in which companies must adopt partially or completely digital business models to compete globally (Palmié et al. 2022; Sedera et al. 2022; Verhoef et al. 2021; Sjödin et al. 2020; Weill and Woerner 2013). Previous research has shown that digital technologies have a key role in the development of new business models, which enable new ways to elevate financial performance through the expansion of offerings, new forms of commerce, and new forms of cross-border organization and relationship-marketing approaches (Li 2020). However, the results of this study do

Table 4 Unstandardized and standardized maximum likelihood estimates

	Estimate (unstandardized)	Estimate (standardized)	S.E	C.R	P-value
Size → Financial performance	−0.178	−0.100	0.095	−1.885	0.059
Industry → Financial performance	0.162	0.091	0.094	1.722	0.085
Digital business model → Financial performance	0.009	0.014	0.039	0.241	0.810
Digital business model → Business renewal	0.056	0.224	0.020	2.857	0.004
Business renewal → Financial performance	1.382	0.526	0.237	5.829	0.000

not entirely support these notions. This study's results are in line with Töytäri et al. (2018), who suggested that in the case of digital business models, it is not obvious that digitalization automatically generates business benefits, but companies can strive for financial benefits by delivering added value to their customers via new types of solutions.

Second, in terms of H2, the results indicate that business renewal positively mediates the relationship between the digital business model and financial performance. This is in line with numerous studies that suggest a more fundamental renewal of business processes and strategies to achieve financial benefits from a digital business model (Coskun-Setirek and Tanrikulu 2021; Warner and Wäger 2019; Matt et al. 2015). Overcoming this challenge may require elements of business renewal, such as activities captured by flexibility, experiments, and innovation undertaken by companies to achieve success or alter their path dependence, which extends their survival and financial success in the long run (Montealegre and Iyengar 2021; Riviere et al. 2018). The results show that in addition to investing in digital technologies to change the business model (Venkitachalam and Bosua 2019), digital business models require a strategic business reform that incorporates the rethinking of organizational processes and culture, business processes, and operations, as well as adjustments of the digital business model to existing product processes (Rummel et al. 2021; Correani et al. 2020; Tabrizi et al. 2019; Warner and Wäger 2019; Matt et al. 2015). The results also suggest that companies with strong dynamic capabilities are likely to successfully possess a strategic business reform and business model change in response to digitization (cf. Witschel et al. 2019). Thus, the digital business model requires broader business renewal than mere changes to the business model in order to make it a pathway for deeply understanding business opportunities through description of value creation, value capture, and financial performance (cf. Xu and Koivumäki 2019; Wirtz et al. 2016).

7 Contribution

7.1 Theoretical Contribution

From a theoretical perspective, this study contributes to research in the field of digital transformation and business models by increasing understanding of business renewal as it relates to digital business models. The aim of this research was to study the conditions under which digital business models affect financial performance. Firstly, the study suggests that digital business models do not directly affect financial success. Digital technologies enable the crossing of geographical borders, which increases global competition. Thus, utilizing digital technologies in business models without more in-depth business analysis is not enough from the perspective of financial performance. Secondly, the study suggest that companies should focus on various elements of business renewal to take full advantage of digital business models from a financial performance perspective. This refers, for example, to rethinking business processes, operations, and dynamic capabilities and aligning them with the company's strategy.

7.2 Practical Contribution

From the perspective of managerial contribution, this study shows that the digital business model itself does not directly affect companies' financial performance in the explored context. This finding demonstrates that while companies adopt digital business models in pursuit of increased performance, it is not obvious that they can improve their financial performance merely by adopting a digital business model. Thus, when seeking improvements in financial performance, companies must pay attention to business renewal. The results of the study show the mediating effect of business renewal between the digital business model and financial performance. This is something companies should focus on while adopting and updating their digital business model. If the goal is better financial performance, they must focus not only on the digital business model, but also on business renewal.

7.3 Limitations and Further Research Directions

A limitation of this study is that the results show empirical evidence from one country, which must be considered before generalizing the results. While the results of the study increase understanding of the interplay between the digital business model, business renewal, and financial performance, there may be some country-specific characteristics that could influence the results. While the results of the study show that digital business models do not affect companies' financial performance directly, the study also raises the need for further studies to increase understanding of the effects of digital business models on companies' performance.

References

Abou-Foul, M., Ruiz-Alba, J.L., Soares, A.: The impact of digitalization and servitization on the financial performance of a firm: an empirical analysis. Prod. Plan. & Control **32**(12), 975–989 (2021)

Al-Debi, M.M., El-Haddadeh, R., Avison, D.: Defining the business model in the new world of digital business. In: AMCIS 2008 Proceedings, vol. 300 (2008)

Al Humaidan, S., Sabatier, V.: Strategic renewal in times of environmental scarcity: the mediating role of technology in business model evolution. J. Organ. Chang. Manag. **30**(1), 106–120 (2017). https://doi.org/10.1108/JOCM-09-2015-0161

Amankwah-Amoah, J., Khan, Z., Osabutey, E.L.: COVID-19 and business renewal: lessons and insights from the global airline industry. Int. Bus. Rev. **30**(3), 101802 (2021)

Armstrong, J.S., Overton, T.S.: Estimating nonresponse bias in mail surveys. J. Mark. Res. **14**(3), 396–402 (1977)

Bentler, P.M., Bonett, D.G.: Significance tests and goodness of fit in the analysis of covariance structures. Psychol. Bull. **88**(3), 588 (1980)

Baines, T., Bigdeli, A.Z., Sousa, R., Schroeder, A.: Framing the servitization transformation process: a model to understand and facilitate the servitization journey. Int. J. Prod. Econ. **221**, 107463 (2020)

Chesbrough, H., Rosenbloom, R.S.: The role of the business model in capturing value from innovation: evidence from Xerox Corporation's technology spin-off companies. Ind. Corp. Chang. **11**(3), 529–555 (2002)

Correani, A., De Massis, A., Frattini, F., Petruzzelli, A.M., Natalicchio, A.: Implementing a digital strategy: learning from the experience of three digital transformation projects. Calif. Manag. Rev. **62**(4), 37–56 (2020)

Coskun-Setirek, A., Tanrikulu, Z.: Digital innovations-driven business model regeneration: a process model. Technol. Soc. **64**, 101461 (2021)

Davenport, T.H., Westerman, G.: Why so many high-profile digital transformations fail. Harv. Bus. Rev. **9**, 15 (2018)

Deprez, J., Leroy, H., Euwema, M.: Three chronological steps toward encouraging intrapreneurship: lessons from the Wehkamp case. Bus. Horiz. **61**(1), 135–145 (2018)

Fernández-Portillo, A., Almodóvar-González, M., Sánchez-Escobedo, M.C., Coca-Pérez, J.L.: The role of innovation in the relationship between digitalisation and economic and financial performance. A company-level research. Eur. Res. Manag. Bus. Econ. **28**(3), 100190 (2022)

Fornell, C., Larcker, D.F.: Evaluating structural equation models with unobservable variables and measurement error. J. Mark. Res. **18**(1), 39-50 (1981)

Foss, N.J., Saebi, T.: Fifteen years of research on business model innovation: how far have we come, and where should we go? J. Manag. **43**(1), 200–227 (2017)

Gebauer, H., Arzt, A., Kohtamäki, M., Lamprecht, C., Parida, V., Witell, L., Wortmann, F.: How to convert digital offerings into revenue enhancement–conceptualizing business model dynamics through explorative case studies. Ind. Mark. Manag. **91**, 429–441 (2020)

Hänninen, M., Smedlund, A.: Same old song with a different melody: the paradox of market reach and financial performance on digital platforms. J. Manage. Stud. **58**(7), 1832–1868 (2021)
Hoang, L., Blank, G., Quan-Haase, A.: The winners and the losers of the platform economy: who participates? Inf. Commun. Soc. **23**(5), 681–700 (2020)
Huikkola, T., Kohtamäki, M., Ylimäki, J.: Becoming a smart solution provider: reconfiguring a product manufacturer's strategic capabilities and processes to facilitate business model innovation. Technovation 102498 (2022)
Iansiti, M., Levien, R.: Strategy as ecology. Harv. Bus. Rev. **82**(3), 68–78 (2004)
Iansiti, M., Lakhani, K.R.: Digital ubiquity: how connections, sensors, and data are revolutionizing business. Harv. Bus. Rev. **92**(11), 19 (2014)
Kohtamäki, M., Parida, V., Oghazi, P., Gebauer, H., Baines, T.: Digital servitization business models in ecosystems: a theory of the firm. J. Bus. Res. **104**, 380–392 (2019)
Kohtamäki, M., Parida, V., Patel, P.C., Gebauer, H.: The relationship between digitalization and servitization: the role of servitization in capturing the financial potential of digitalization. Technol. Forecast. Soc. Chang. **151**, 119804 (2020)
Latifi, M.A., Nikou, S., Bouwman, H.: Business model innovation and firm performance: exploring causal mechanisms in SMEs. Technovation **107**, 102274 (2021)
Li, F.: The digital transformation of business models in the creative industries: a holistic framework and emerging trends. Technovation **92**, 102012 (2020)
Matarazzo, M., Penco, L., Profumo, G., Quaglia, R.: Digital transformation and customer value creation in Made in Italy SMEs: a dynamic capabilities perspective. J. Bus. Res. **123**, 642–656 (2021)
Matt, C., Hess, T., Benlian, A.: Digital transformation strategies. Bus. Inf. Syst. Eng. **57**(5), 339–343 (2015)
Montealegre, R., Iyengar, K.: Managing digital business platforms: a continued exercise in balancing renewal and refinement. Bus. Horiz. **64**(1), 51–59 (2021)
Muzyka, D., De Koning, A., Churchill, N.: On transformation and adaptation: building the entrepreneurial corporation. Eur. Manag. J. **13**(4), 346–362 (1995)
Nunnally, J.C., Bernstein, I.H.: Psychometric theory, McGraw Hill, New York. The role of university in the development of entrepreneurial vocations: a Spanish study, pp. 387–405 (1978)
Pagani, M., Pardo, C.: The impact of digital technology on relationships in a business network. Ind. Mark. Manage. **67**, 185–192 (2017)
Palmié, M., Miehé, L., Oghazi, P., Parida, V., Wincent, J.: The evolution of the digital service ecosystem and digital business model innovation in retail: the emergence of meta-ecosystems and the value of physical interactions. Technol. Forecast. Soc. Chang. **177**, 121496 (2022)
Parida, V., Sjödin, D., Reim, W.: Reviewing literature on digitalization, business model innovation, and sustainable industry: past achievements and future promises. Sustainability **11**(2), 391 (2019)
Podsakoff, P.M., MacKenzie, S.B., Lee, J. Y., Podsakoff, N.P.: Common method biases in behavioral research: a critical review of the literature and recommended remedies. J. Appl. Psychol. **88**(5), 879 (2003)
Porter, M.E., Heppelmann, J.E.: How smart, connected products are transforming companies. Harv. Bus. Rev. **93**(10), 96–114 (2015)
Rabetino, R., Kohtamäki, M., Brax, S.A., Sihvonen, J.: The tribes in the field of servitization: discovering latent streams across 30 years of research. Ind. Mark. Manag. **95**, 70–84 (2021)
Remane, G., Hanelt, A., Nickerson, R.C., Kolbe, L.M.: Discovering digital business models in traditional industries. J. Bus. Strat. **38**(2), 41–51 (2017)
Riviere, M., Suder, G., Bass, A.E.: Exploring the role of internationalization knowledge in fostering strategic renewal: a dynamic capabilities perspective. Int. Bus. Rev. **27**(1), 66–77 (2018)
Rummel, F., Hüsig, S., Steinhauser, S.: Two archetypes of business model innovation processes for manufacturing firms in the context of digital transformation. R&D Manag. (2021)
Schallmo, D., Williams, C.A., Boardman, L.: Digital transformation of business models—best practice, enablers, and roadmap. Int. J. Innov. Manag. **21**(8), 1740014 (2017)

Schmitt, A., Barker, V.L., III., Raisch, S., Whetten, D.: Strategic renewal in times of environmental scarcity. Long Range Plan. **49**(3), 361–376 (2016)
Schumacker, E., Lomax, G.: A Beginner's Guide to Structural Equation Modeling, 4th edn. (2016)
Sedera, D., Tan, C. W., Xu, D.: Digital business transformation in innovation and entrepreneurship. Inf. & Manag. 103620 (2022)
Shapiro, C., Varian, H.R.: Information Rules: A Strategic Guide to the Network Economy. Harvard Business School Press, Boston (1999)
Sjödin, D., Parida, V., Jovanovic, M., Visnjic, I.: Value creation and value capture alignment in business model innovation: a process view on outcome-based business models. J. Prod. Innov. Manag. **37**(2), 158–183 (2020)
Tabrizi, B., Lam, E., Girard, K., Irvin, V.: Digital transformation is not about technology. Harv. Bus. Rev. **13**, 1–6 (2019)
Talaoui, Y.: BI-in-Practice: a look at how bi enacts framing contests and affects the service transition path. Eds. In: Kohtamäki, M., Baines, T., Rabetino, R., Bigdeli, A. (eds.) Practices and Tools for Servitization, pp. 233–247. Springer International Publishing, Cham (2018)
Töytäri, P., Turunen, T., Klein, M., Eloranta, V., Biehl, S., Rajala, R.: Aligning the mindset and capabilities within a business network for successful adoption of smart services. J. Prod. Innov. Manag. **35**(5), 763–779 (2018)
Teece, D.J.:Explicating dynamic capabilities: the nature and microfoundations of (sustainable) enterprise performance. Strateg. Manage. J. **28**(13), 1319–1350 (2007)
Teece, D.J.: Business models, business strategy and innovation. Long Range Plan. **43**(2–3), 172–194 (2010)
Vargo, S.L., Lusch, R.F.: Service-dominant logic: continuing the evolution. J. Acad. Mark. Sci. **36**(1), 1–10 (2008)
Vaska, S., Massaro, M., Bagarotto, E.M., Dal Mas, F.: The digital transformation of business model innovation: a structured literature review. Front. Psychol. **11**, 3557 (2021)
Venkitachalam, K., Bosua, R.: Perspectives on effective digital content management in organizations. Knowl. Process. Manag. **26**(3), 202–209 (2019)
Verhoef, P.C., Broekhuizen, T., Bart, Y., Bhattacharya, A., Dong, J.Q., Fabian, N., Haenlein, M.: Digital transformation: a multidisciplinary reflection and research agenda. J. Bus. Res. **122**, 889–901 (2021)
Warner, K.S., Wäger, M.: Building dynamic capabilities for digital transformation: an ongoing process of strategic renewal. Long Range Plan. **52**(3), 326–349 (2019)
Weill, P., Woerner, S.L.: Optimizing your digital business model. MIT Sloan Manag. Rev. **54**(3), 71 (2013)
Wirtz, B.W., Pistoia, A., Ullrich, S., Göttel, V.: Business models: origin, development and future research perspectives. Long Range Plan. **49**(1), 36–54 (2016)
Witschel, D., Döhla, A., Kaiser, M., Voigt, K.I., Pfletschinger, T.: Riding on the wave of digitization: Insights how and under what settings dynamic capabilities facilitate digital-driven business model change. J. Bus. Econ. **89**(8), 1023–1095 (2019)
Xu, Y., Koivumäki, T.: Digital business model effectuation: an agile approach. Comput. Hum. Behav. **95**, 307–314 (2019)

Minna Saunila (D.Sc. Tech.) is an Associate Professor at LUT University, School of Engineering Sciences, Department of Industrial Engineering and Management. Since 2018, she is also a docent of the University of Jyväskylä School of Business and Economics. Her research covers topics related to performance management, innovation, service operations, as well as sustainable value creation. Recently, her research projects have been related to digitization of services and production. She has previously published in International Journal of Operations and Production Management, Technovation, and Computers in Industry among others.

Juhani Ukko (D.Sc. Tech.) is a Professor at LUT University, School of Engineering Sciences, Department of Industrial Engineering and Management. He is also an adjunct professor at Tampere University. His current research focuses on performance measurement, operations management, digital transformation, digital services and corporate sustainability performance. In recent years, he has managed and participated in research projects related to digital transformation in companies and society. His work has been published in journals such as Information Systems Frontiers, Computers in Industry, International Journal of Operations and Production Management and International Journal of Production Economics.

Tero Rantala (D.Ss. Tech.) is a Postdoctoral Researcher at LUT University, School of Engineering Sciences. His current research focuses on performance management and measurement in digital business environments and sustainable business contexts. He has previously published in journals such as Technology Analysis & Strategic Management, European Journal of Operational Research, Technovation, Journal of Cleaner Production, Information Technology & People, and Education and Work.

Mira Holopainen (M.Sc. Tech.) is a Doctoral Student and Junior Researcher in the School of Engineering Sciences at LUT University, Finland. Her research is related to performance measurement and management as well as digital transformation of industrial companies.

Mina Nasiri received her D.Sc. degree from LUT university in February 2021 in the field of Industrial Management. Her research interests lie in digital business strategy, digital supply chain, digital transformation, digital innovation, corporate sustainability, smart technologies, performance measurement and management, operations management, and sustainable strategies. Her works have been published in different journals such as Technovation, Information system frontiers, Technology analysis and strategic management, Sustainable development, Computers in industry, and Journal of cleaner production, International journal of operations and production management.

Digital Innovations and Transformation in the Public Sector of Panama

Laura Martinez

Abstract Digital innovations and transformation have changed the way in which the public sector works, whilst massive digital disruption took place during the pandemics. The research gap that this article looks at is the lack of academic research on this phenomenon in Panama. The paper presented here is as a qualitative case study of 9 public organizations in Panama and aims to the explore the issue from the theoretical framework of the theory of affordances using semi structured interviews and focus group as well as to serve as a steppingstone for further research of the subject in Panama and in the rest of the Latin American region.

Keywords Digital · Transformation · Innovation · Disruption · Developing country · E-government · Women · Public sector · STEM · Public management

1 Introduction

This research paper was presented at the XXXIII ISPIM Innovation Conference "Innovating in a Digital World" Copenhagen, Denmark in June 2022. It concerns public sector digitalization, presenting a literature review of the current state of the art and contributing areas for further research and exploration. Moreover, the objective of this paper is to share the theoretical background, explain the problem addressed, the research objective and questions, the research design, an overview of the findings, contribution, practical implications, limitations and a recommendations section.

L. Martinez (✉)
University of Birmingham, Edgbaston, Birmingham B15 2TT, UK
e-mail: lem209@student.bham.ac.uk

© The Author(s), under exclusive license to Springer Nature Switzerland AG 2024
D. Schallmo et al. (eds.), *Digital Disruption and Transformation*, Springer Proceedings in Business and Economics, https://doi.org/10.1007/978-3-031-47888-8_5

2 Theoretical Background

Digital transformation refers to the social and economic undertaking of online operations and the overall change in the way organizations work to the online arena (Ciuriak and Ptashkina 2019, p. 1). Moreover, according to an article about this issue in the energy sector, digital disruption is caused by digital transformation though it brings "new and important opportunities for our societies, both in strengthening the reliability and resilience of our grids and even highly ambitious climate change goals" (Chase and Berzina 2018, p. 48). The core idea here could be transversal to other sectors of society. Thus, it is essential to consider how the public sector is coping with digital disruption and how besides the challenges it might present, it also may open opportunities.

Digital transformations might produce status quo disruption in the organization internal procedures, changes may occur in the way power is held by stakeholders and, the very core of the organization might completely change. Management needs to consider the pro and cons and make sure they have the right tools to face the complications that going digital could bring (Von Kutzschenbach and Brønn 2017, p. 1). In the midst of this need of change from traditional procedures to digital ones digital innovation will be catalysed. For managers the challenge is "successfully managing the transition from where the organization is toward a desired future state" (Li 2020, p. 809).

According to Nambisan et al., digital innovation is "the use of digital technology during the process of innovating. Digital innovation can also be used to describe fully or partly, the outcome of innovation" (Nambisan et al. 2017, p. 223). In this manner new digital solution may emerge to new or old problems. It also puts together digital and physical aspects in order to develop new solutions (Yoo et al. 2010, p. 725). As mentioned here, the physical aspect is also important to consider, given that there is physical equipment that is necessary to develop digital innovation and capacity building of it is also required so that the backend users (public servants) and end users (citizens) are comfortable with it.

Furthermore, when considering digital innovation in the public sector, it could be important to analyze it in a wider context. Avgerou and Bonina suggest that public sector technology professionals need to consider the social aspect to be able to fully grasp the objectives of the IT projects that are assigned to them. This is especially important in developing countries where resources are more limited and unstable political condition can put IT implementation at risk faster (Avgerou and Bonina 2019, p. 91). This might be a highly important reflection to this research project considering that Panama is still categorized as a developing country and most of the countries of the Latin American region are too.

Additionally, in an article about digital affordances, the authors point out that they are based in the "technical architecture of digital infrastructures, and they support an economy-wide redesign of value creation, delivery and capture processes" (Autio et al. 2018, p. 74). Therefore, it could be inferred that because of the rapid technological change the world is facing right now, there is the possibility that the perception of digital affordances also changed.

Another interesting aspect to look at is the participation of women in all of these, according to a study about gender gaps in Research and Innovation of the European Commission, women represent "48% of Ph.D. graduates, 33%o f researchers, 24% of Top-level researchers (grade A) and, 22% of Heads of higher-education institutions" in the European Union as of 2020 (European Union 2020, p. 1). This could be an indication of how the gender gap grows as the complexity or the level of seniority increases. It also elucidates that even though this particular study shows a gap, there is a presence of women in the field therefore, their perspective is relevant.

Meanwhile regarding the gender gap in sciences, technologies, engineering and mathematics (STEM) in Latin America, Arredondo Trapero, Vásquez and Velásquez mention that social and cultural factors related to women must be considered in order to be able to diminish the gender gap in the region, thus providing the conditions for Latin American women to change their own perspective and see themselves as part of the science and technology field (Arredondo Trapero et al. 2019, p. 154).

Moreover, it seems that the root cause of this issue goes beyond the problem itself. In fact, "some gender and IS research imports gender theories from disciplines such as feminism, sociology and psychology to study both gender and IT use, and gender in the workforce" (Trauth 2013, p. 285). This is a very complex area of analysis that requires efforts from different areas of study.

An author notes as part of the conclusions of her study, that social, political and economic conditions are decisive factors for women in innovation leadership positions and, that there should be policies that take these factors into account (Carrasco 2014, p. 421). Thus, it's possible that having the perspective of women on such issues and particularly on digital innovation could help broaden its understanding as a topic and perhaps even help empower women to get involved in this field somewhere in the future.

Looking at innovation through the gender lens makes it possible to understand the particular gender concepts within the area of innovation and, the ways in which they are deep within the mindset of those developing innovation (Pecis 2016, pp. 2119–2020). Incorporating this lense to this research project, even in a small way could also provide a deeper comprehension which would enrich the analysis.

3 Problem

Public sector organizations have been relatively slow in their adoption of digital innovation with it being even a novel idea until recent years. However, rapid technology development in digital innovation alongside the effect of rapid adoption to counter the global pandemic, digitalization has become a global necessity with increasing policy calls for adoption. To keep citizens safe through the pandemic, countries implemented several new technologies thus, digital transformation took place, bringing with it digital disruption in the areas where these changes happened too suddenly. In Panama, this was also the case, and the speed of digital transformation provided research opportunity. This is where this study is focused.

4 Research Objective and Questions

Research question: How do managers in Panamanian public sector perceive the affordance of digital innovation?

And my sub questions are:

- What is the understanding of digital innovation in the public sector?
- What is the perception of women and women in management positions of digital innovation in the public sector?
- How is digital innovation in the public sector developed and implemented?

5 Research Design

Regarding the research methodology for this project, I am conducting a qualitative and exploratory type of research. The goal is to understand the research topic and explore it, instead of aiming to study large samples in order to have outcomes that are representative of some area (Ambert et al. 1995, p. 880). Also, I will be using the inductive approach for this endeavor, the general idea is to gain insight on the participants perceptions regarding the research topic and questions and, to provide a description of it (Yilmaz 2013, p. 313) to be able from to gain understanding from the research participants views. The intent is that my research can also help other researchers on the future, thus also building on it and looking further other more specific interest areas.

In reference to my research philosophy choices, ontologically I have chosen constructionism which "refers to the construction of knowledge through active interaction with environments, emphasizing the purposeful production of knowledge" (Trainor and Graue 2013, p. 13) and, that interaction with the environment is part of the learning process which leads to construction (Packer and Goicoechea 2000, p. 3). In other words, knowledge is constructed from different interpretations of realities therefore the idea is that there is not one single truth.

Moreover, epistemologically I am using hermeneutics, an approach that "provides insight into ways of interpreting textual material, which can comprise both formal written texts and spoken words that can be recorded (Easterby-Smith et al. 2012, p. 170). As an epistemology, hermeneutics "maintains interest in issues of human knowledge: it does help to explain how humans come to know" (Bineham 1994, p. 307). Thus, the interest is to understand the topic from human experience and to have different views according to the perspectives of the participants gathered from the data collection, which will enable the possibility of making a wholesome analysis.

It is important to mention that I will use of secondary data and of comparing the results from the data collection in Panama with research from other countries in the Latin American region, the larger scope of the context will help understand better the experiences from the Panamanian participants and find perhaps some commonalities or differences which could enhance the depth of the analysis and reflections for the research project.

Also, it is relevant to highlight that the Theory of Affordances provides an interconnection structure from which to analyze the different aspects of technology which can possibly change (Evans et al. 2017, p. 36). Thus, this theory would be very relevant to the analysis part of this study given as it provides a specific ground where this research project attempts to contribute to knowledge.

This is a qualitative multiple case study of the affordances of digital innovations in the public sector of Panama. I am using the case study method which according to Simmons "is an in-depth exploration from multiple perspectives of the complexity and uniqueness of a particular project, policy, institution, programme or system in a´real life´ context" (Simons 2009, p. 21) which aligns exactly with the intention of this project.

It is also relevant to mention that I chose to use this method over others such as surveys, because the case study seeks to explain the items of study and surveys attempt to indicate the occurrence of certain events and to predict possible results (Yin 2003, p. 7) and the intention of my study has been from the beginning to understand the topic at depth. On the other hand, even though ethnography is another qualitative method that has a similar approach, I did not choose it mainly because it's a type of study that requires long periods of time to undertake and the researcher spends most of its time immersed in one organization carrying out observations and informal interviews (Reeves and Hodges 2008, p. 514) Therefore, ethnography was not a suitable method for this research project, given that I would like to contact more than one public institution in order to compare the results and the long term required access to a public institution would probably be a sensitive matter.

Regarding the data collection, I used mainly semi structured interviews in 9 public institutions and was able to carry out one focus group in one of the organizations. Whilst the data for this research project will be gathered in these two manners, I will also rely on secondary data, using research from the topic of study focusing on other Latin American countries for comparison, specifically Brazil and Mexico given that they are two of the biggest countries in our geographical area and Costa Rica and Chile which are some of the most technologically advanced countries of the region. Nevertheless, I might also use research from other parts of the world as a reference especially in the context part of the thesis.

The aim of the interviews was to get insight in regards of the perception on organizational change of digital innovations in the public sector and, to get people´s overall view, thoughts, and even personal experiences regarding this issue, also following the lines of my sub questions specific areas of interest. And for the focus group, they had the same general objective, with the difference of aiming to get their viewpoints the implementation processes and adoption of digital innovation which might differ from the perceptions of their own managers, and to see the interaction amongst the group, which could also lead to more a more in-depth grasp of the topics discussed. The samples were small, given that the interest was to dig deeper into each person's perspective rather than to get information that would be representative of some niche.

6 Findings

9 semi structured interviews with senior public managers were carried out in 9 public institutions in Panama, and 1 focus group with the team members of one of those public managers.

It´s important to mention that it was the original intention of the Project to have a focus group which each of the team members of each public manager, however it was not possible mainly due to their preference to keep their participation in the study completely anonymous even from their own team.

The data collection took place in two parts, 1st part during the last 3 months of year 2021 in which 5 semi structured interviews and 1 focus group were carried out, and the 2nd part during the first 3 months of year 2022. The interviews conducted lasted between 45 and 60 min, and the focus group, about 90 min.

The participants were approached by sending them an invitation letter to participate in the study which was addressed directly to them, the communication with the public managers and coordination of the meetings was facilitated by the fact that I personally knew most of them, given that I had worked as a public manager for almost 5 years at that moment. Thus, not long after the invitations were issued, I was able to start the data collection.

Regarding to the data analysis framework for this study, it's based on the Gioia methodology, which intends to improve qualitative strictness in its "approach to analyses, especially in terms of organizing the data into 1st- and 2nd-order categories to facilitate their later assembly into a more structured form" (Gioia et al. 2013, p. 20). This allows to see the qualitative data in a much more organized way, which might make it easier to understand for both the researcher and the reader.

The first step towards the analysis, was to transcribe the interviews, and to translate them. Then the information was coded by common themes, concepts and later on creating categories. Following the Gioia methodology, 1st and 2nd order concepts related to 3 different aggregate dimensions came up, which are: digital innovation development, gender gap perceptions and digital innovation affordances. Moreover, the interviews with the participants provided much in-depth information from their own experience regarding digital innovations and transformation in the public sector in Panama.

7 Contribution

This research aims to contribute to the theory of affordances, by giving insight on its application on digital innovation and transformation research analysis and how understanding what the subject affords to the public sector provides value to a qualitative type of analysis.

The paper also expects to contribute practically to public policy, hoping that the case of Panama could serve as a reference for further study in other Latin American countries, and/or into more specific subjects of digital innovation and transformation in the public sector, such as: artificial intelligence, open innovation and, cybersecurity.

8 Practical Implications

Challenges to the adoption and implementation of digital innovations were identified, which could have practical implications for decision makers and can be used as lessons to learn.

Some of the challenges identified in the data analysis so far are: having an adequate IT infrastructure throughout the whole country in order that all of the population may have internet access, not enough prepared professionals in digital innovation and transformation related areas, acceptance of change, new cybersecurity threats and the need of citizen centred digital innovation developments, among others. These represent serious challenges to a government (and its managers) that is still trying to process very rapid digital transformation processes, and to citizens who are still trying to learn how to use new technological developments, or to find a way access them. Bearing in mind the ongoing health crisis, which still requires many resources from the government.

9 Limitations

The main limitation for this research was that it was not possible to carry out a focus group with the team of each public managers interviewed, given that most of them had a strong preference of their participation in the study remaining anonymous even from their own team. Given that this was considered in the original research design, this issue presented an interesting finding, which can be related to the fact that all of the interviewees were senior managers, and had many years devoted to public service, which caused them to be more apprehensive towards keeping their opinions and insights completely private and knowing that what they would share with the author would not affect them or their post in any way, and this could be only secured by providing total anonymity.

Another aspect that can be considered as a limitation worth mentioning, was just how broad the subject of digital innovation and transformation in the public sector has become, and as the empirical data collection took place, it came to be obvious how it has affected many different aspects and how the research could only be but a small general steppingstone for a research subject that will require much attention and detailed research into various specific areas of study. However, this limitation also became an opportunity to highlight these areas in the coming recommendation section, so they can be considered by other researchers.

10 Recommendations

Digital innovations and transformation in the public sector of Panama in the context of the pandemics, rapidly increased the speed at which digital disruption took place, and it also opened the way for more specific sub areas of development and research, such as: artificial intelligence, open innovation and cybersecurity. It is true that in concept they already existed, but at a practical level, perhaps only partially and in terms of academic research on it in Panama and in the Latin American region, it was almost unexplored. However, as the adoption of these new technologies have been implemented throughout the public sector it is important to continue to research on them, so that countries may strategically consider them when public policy planning is taking place and when resources are being distributed, hopefully as a priority.

Other areas that were brought to conversation during the empirical data collection by the participants that are interesting to develop further research on them, are: the age gap and the difficulty of the older generations to adapt to digital transformation and, the lack of access of indigenous communities to the internet which leaves them excluded from any and all digital government initiatives, and the importance of adequate infrastructure for information technologies in urban and rural areas as well.

Appendix

See Figs. 1, 2 and 3.

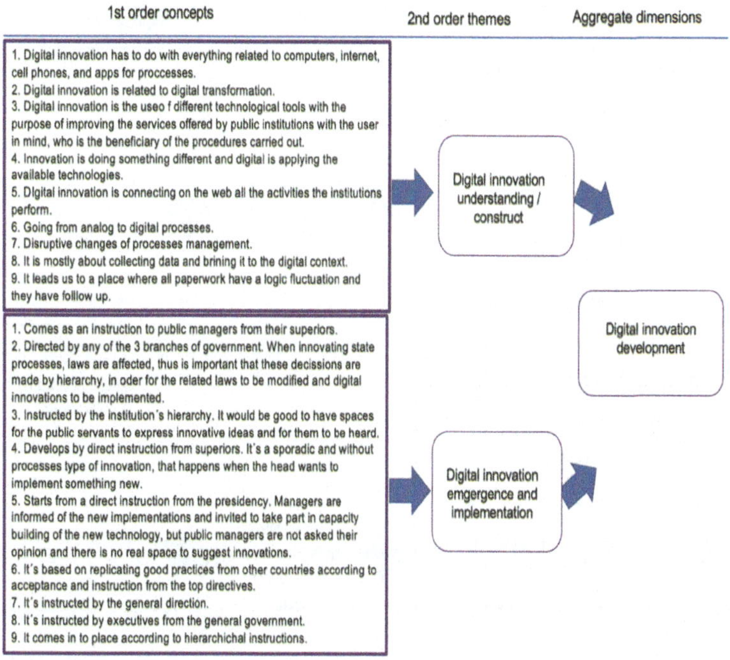

Fig. 1 Graphic. Data structure

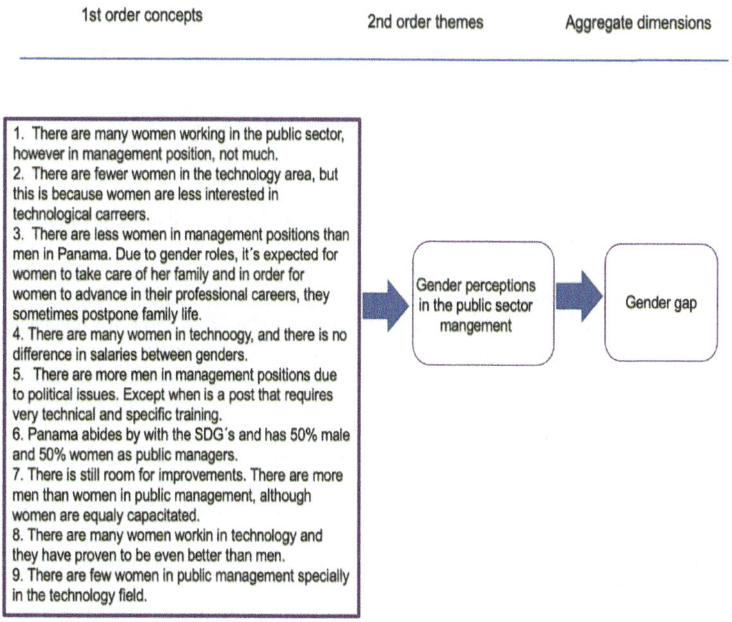

Fig. 2 Graphic. Data structure 2

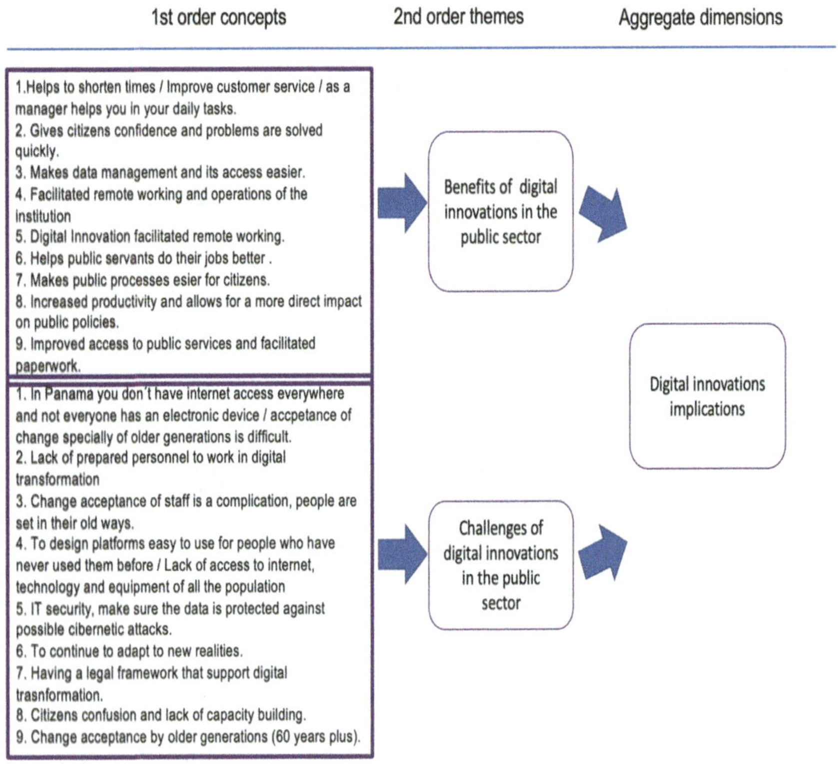

Fig. 3 Graphic. Data structure 3

References

Ambert, A., Adler, P.A., Adler, P., Detzner, D.F.: Understanding and evaluating qualitative research. J. Marriage Fam. **57**(4), 880 (1995)

Autio, E., Nambisan, S., Thomas, L.D.W., Wright, M.: Digital affordances, spatial affordances, and the genesis of entrepreneurial ecosystems. Strateg. Entrep. J. **12**(1), 74 (2018)

Arredondo Trapero, F.G., Vázquez Parra, J.C., Velázquez Sánchez, L.M.: STEM y brecha de género en latinoamérica. Revista De El Colegio De San Luis **9**(18), 154 (2019)

Avgerou, C., Bonina, C.: Ideologies implicated in IT innovation in government: a critical discourse analysis of mexico's international trade administration. Inf. Syst. J. (oxford, England) **30**(1), 91 (2019)

Bineham, J.L.: Displacing descartes: philosophical hermeneutic and rhetorical studies. Philos. Rhetor. **27**(4), 307 (1994)

Carrasco, I.: Gender gap in innovation: an institutionalist explanation. Manag. Decis. **52**(2), 421 (2014)

Chase, P., Berzina, K.: Digital Transformation Policy Issues. German Marshall Fund of the United States, p. 48 (2018)

Chesborough, H.: The logic of innovation: managing intellectual property. Calif. Manag. Rev. **45**(3), 37 (2003)

Ciuriak, D., Ptashkina, M.: Leveraging the digital transformation for development: a global south strategy for the data-driven economy, p. 1–2. Centre for International Governance Innovation (2019)

Easterby-Smith, M., Thorpe, R., Jackson, P.: The philosophy of management and business research (Chap. 3). In: Management Research, pp. 170. SAGE, London (2012)

European Union: Horizon 2020: Closing Gender Gaps in Research & Innovation, p. 1. Luxembourg: Publications Office, Luxembourg (2020)

Evans, S.K., Pearce, K.E., Vitak, J., Treem, J.W.: Explicating affordances: a conceptual framework for understanding affordances in communication research. J. Comput.-Mediat. Commun. **22**(1), 36 (2017)

Gioia, D.A., Corley, K.G., Hamilton, A.L.: Seeking qualitative rigor in inductive research. Organ. Res. Methods **16**(1), 20 (2013)

Li, F.: Leading digital transformation: three emerging approaches for managing the transition. Int. J. Oper. Prod. Manag. **40**(6), 809 (2020)

Nambisan, S., Lyytinen, K., Majchrzak, A., Song, M.: Digital innovation management: reinventing innovation management research in a digital world. MIS Q. **41**(1), 223 (2017)

Packer, M., Goicoechea, J.: Teorías socioculturales y constructivistas del aprendizaje: Ontología, no solamente epistemologíal, p. 3. Universidad del Valle, Psicología Cultural (2000)

Pecis, L.: Doing and undoing gender in innovation: femininities and masculinities in innovation processes. Hum. Relat. (n. Y.) **69**(11), 2119–2120 (2016)

Reeves, S., Hodges, B.D.: Ethnography, p. 514 (2008)

Simons, H.: Case Study Research in Practice, p. 21. SAGE Publications, London (2009)

Trainor, A., Graue, E.: Standing at the Corner of epistemology ave, theoretical trail, methodology Blvd, and methods street: the intersections of qualitative research. In: Anonymous Reviewing Qualitative Research in the Social Sciences, p. 13. Routledge (2013)

Trauth, E.M.: The role of theory in gender and information systems research. Inf. Organ. **23**(4), 285 (2013)

Von Kutzschenbach, M., & Brønn, C.: Education for managing digital transformation: a feedback systems approach. J. Syst. Cybern. Inf. **15**(2), 1 (2017)

Yoo, Y., Henfridsson, O., Lyytinen, K.: Research commentary: the new organizing logic of digital innovation: an agenda for information systems research. Inf. Syst. Res. **21**(4), 275 (2010)

Yilmaz, K.: Comparison of quantitative and qualitative research traditions: epistemological, theoretical, and methodological differences. Euro. J. Edu. **48**(2), 313 (2013)

Yin, R.: Case Study Research Design and Methods, 3rd edn., p. 7. SAGE, London (2003)

Laura Martinez is a Management Ph.D. Candidate from the University of Birmingham working on her thesis of Digital Transformation in the Public Sector in Panama, who is also currently pursuing a master's degree in Higher Education from the Latin University of Panama, has an MBA from the University of Chile, and a bachelor's degree in international affairs from Florida State University. She is management professional with 10 years of work experience in the private and public sector as well as in INGO's.

Platform-Based Interorganizational Learning for Business Model Innovation: Case Study AgilHybrid

Thomas Trabert, Caroline Große, Sebastian Beiner, Tobias Göcke, Claudia Lehmann, and Steffen Kinkel

Abstract The research project AgilHybrid aims to support SMEs and traditional industrial companies in innovating digital and hybrid business models. The focus of the project lies on needed processes, structures and competences for the successful innovation of digitally networked business models in the era of digital transformation. To this end, an interorganizational learning platform was developed during the project which is examined in this paper. Consisting of two parts named iCourious (being an online course) and iAccelerator (as a business model innovation tool), the platform connects learners from varying organizations. As a practice-oriented contribution, the paper elaborates on how different learners have developed their competences when using the platform. Whereas digital experts improve their skills from a good competence level to a slightly higher level, it is digital beginners that benefit most from learning on the platform.

T. Trabert · C. Große (✉)
HHL Leipzig Graduate School of Management, Center for Leading Innovation and Cooperation, Jahnallee 59, 04109 Leipzig, Germany
e-mail: c.grosse@hhl.de

T. Trabert
e-mail: thomas.trabert@hhl.de

S. Beiner · S. Kinkel
Hochschule Karlsruhe, Institut Für Lernen Und Innovation in Netzwerken, Moltkestr. 30, 76133 Karlsruhe, Germany
e-mail: sebastian.beiner@hka.de

S. Kinkel
e-mail: steffen.kinkel@hka.de

T. Göcke
SupraTix GmbH, Bautzner Str. 45-47, 01099 Dresden, Germany
e-mail: tobias.goecke@supratix.com

C. Lehmann
HHL Leipzig Graduate School of Management, LF Group Chair of Digital Innovation in Service Industries, Jahnallee 59, 04109 Leipzig, Germany
e-mail: claudia.lehmann@hhl.de

© The Author(s), under exclusive license to Springer Nature Switzerland AG 2024
D. Schallmo et al. (eds.), *Digital Disruption and Transformation*, Springer Proceedings in Business and Economics, https://doi.org/10.1007/978-3-031-47888-8_6

Keywords Business model innovation · Product-service-systems · Digital business models · Interorganizational learning · Blended learning · Competence development · Learner persona

1 Introduction

The digital transformation goes hand in hand with fast changing market conditions. With respect to that, especially SMEs and traditional industrial companies face some challenges since they often lack in terms of competences for digitalization and business model innovation. However, digitalization offers several opportunities to optimize processes by using new technologies or for business model innovation (Araujo and Spring 2006; Windahl et al. 2004).

Against the background of the rising importance of digital and service-based business models across all over the world, traditional industrial companies have to develop their business model innovation capabilities if they do not want to be left behind (Hess et al. 2016; Ramdani et al. 2021). The aim of the research project AgilHybrid was to help those companies and their employees to arrive in the digital age. The following conference contribution shows an important project result in the field of interorganizational collaboration, namely it describes a learning platform that connects learners from varying organizations. The paper focusses on how different learner types can develop their competences when using the platform for interorganizational learning. For this purpose, a categorization of the learning types based on the collected data after completion of the learning platform was determined.

The remainder of the paper is structured as follows: The second chapter provides some theoretical underpinnings and insights on prior studies, especially from our AgilHybrid project. Subsequently, the third chapter describes the platform for interorganizational learning, consisting of the two parts iCourious, which is a Massive Open Online Course (MOOC) on the basics of digital transformation, and iAccelerator, as a tool of business model innovation. The fourth chapter elaborates on how different learner types have developed their competences using the platform, whereas the fifth chapter reflects on the results. The sixth and last part finalizes the paper with some concluding remarks.

2 Insight on Prior Studies

The research project AgilHybrid studied on requirements that industrial companies have to meet in order to successfully develop digitally networked business models (DNBM). Those requirements range from suitable processes and organizational structure to necessary competences for developing teams and leadership competences. This study shows how AgilHybrid merged these requirements into a practical online tool that brings learners and business model developers of different organizations together to develop their competences while working on business model innovation projects. This exciting point highlights the unique nature of this format—a high diversity of learners, resulting in the identification of a wide variety of personas.

To provide a short theoretical introduction to the development of competences related to the development of digitally networked business models, this section briefly considers key aspects and definitions.

Competences and Competence Management. According to Erpenbeck (2017), competences are described as the ability to act creatively and self-organized in open, unmanageable, complex, dynamic, and sometimes chaotic situations (Erpenbeck 2017). This results in differentiation to qualifications described as being externally organized to fulfill given goals, while competences refer to self-organized problem solving (Arnold 2001). Only by solving real problems or receiving feedback from partners, learners can internalize values and develop competences (Erpenbeck 2017).

Competence management makes an essential contribution to corporate and human resources development (Rost 2020) by systematically describing, synchronizing, and developing individual competences and organizational skills (North et al. 2013). Specifically, strategic competence management can promote the implementation of a corporate strategy by using competence models to target employees' behaviour in line with the strategy (Meifert 2013). Strategic competence models bundle professional, social, and methodological competences that have been identified as critical to success across different roles and organizations, considering future requirements resulting from the corporate strategy (Meifert 2013).

Digitally Networked Business Models (DNBM). Digitally networked business models combine physical products and services to hybrid Product-Service-Systems. Digitalization of products, processes and actors enable the producer to individually adapt features and meet every customer's demand. Thus, the customer is involved in the design and value creation process of the Product-Service-System. Suppliers are able to raise the added value and therefore profit in terms of revenue (Kinkel et al. 2020).

Innovation of DNBMs. The innovation process of DNBMs demands different requirements compared to classical business model innovation (BMI) of physical products. There are more interdependencies of the demands of the actors (Parviainen et al. 2017; Matt et al. 2015). It is necessary to adapt the features closer to the needs of the customers. In addition, DNBMs combine various digital elements that are developed differently than physical products or features.

Therefore, AgilHybrid developed a 4-phase-process model that combines elements of agile software development, hybrid BMI and the requirements of industrial companies that aim to develop DNBMs (Trabert and Beiner 2021). The four phases are: (1) problem identification, (2) idea creation, (3) validation and (4) realization. The innovation process takes place in iterative recursions, which allow the developers to test their ideas at an early stage, to adapt prototypes considering customer feedback and to throw away ideas, if the customers do not like them (Fig. 1).

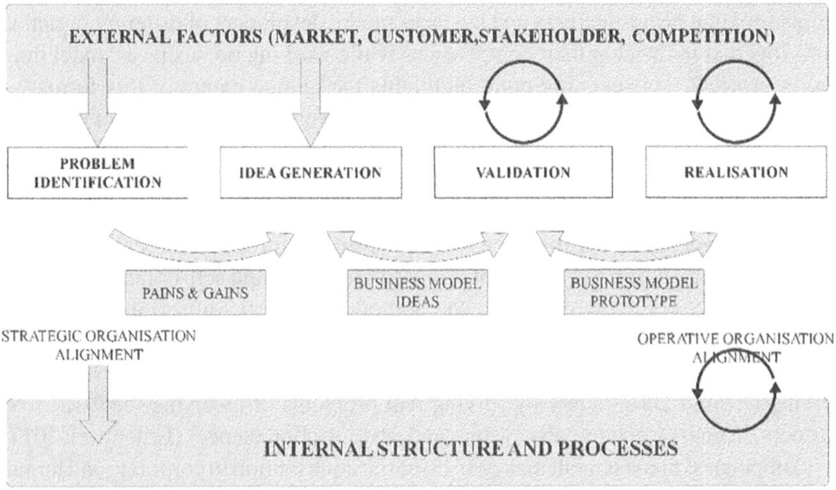

Fig. 1 4-phase-process model of business model innovation (*Source* Trabert and Beiner 2021)

Competences for DNBM developing teams. One core result of the AgilHybrid project is the fact that successful innovation processes not only need suitable methods and organizational prerequisites but rather the right people with the right competences and ideas. Following this idea, AgilHybrid developed and validated a 20-competence model structured in five different competence categories, as shown in Table 1. Those categories are entrepreneurship capabilities, mutability, agile capabilities, interoperability and digital capabilities (Beiner et al. 2021).

Prior studies show the necessity to develop these competences if companies aim to innovate DNBMs. We could notice a difference between the actual competence levels of the employees and the aimed competence levels for successful DNBM innovation. Asked for the way leaders of companies wish to develop those competences, learning

Table 1 AgilHybrid 20-competence-model for teams

Entrepreneurship capabilities	Mutability	Agile capabilities	Interoperability	Digital capabilities
Openness to coincidences	Willingness to change	Design thinking	Interdisciplinary collaboration	Digital thinking
Business model thinking	Creative problem solving	Mastering complexity	Networking	Data comprehension
Ecosystem thinking	Enthusiasm for innovation	Self-management and reflection	Open communication	IT security, law and data protection
Initiative	Overview competence	Customer orientation	Teamwork	Digital collaboration

Source Beiner et al. (2021)

on-the-job and digital solutions are considered to play a major role (Beiner et al. 2021). This is why AgilHybrid, especially the learning specialist SupraTix developed a two-stage online platform for interorganizational learning that combines the advantages of online learning with project-oriented and interorganizational business model innovation.

3 Platform for Interorganizational Learning

The blended learning course iCourious represents the first stage of the innovation learning journey in the SupraWorx ecosystem provided by SupraTix. Its focus is to enable people to understand what is essential while challenging digital transformation and business model innovation processes. Background knowledge and valuable methods are presented in web sessions and with the help of video content. iCourious also has an active and practical level, where participants can test their newly gained knowledge and have to solve different tasks. For example, they have to write blog entries describing how they used different methods of BMI. Furthermore, they use a checklist or a workbook to solve individual and organization related challenges. In addition, they can get in touch with various experts and other participants. Alone, in learning tandems, or in a learning group with a maximum size of 5 participants, the learners use the integrated network, chat and video call capabilities to work together and ask questions to the experts in expert hours or collaborate on a virtual whiteboard.

A cohort of iCourious takes about four weeks in terms of time. At the end of a session, the tasks are handed over so that the learners can work out steps towards digitization independently with our help channels. For elaborating the tasks, we do not expect more than 7 h in the four weeks. All webinars are recorded so that the learners can join in after a live session.

In the following, we like to provide an overview of the sessions and learning process of the iCourious course. These sessions are structured as follows:

1. The three stages of digitization
2. What are digitally networked business models?
3. Actual challenges of business model innovation
4. Discussion of ideas, hurdles and success factors for BMI.

At the end of the course, a certificate is issued for successful participation.

Before and after participation of the learners, their competence maturity level is calculated based on a questionnaire. To this end, the AgilHybrid competence model with behaviour anchors is applied. The SupraTix team sees the individual and current state of competence expression from the calculations and assembles the learning teams according to this data and the learner's preferences. Each session, task and learning content defines a learning aim.

Using SupraTix AI, adaptive learning was tested. In adaptive learning, knowledge transfer is adapted to the current state of knowledge, i. e. participants received an individual learning path. It turned out that this group of people was about 40% faster than the rest of the group while the average learning time was 195 h. In total, 70 learners from different companies were attending the iCourious program.

After completing iCourious, the learners are ready to start innovating their business model by using the iAccelerator. It is an internet platform where companies can design, develop, test and plan digitally networked business models through to realization. They can develop a new business model to "pitch readiness" with different tools, e.g., creativity methods. The participants bring their business model so far to test it on potential customers. It aims to support DNBM innovating companies and single persons with practical methods and to lead through the process, oriented at the above-mentioned 4-phase-process model. One of the central features of iAccelerator is selecting and assembling teams for innovation projects while taking the participant's competences into account. It is possible to provide interorganizational teams with innovative new business models with that feature. The iAccelerator combines various tools in an innovative way.

One of the central elements is a project management software that guides purposefully through the steps of a business model development for digital business models. At the same time, the system provides the necessary tools for interactive collaboration and structuring of the content and the project team.

In addition to the collaborative work tools, the platform includes more than 20 design thinking methods used within the context of BMI to identify customer problems and develop ideas and prototypes. Unique about the iAccelerator platform is that the people during the business model development are supported by an AI, which suggests the appropriate methods for the current problem and ensures the selection of the most promising business ideas. As part of the iAccelerator, participants are empowered to develop new business models and acquire necessary skills simultaneously, supported by an AI-enabled governance process.

4 Competence Development of Different Types of Learners

Generally, for the development of digital business models, both managers and development teams must be equipped with a broad range of competences. Only teams with a broad range of different competences can succeed in digital transformation. Competence development depends on the actual level at which learners start the learning process. Beginners perform differently compared to experienced innovators or experts for digitalization. This is the reason why we compare different stereotypes of learners using the presented platform.

Identification of Learner-Personas. Prior to the participation on the platform, learners assessed themselves regarding the 20-competence-model. To that intend, we queried so called behavioural anchors that describe typical actions for people with distinct competences. This enables us to define and compare different participants' competence profiles. By doing so, we were able to identify some stereotypical learner profiles. We added them to two heterogenous groups of different homogenous competences. Figures 2 and 3 show selective examples for two of those stereotypes.

The following competence development relates to learning activities of the iCourious online course. Those results are used to adapt and improve aspects of the iAccelerator tool.

Competence development of different learners. The so-called digital beginners (Fig. 2) exhibit rather high (≥80%) interoperability, agile capability and mutability, medium (60–70%) entrepreneurship capabilities and just low digital capabilities (20–30%). These learners are characterized as traditional engineers. The digital beginner is able to develop new products in a traditional, but also in an agile way. They are

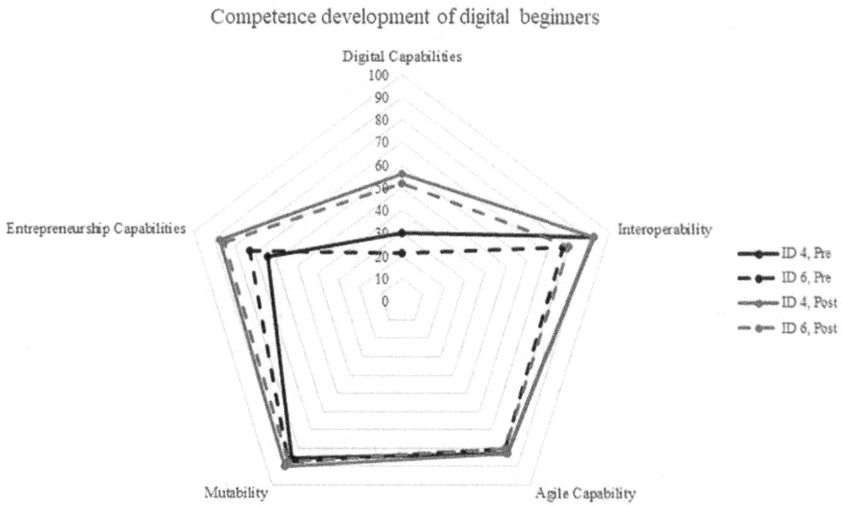

Fig. 2 Competence development of persona 1—digital beginner (*Source* own illustration)

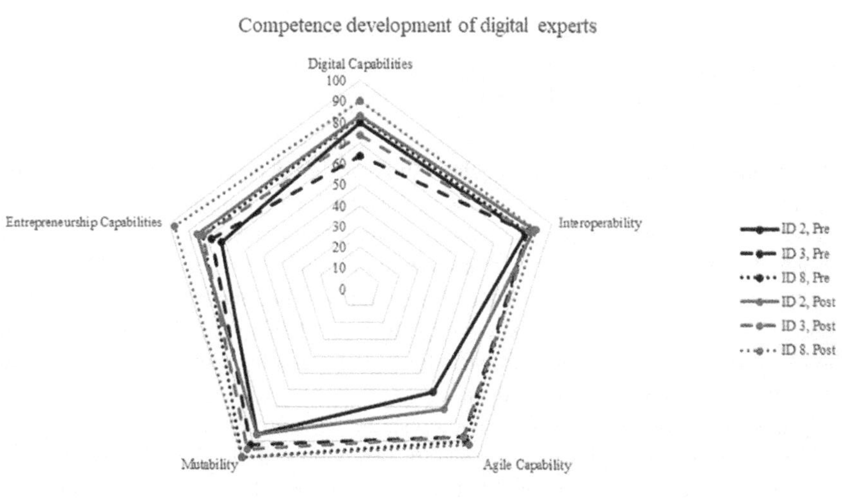

Fig. 3 Competence development of persona 2—digital expert (*Source* own illustration)

good team workers and know how to work in interdisciplinary teams. Raising their scope from developing products to develop business models is not easy for them. But most significantly, they lack of digital competences. Especially when it comes to the innovation of digital business models, digital beginners struggle by understanding the specific demands.

After completing the iCourious course, learners assessed their competences a second time. One can recognize a development in the competence groups of entrepreneurship capabilities and digital capabilities. The other competence groups did not change noticeably. This effect seems plausible, because these increased competences are the ones that were the least distinct ones. Focussing entrepreneurship capabilities, the learners increased their competences on a higher level than agile capabilities. The latter did not increase at all.

These high effects on digital beginners lead to the assumption, that the course only raises competence levels, that are less distinct. This is why we also studied the effects of the course on digital experts.

In comparison to the digital beginners, digital experts show at least medium, but mostly high abilities in every group of competences (Fig. 3). The digital capabilities for instance, show values from 65 to 80% prior to the participation. The three exemplary learners seem to be able to take part in DNBM developing teams. They know something about agile methods and digital solutions, they are able to collaborate in interdisciplinary teams and understand the systematics of business models. It is therefore of interest to compare whether the use of the platform has further improved these competences.

Observing the competence development of digital experts, one can recognize positive effects. All the learners increased their competences at the sections of digital capabilities, agile capabilities and entrepreneurship capabilities. Some learners raised their competence levels when it comes to mutability, others remained on their prior level. Interoperability did not change noticeably.

5 Discussion and Reflection

After comparing the competence development of different types of learners, it became apparent that the benefit of the course iCourious for competence development is visible. The detailed comparison of mean competence levels over both types of learners before and after the course is shown in Fig. 4.

In particular, the fact that German companies are lagging behind in the use of agile or innovative methods for knowledge transfer (Kinkel et al. 2020) means that the two formats provide a targeted basis for training employees to drive forward the development of new business models.

Finally, the training of employees represents the central point within an organization to enrich the (digital) value creation (Trabert et al. 2022). When looking at the identified learner types, it quickly becomes clear that these groups are present in almost every organization. Therefore, the developed formats are a new way to build

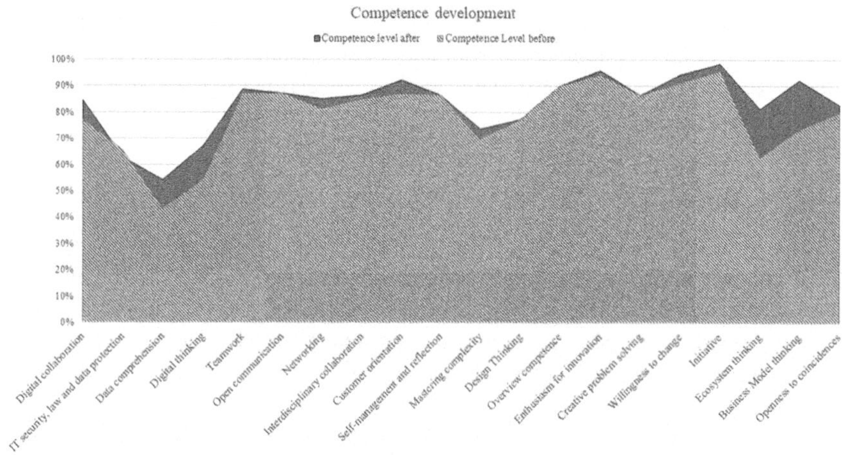

Fig. 4 Cumulated competence development (*Source* own illustration)

up digital collaboration skills especially for digital beginners, as well as to consolidate or slightly improve them for digital experts. From this point of view, iCourious primarily offers the opportunity for beginners to expand their skills. Thereby a clear impact on digital skills could be noticed.

It was also recognizable that skills showed improvement when they were already at a high level. Interoperability is the exception here. These competences did not increase and rather remained at the same level. However, the interorganizational platform iAccelerator can support this and enable an increase in competences. The iAccelerator in particular can bring even more benefits due to its practical relevance on real problems, so that more value is being created and competences are developed. (Erpenbeck 2017).

The use and consideration of blended learning approaches in interaction with the validated competence fields, enabled a target-oriented design of the courses. Furthermore, the approaches presented here are a good instrument to ensure the competitiveness of SMEs in particular. In addition, all participating companies can benefit from a cooperation that goes beyond their own company boundaries. Ideas can thus be processed across organizations.

Especially the scientifically based analysis of the necessary competences and embedding them into the 4-phase-process model, proves to be an innovative integration into the course format. The specific focus on business model innovation provides a validated added value for companies, especially for their products and services, by empowering their employees to develop hybrid and digital business models.

Therefore, both tools aim for professionals with an interest in developing competences for being enabled to innovate digital and hybrid business models. We especially want to address SMEs that struggle in the era of digital transformation. SMEs often show a low degree of digitalization. They could benefit from interorganizational collaboration and learn from our recommendations.

Nevertheless, the application of both formats is still in its beginning stages and needs to be further complemented with participating companies. As a result, more data is needed to concretize or possibly expand the learning type categorization.

6 Conclusion

All in all, we want to disseminate our project results and show the potential of interorganizational learning by using the developed platform to a broad audience. By using the platform, SMEs can benefit in particular from the cross-organizational increase in knowledge and further enhance the development of innovative business models.

During the review and validation of the developed format, it became clear that there is an increase in competence with regard to the development of DNBM. In addition, MOOCs also appear promising for further investigation, as they represent an attractive combination of online and collaborative learning environments. This hybridity will continue to increase in the course of digitization due to the need for interaction between the physical and virtual world of work.

The AgilHybrid project was funded by the German Federal Ministry of Education and Research (BMBF) and the European Social Fund (ESF) within the Future of Work funding program and implemented by the Project Management Agency Karlsruhe (PTKA). The authors are responsible for the content of this publication.

References

Araujo, L., Spring, M.: Services, products, and the institutional structure of production. Ind. Mark. Manag. **35**(7), 797–805 (2006)

Arnold, R.: Wörterbuch Erwachsenenpädagogik. Klinkhardt, Bad Heilbrunn/Obb. (2001)

Beiner, S., Trabert, T., Kinkel, S., Müller, J., Cherubini, E., Lehmann, C.: Identifikation und Validierung von Teamkompetenzen für die Entwicklung digital vernetzter Geschäftsmodelle. Gruppe Interaktion Organisation, pp. 1–17 (2021)

Erpenbeck, J.: Handbuch Kompetenzmessung. Erkennen, verstehen und bewerten von Kompetenzen in der betrieblichen, pädagogischen und psychologischen Praxis, 3rd edn. Schäffer-Poeschel, Stuttgart (2017)

Hess, T., Matt, C., Benlian, A., Wiesböck, F.: Options for formulating a digital transformation strategy. MIS Q. Exec. **15**, 123–139 (2016)

Kinkel, S., Cherubini, E., Kopp, T., Beiner, S.: Entwicklung digital vernetzter Produkte und Geschäftsmodelle. Z. für Wirtschaftlichen Fabrikbetrieb **115**(6), 376–380 (2020)

Matt, C., Hess, T., Benlian, A.: Digital transformation strategies. Bus. Inf. Syst. Eng. **57**(5), 339–343 (2015)

Meifert, M.: Strategische Personalentwicklung. Springer Fachmedien Wiesbaden, Wiesbaden (2013)

North, K., Reinhardt, K., Sieber-Suter, B.: Was ist Kompetenz? In: Kompetenzmanagement in der Praxis, pp. 43–91. Gabler, Wiesbaden (2013)

Parviainen, P., Tihinen, M., Kääriäinen, J., Teppola, S.: Tackling the digitalization challenge: how to benefit from digitalization in practice. Int. J. Inf. Syst. Proj. Manag. **5**, 63–77 (2017)

Ramdani, B., Raja, S., Kayumova, M.: Digital innovation in SMEs: a systematic review, synthesis and research agenda. Inf. Technol. Dev. **28**(1), 56–80 (2021)

Rost, M.: Mit Kompetenzmanagement die Strategie und Innovationsfähigkeit des Unternehmens unterstützen. In: Pfannstiel, M., Steinhoff, P. (eds.) Transformationsvorhaben mit dem Enterprise Transformation Cycle meistern, pp. 283–299. Springer Fachmedien Wiesbaden, Wiesbaden (2020)

Trabert, T., Beiner, S.: Gestaltung eines agilen Phasenmodells zur Entwicklung und Erprobung digital vernetzter Geschäftsmodelle. Paper presented at the Frühjahrskongress 2021 of the Gesellschaft für Arbeitswissenschaft (GfA). Arbeit HUMAINE gestalten, Bochum (2021)

Trabert, T., Beiner, S., Lehmann, C., Kinkel, S.: Digital value creation in sociotechnical systems. Procedia Comput. Sci. **200**, 471–481 (2022)

Windahl, C., Andersson, P., Berggren, C., Nehler, C.: Manufacturing firms and integrated solutions: characteristics and implications. Eur. J. Innov. Manag. **7**(3), 218–228 (2004)

Thomas Trabert studied industrial engineering with a focus on production and logistics. In doing so, he was able to gain valuable experience with the integration of technical innovation at high-tech companies from industry. During his time as a research assistant, he explored the agile development of competencies and business models in the context of digital transformation. His research focus within his dissertation is on human-centered organizational design of small and medium-sized enterprises as well as competence development with regard to business model innovation.

Caroline Große is a senior researcher at HHL Leipzig Graduate School of Management where she mainly works on projects around digital transformation and female entrepreneurship. Prior to joining HHL in June 2021, she held various positions at the Institute for Service and Relationship Management at Leipzig University and the Fraunhofer Center for International Management and Knowledge Economy IMW in Leipzig. Caroline received her doctoral degree in Business Administration from the Faculty of Economics and Management Science at Leipzig University in 2021. She holds a B. A. in Service and Marketing Management and a M. Sc. in Management Science.

Sebastian Beiner is an industrial engineer (B. Eng.) and technology manager (M. Sc.). Since 2019, he has been conducting research as a scientific assistant at the Institute for Learning and Innovation in Networks (ILIN) at Karlsruhe University of Applied Sciences on challenges and opportunities of digital transformation in organizations. Here, he focuses on topics such as sustainable industrial production, the agile development of digitally networked business models, and the sociotechnical development and application of artificial intelligence in the context of business operations.

Tobias Göcke As a chemical engineer, Tobias Göcke brings his visions to life with the company he and his wife founded, SupraTix GmbH. Previously, he gained experience in companies with rigid structures that could not do justice to his ideas and solutions, which he underpinned with successful participation in competitions, such as the ChemCar competition, with first places. Tobias passionately supports medium-sized companies in the development of digital business models, in the optimization of work processes, and in finding new approaches to solutions in unclear and complex subject areas.

Claudia Lehmann is Professor of Digital Innovation in Service Industries and Executive Director of the Center for Leading Innovation and Cooperation (CLIC) at HHL Leipzig Graduate School of Management. Her work focuses on methods and tools for the development and provision of digitally enabled services and business models. In particular, the focus is on the interdisciplinary and interactive communication of innovation competence for service engineering in digital transformation with the aim of enabling companies to design and implement digital services and business models. Claudia has been involved in numerous publications as author/co-author as well as editor/co-editor.

Steffen Kinkel is Professor for Innovation Management and International Management at Karlsruhe University of Applied Sciences. He is founder and director of the Institute for Learning and Innovation in Networks (ILIN). Steffen has coordinated numerous national and international research projects. His research focuses on human-centred work design and technology introduction, sustainable work and production systems, AI-supported work and learning systems, digitally supported competence development, digital business models, global and local value chains, resilient supply chains, re/backshoring, production and innovation networks, and technology planning and foresight.

Data-Driven Foresight in Life Cycle Management: An Interview Study

Marie Scheuffele, Niklas Bayrle-Kelso, and Leo Brecht

Abstract Discontinuities in the market create space for disruptive business opportunities. A promising approach for companies to proactively identify future competitive advantages is Data-Driven Foresight (DDF). By using different data sources from various perspectives, DDF can derive solid statements about trend-driven developments in the future. As technology life cycles accelerate, industrial firms increasingly want to incorporate foresight activities into their Life Cycle Management to foster digital transformation. This raises the following research question: How do companies obtain their data for DDF in Life Cycle Management, and what alternative data sources are recommended? By conducting a systematic literature review, the state-of-the-art data sources are described and classified along the life cycle. Twenty semi-structured expert interviews with practitioners from different types of companies show valid premises for data selection and for the practical implementation of DDF. Regarding this, a recognizable difference between technology leaders and followers exists, which opens another gap for future research.

Keywords Data-driven foresight · Trends research · Data sources · Foresight methods · Technology life cycles · Life cycle management · Literature review · Expert interviews

M. Scheuffele (✉) · N. Bayrle-Kelso · L. Brecht
Universität Liechtenstein, Fürst-Franz-Josef-Strasse, 9490 Vaduz, Liechtenstein
e-mail: marie.scheuffele@uni.li

N. Bayrle-Kelso
e-mail: niklas.bayrle@uni.li

L. Brecht
e-mail: leo.brecht@uni.li

© The Author(s), under exclusive license to Springer Nature Switzerland AG 2024

D. Schallmo et al. (eds.), *Digital Disruption and Transformation*, Springer Proceedings in Business and Economics, https://doi.org/10.1007/978-3-031-47888-8_7

1 Introduction

> Why do we talk of foresight rather than vision? Vision connotes a dream or an apparition, and there is more to industry foresight than a blinding flash of insight. Industry foresight is based on deep insights into trends in technology, demographics, regulations, and lifestyles, which can be harnessed to rewrite industry rules and create new competitive space. While understanding the potential implications of such trends requires creativity and imagination, any "vision" that is not based on a solid foundation is likely to be fantastical. (Hamel and Prahalad 1994)

In their text "Competing for the Future", Hamel and Prahalad (1994) ask their readers whether their companies have a clear shared vision of what their own industry might look like in the future. Although this work dates back several years, the question seems more relevant than ever in the current global economic situation. If the past few years have made one thing clear, the market is inevitably changing, and tomorrow's competitive advantages will be different from today's. However, just as discontinuities in the market can lead to uncertainty, they also offer scope for new disruptive business opportunities. Data-Driven Foresight is a promising approach for companies to proactively identify and seize future competitive advantages (Rohrbeck et al. 2015). Data-Driven Foresight (DDF) uses various data sources to make statements about trend-driven developments in the future. By applying suitable analysis methods, the data is processed and interpreted so that concrete measures for action can be derived from it (John 2022). DDF in companies primarily deals with technology and market trends. It provides a better understanding of the future and thus opens an opportunity to influence it. At the same time, DDF expands the diversity of perspectives in the company and helps to achieve more flexibility and participation in decision-making (Blind et al. 1999). Business practice has always been concerned with looking into the future and planning activities in advance. However, due to increasing competitive dynamics, fuelled by advancing globalization and digitalization, future-oriented decision-making in Technology and Innovation Management (TIM) and Product Management (ProMM), including Life Cycle Management (LCM), is becoming increasingly complex (Martin 1995). In this context, an increasing number of studies on digital transformation in LCM is entering the field, striving to get a hold on incorporating new digital technologies, changing customer requirements, and big data insights into product development and life cycle considerations (Holler et al. 2019; C.-H. Lee et al. 2021; Li et al. 2015). Developments in science and technology are interdependent with social change and global economic success. Moreover, innovations are increasingly emerging in large, heterogeneous innovation ecosystems with numerous stakeholders and multi-layered interest groups. Rapid improvement counters this in data collection, processing, and analysis. Therefore, DDF promises to provide an ever-better picture of the future regarding long-term challenges and opportunities (Becker 2002). This publication aims to provide the current state of the art on DDF in science and practice. Furthermore, the paper strives to make a scientific contribution to the application of DDF in LCM with regard to increasing digital support in LCM decision-making.

2 Research Methodology

The research methodology of this paper comprises a systematic literature review and the collection and evaluation of qualitative data employing semi-structured expert interviews. From the current need for research in the field of DDF, the following research question arises and will be answered in this paper: How do companies obtain their data for DDF in LCM, and what alternative data sources are recommended?

The systematic literature review follows a three-step process, which includes first, planning the literature review; second, conducting the literature review; and third, formulating and disseminating the results (Tranfield et al. 2003). The relevance and scope of the topic-specific literature were delineated by an initial filtered search in the Web of Science, which resulted in 2,720 hits. The following search terms and filter settings were used as a basis for this initial search: data-driven foresight (All Fields) or foresight methods (All Fields), or data sources foresight (All Fields). To refine the search results the following search query was added to the keywords during the second process step: (Data OR Method* OR Algorithm*) AND foresight AND (compan* OR firm* OR corporate*) (Topic). This search query resulted in 288 hits on the Web of Science. After an initial review of the literature base data and a subsequent detailed analysis of the full texts, those works were included in the final list, which both addressed a research question relevant to the subject and demonstrated a high degree of internal validity in their methodological approach. Resources that did not meet the above criteria were excluded from the list. The next section of this publication contains the results of the literature analysis. It presents the state of the art of DDF data sources and methods together with its leading authors in a tabular form.

Since it is beneficial to use a qualitative research method to investigate young research areas with a limited knowledge base, the present work relies on semi-structured expert interviews (Rohrbeck and Gemünden 2011). To meet the basic criteria for a high-quality qualitative study, the current work considers the subjective meaning that the interviewed experts attach to specific experiences and events. This also preserves the necessary degree of flexibility that a qualitative method requires to be able to collect context-specific data. The sampling strategy is described in section four of this paper and fulfills the conditions of theory- and context-relatedness. By interviewing several independent experts, data triangulation could be established, which facilitates the generalizability of the findings obtained (Popay et al. 1998).

In a concluding discussion in the last section, the findings from the literature review are contrasted with the results of the semi-structured expert interviews. This makes it possible to uncover existing similarities and any discrepancies between theory and practice and to find a well-founded answer to the research question.

3 Literature Review

3.1 State-of-the-Art Data Sources for Data-Driven Foresight

In the theoretical part of this paper, the focus is entirely on the data sources and methods available for Data-Driven Foresight. Since the outcome of a foresight project depends mainly on the selection of suitable data sources, these will be described first in the further course of this chapter before some well-known and proven foresight methods are explained in more detail.

To ensure a structured presentation of the data sources, this study follows a simple STEEP (Society, Technology, Economy, Environment, Politics) approach. The STEEP analysis, as such, is an external environmental analysis. By listing all the factors or trends per perspective that have a significant influence on a unit under investigation, a holistic view of the industrial dynamics in a business environment is created (Saritas et al. 2019). Just as trends and their drivers can be classified using a STEEP analysis, the data sources on which the DDF is based can also be classified in these perspectives. Throughout this chapter, the relevant data sources for each perspective are displayed with mention of the most influential authors. Additionally, their types (textual, numerical, verbal) and structures (structured, semi-structured, unstructured, mobile/sensor-based data) as well as their positions along the technology life cycle are described. As a basis for the latter serves Table 1 by Martino (2003), who started to position the DDF data sources according to their informative value in an earlier work.

According to the author, emergent technologies that are still at the very beginning of their life cycle can be derived from scientific publications. On the other hand, the analysis of newspaper and press data makes it possible to identify trends that relate to technologies and products that are already in the application phase or the social impacts phase (Martino 2003). For some of the established data sources, a valid assignment to the life cycle phases already exists according to the current state of research (Mikova and Sokolova 2019). In such cases, the present work adopts the proposed positioning. In the case of newer data sources, which have not yet been comprehensively studied, the evidence-based classification by previous research work is partly missing. Here, the present work takes its own positioning of the data

Table 1 Sources for lifecycle data

R&D stage	Typical source
Basic research	Science citation index
Applied research	Engineering index
Development	US patents
Application	Newspaper abstracts daily
Social impacts	Business and popular press

Source Martino (2003)

source along the technology life cycle. This is done based on the proven informative value of the respective data source and should be validated in the context of future research. Table 2 provides an overview of data sources that, according to the current state of literature, are suitable for analyzing the societal factors influencing the future of a business field.

Table 3 contains the data sources of the technological perspective and briefly describes and typologizes them.

Table 4 shows the state of the art of data sources that, according to the current state of research, are suitable for analyzing economic trend drivers.

Table 5 contains the state-of-the-art data sources from the environmental perspective.

Table 2 Overview of DDF data sources for the social perspective

Data source	Database/Data collection	Typology	Authors
Expert opinions	Experts from academia and practice Interviews (semi-structured) Surveys (semi-structured)	Unstructured, verbal, and textual data Life cycle stages: development and application	Dransfeld et al. (2000) Reger (2001)
Customer reviews	Complaint Management Online-customer reviews	Semi-structured, numerical, and textual data Life cycle stages: application and social impacts	Becker (2002) Chen et al. (2012) Reger (2001) Zhang et al. (2014) Zhang et al. (2015)
Media/press	Factiva LexisNexis Newspapers and articles	Un-structured, textual data Life cycle stages: application and social impacts	Daim et al. (2006) Mikova and Sokolova (2019) Reger (2001) Segev et al. (2015)
Job postings	Bundesagentur für Arbeit, Indeed, Burning Glass Technologies, Job portals	Un-structured, textual data Life cycle stage: development	Costa Dias et al. (2020) Deming and Kahn (2018) Hirudayaraj and Baker (2018) Reger (2001)
Web sources	News pages e.g., New York Times Websites and blogs RSS Feeds Wikipedia Search engine inquiries e.g., Google Trends	Un-structured and semi-structured, textual data Life cycle stages: application and social impacts	Bonaccorsi et al. (2020) El Akrouchi et al. (2021) Ferragina and Scaiella (2012) Mühlroth and Grottke (2018) Segev et al. (2015)

Table 3 Overview of DDF data sources for the technological perspective

Data source	Database/Data collection	Typology	Authors
Awards and funding programs (in research)	RaDiUS Förderkatalog (BMBF) National research institutions	Semi-structured, textual data Life cycle stages: basic research and applied research	Cozzens et al. (2010)
Conferences	Ei Compendex INSPEC Conference websites	Un-structured and semi-structured, textual data Life cycle stages: basic research et seq	Mikova and Sokolova (2019) Porter and Cunningham (2005) Rohrbeck et al. (2015)
Gartner Hype Cycles	Gartner Inc.	Un-structured, textual, and numerical data Life cycle stage: any	Segev et al. (2015) Wustmans et al. (2022)
Collaborations	Press releases Förderkatalog (BMBF) Corporate and university websites	Un-structured, textual data Life cycle stage: applied research and development	Fritsch et al. (2020) Reger (2001)
Patens	European patent office World intellectual property organization Derwent world patent index Questel orbit intelligence PatBase National patent offices	Semi-structured, textual data Life cycle stage: development	Mikova and Sokolova (2019) Mühlroth and Grottke (2018) Segev et al. (2015) Wustmans et al. (2022)
Scientific publications	Web of Science Scopus Ei Compendex INSPEC Subject-specific journals	Semi-structured, textual data Life cycle stages: basic research and applied research	Cozzens et al. (2010) Mikova and Sokolova (2019) Mühlroth and Grottke (2018) Stelzer et al. (2015)

In Table 6, the data sources for the political perspective are listed as well as described and typologized.

To increase both the effectiveness and efficiency of foresight activities, researchers and practitioners are constantly searching for new data sources and improved analytical methods for DDF. In this context, there is a strong focus on reducing human bias in decision-making under uncertainty. Therefore, improving search strategies and keyword definitions can be vital to increase the data quality in future foresight projects. In addition, it is recommended to stronger rely on automation and machine

Table 4 Overview of DDF data sources for the economic perspective

Data source	Database/Data collection	Typology	Authors
Foresight projects	European Foresight Monitoring Network (EFMN)	Un-structured, textual data Life cycle stage: any	Crehan et al. (2008) Mikova and Sokolova (2019) Reger (2001)
Business reports	EDGAR/U.S. Securities and Exchange Commission (SEC) Company registers of German Federal Gazette	Semi-structured, numerical, and textual data Life cycle stages: development and application	Kloptchenko et al. (2004) Qiu et al. (2006)
Start-ups	Crunchbase Inc. Deutscher Startup Monitor	Un-structured and structured, textual, and numerical data Life cycle stages: applied research and development	Cozzens et al. (2010) Kortum and Lerner (2000) Mikova and Sokolova (2019) Reger (2001) Remané et al. (2016) Zhou et al. (2016)
Trend data	TRENDONE Trendexplorer	Semi-structured, textual data Life cycle stage: any	Wustmans et al. (2022)
Venture Capital	Thomson Reuters VentureXpert S&P Capital IQ Pitchbook Preqin VCExperts Crunchbase Inc.	Un-structured and structured, textual, and numerical data Life cycle stage: applied research and development	Cozzens et al. (2010) Kaplan and Lerner (2017) Kortum and Lerner (2000) Mikova and Sokolova (2019) Reger (2001)

Table 5 Overview of DDF data sources for the environmental perspective

Data source	Database/data collection	Typology	Authors
Sustainability reports	Global Reporting Initiative (GRI) Corporate register	Semi-structured, textual, and numerical data Life cycle stages: application and social impacts	Freundlieb and Teuteberg (2013) Kolk (2004) Liew et al. (2014) Székely and vom Brocke (2017)
Traffic data	BayernInfo ADAC	Mobile/sensor-based, numerical data Life cycle stages: application and social impacts	Leduc (2008) Maarala et al. (2015) Mikova and Sokolova (2019) van Lint and Hoogendoorn (2010)

Table 6 Overview of DDF data sources for the political perspective

Data source	Database/data collection	Typology	Authors
Calls for tenders	Tenders electronic daily (European Commission) Deutscher Auftragsdienst (DTAD)	Structured, textual, and numerical data Life cycle stage: application	Ebener and Ebener (2017) Klien and Hölzl (2019)
Political debates	Hansard (UK Parliament) GovTrack.us (US Congress) Dokumentations-und Informationssystem für Parlamentsmaterialien (DIP)	Un-structured, textual data Life cycle stages: development et seq	Balahur et al. (2009) Mackieson et al. (2019) Vilares and He (2017)
Regulations (planned)	Regulatory foresight projects Sigma Scan Project	Semi-structured, textual data Life cycle stages: development et seq	Blind (2008) Ladegaard and Konvitz (2003) MacDonald et al. (2011)
Social Media	Online communities, blogs, and forums Twitter Facebook Instagram Notified (social listening and media monitoring)	Un-structured, textual data Life cycle stages: development ff	Ehls et al. (2020) Grubmüller et al. (2013) Laurell and Sandström (2022) Mühlroth and Grottke (2018)

learning to detect weak signals better and earlier (Mühlroth and Grottke 2018). A restructuring of the foresight process in a way that the human component is moved from the beginning of the process (data collection) to the end (interpretation and decision-making) appears to make sense in this context (Keller and Gracht 2014). Similarly, collaboration with other companies in the innovation ecosystem is seen as a way to increase and improve the database for Data-Driven Foresight (Becker 2002). Again, digital transformation comes into play, with its ability to support networking and cooperation, for example, through the exchange of data. Coming from existing research, it can even be deduced that parts of established foresight processes are suitable for digital transformation (Schallmo et al. 2017), supporting the above-mentioned need to restructure foresight processes. The specific data sources and methods used for a foresight project depend on several factors. As already indicated, the life cycle phase of the technology to be monitored plays an important role. But also, the goal of the foresight, the resources available, and the desired scope of the analysis determine which data sources and methods are used (Mikova and Sokolova 2019). For a Data-Driven Foresight, which is intended to cover the entire life cycle, it is, therefore, advisable to combine several data sources and methods in such a way that valid trend statements can be made for each phase of the life cycle. In this way, companies can not only conduct a stage-specific foresight for each of their existing

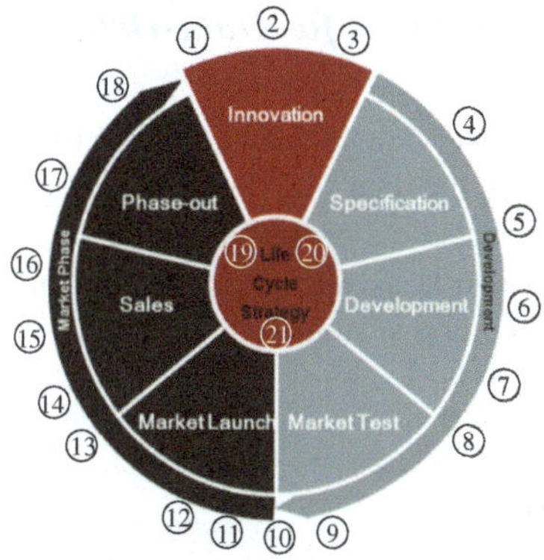

(1) Scientific Publications	(8) Expert opinions	(15) Traffic data
(2) Conferences	(9) Social Media	(16) Sustainability reports
(3) Awards and funding programs	(10) Political Debates	(17) Web sources
(4) Collaborations	(11) Regulations (planned)	(18) Media / Press
(5) Start-ups and Venture Capital	(12) Business reports	(19) Gartner Hype Cycles
(6) Patents	(13) Customer reviews	(20) Foresight projects
(7) Job postings	(14) Call for tenders	(21) Trend data

Fig. 1 Graphical allocation of DDF data sources to the lifecycle stages. *Source* Osswald et al. (2015)

technologies, rather they can accompany their technologies as they move into the next lifecycle stage.

Figure 1 shows a product or technology life cycle model containing a graphical allocation of the identified DDF data sources above to the individual life cycle phases.

The literature-based allocation of DDF data sources to individual life cycle phases, as depicted in the extended life cycle model above, cannot be made with pure accuracy. Primarily since most existing foresight studies mainly focus on the derivation of trends and not on the life cycle expressiveness of data sources. The few life cycle considerations are only made with a rough classification into higher-level phases, such as the development or market phases. Additionally, some data sources can provide meaningful results across multiple lifecycle stages. Because this condition is difficult to depict graphically, the chosen form of representation greatly simplifies the complexity of the actual interrelationships. The model extension does not imply that the individual data sources may be used exclusively in the lifecycle phases assigned above. Rather, it builds on the fact that different data sources have different foresight horizons and provides a first graphical representation of this phenomenon. However, Fig. 1 shows that according to the current state of research, enough data sources are available to cover the entire technology or product lifecycle with a DDF process. These findings are not only relevant for integrating foresight activities into LCM but hold the potential to support digital transformation in LCM as well as corporate foresight processes. The later proves to be particularly relevant, coming from studies that show how the digital transformation of foresight processes can even amplify corporate digital transformation strategies arching across multiple management practices (Peter 2019).

3.2 State-of-the-Art Methods for Data-Driven Foresight

Table 7 provides a compact overview of the literature-based state-of-the-art foresight methods available to analyse the data sources identified so far. In addition to listing the DDF methods in an alphabetical order, Table 7 also contains a brief description of how the listed methods work, as well as an assignment of the data sources and types for which the DDF method is suitable.

4 Expert Interviews

4.1 Data Collection

The selection of experts follows a targeted sampling strategy. This is based on both the objective of the paper and the findings obtained from the systematic literature review. The goal of the sampling strategy was to select typical members of the interest group while maintaining some variation in the population (Starr 2014). The criteria for choosing the experts were defined in advance and recorded in an interview guide. Accordingly, the experts were required to represent a company with established foresight practices in the fields of product, technology, or innovation development. In addition, the respective expert should be actively involved in the selection of data and methods or at least be kept informed about them. Based on this and following the current state of literature, three stakeholder groups emerged whose members could be considered as conversation partners for the semi-structured expert interviews. First, the foresight managers, who are responsible for the foresight projects in the company. Secondly, the foresight team, which is made up of all employees who are involved in the practical implementation of foresight. And finally, the internal foresight customers, i.e., those employees who use the foresight results (Rohrbeck and Gemünden 2011). The experts were initially contacted by e-mail. Twenty-two experts from twenty different companies responded with a commitment and were subsequently interviewed with the help of a predefined and literature-based interview guide. This approach enabled a certain degree of structure while remaining open to new insights. To ensure the validity and replicability of the data collection, all interviews were recorded after prior approval by the experts and then transcribed. The duration of the individual interviews varied depending on the interviewee but was generally between 45 and 75 min. Table 8 provides an overview of the experts interviewed together with a short classification of their represented company types.

Table 7 Overview of DDF methods per data source and type

Method	Functionality	Data source/type	Authors
Bibliometrics	Bibliographic coupling; identifying research fronts Co-citation; identifying knowledge bases	Semis-structured, textual data Data source: scientific publications	Hanisch and Wald (2012) Persson (1994) Stelzer et al. (2015)
Delphi	Surveys and discussion boards; finding consensus on a question	Un-structured, verbal, and textual data Data source: expert opinion	Dransfeld et al. (2000) Segev et al. (2015)
Futures images	Interviews (semi-structured) and workshops; developing images of the future Transcription and coding; enabling text analysis	Un-structured, verbal, and textual data Data source: expert opinion	Ahlqvist and Uotila (2020) Jokinen et al. (2022) Rossel (2012)
Patent analysis	Patent mapping; developing a patent map Morphological analysis; exploiting the technology system Network and citation analysis	Semi-structured, textual data Data source: patents	Chang et al. (2010) Lee et al. (2020) Lee et al. (2011)
Systems dynamics modelling	Feedback loops; modelling complex systems	Cause and effect relationships Data source: results of other foresight methods	Daim et al. (2006) Sterman (2000)
Scenario analysis	Multi-stage analysis process; deriving three scenarios Systems thinking and PESTEL; determining the focus of analysis Quantitative trend analysis; formulating forecasts Systems dynamics modelling and cluster algorithms; bundling topic clusters	Un-structured, verbal data and semi-structured, textual data Data sources: expert opinions in combination with scientific publications, patents etc.	Amer et al. (2013) Drew (2006) Mietzner and Reger (2005) Piirainen and Kortelainen (2010) Saritas and Aylen (2010) Stelzer et al. (2015)
Technology road mapping	Time-based multilevel diagrams; representing the co-evolution of markets, products, and technologies	Any textual, numerical, and verbal data Data sources: expert opinions, results of other foresight methods etc.	Bray and Garcia (1997) Phaal et al. (2004)

(continued)

Table 7 (continued)

Method	Functionality	Data source/type	Authors
Text mining (esp. Natural language processing)	Latent Dirichlet allocation; topic modelling Term frequency; word frequency analysis Word2Vec; word similarity analysis Sentires; sentiment analysis at phrase level	Un-structured, textual data Data sources: web sources, social media data, customer reviews, sustainability reports etc.	Blei et al. (2003) El Akrouchi et al. (2021) Kim et al. (2020) Maitre et al. (2019) Mikolov et al. (2013) Zhang et al. (2014)
Growth curves	Fisher-Pry model; calculating the substitution rate Gompertz function Lotka-Volterra equations	Structured, numerical data Data source: sales figures	Daim et al. (2006) Porter (2010) Roper et al. (2011)

4.2 Data Analysis

When analyzing qualitative data, it is always important to recognize clear patterns in the data set and to interpret them correctly. To ensure validity, the present study applies the so-called "Reasonable Person Standard," based on a level of care and systematic approach to data analysis that would be applied by any reasonable person concerned with scientific validity. With the help of this narrowly defined analysis approach, it can be ensured that the personal views of the researcher do not find their way into the evaluation and interpretation of the results (Starr 2014). It is advantageous for the data analysis that the underlying interview guide was structured in a way that simplifies the derivation of causalities.

5 Findings and Discussion

Comparing the results of the systematic literature analysis and those of the semi-structured expert interviews, various similarities and discrepancies between foresight theory and foresight practice can be derived. Based on the thematic scope of the foresight activities described by the experts, it can be seen that the theory-based classification of data sources into STEEP perspectives has tremendous practical relevance. All experts state that their foresight process is somehow guided by the STEEP perspectives (or PESTEL), even if they weigh the perspectives differently. Nevertheless, the companies interviewed use a variety of data sources and types, some of which differ from the data sources explained in the theory section.

It is noticeable that the typical data sources of the early life cycle phases, which are very popular in research, such as scientific publications or patents, are rather

Table 8 Overview of interviewed experts and their represented companies

Experts	Position	Company type
1	Head of foresight management	Industrial firm
2	Senior management consultant for digital foresight and trends evaluation	Industrial firm
3 & 4	Vice president engineering Senior manager market intelligence	Industrial firm
5	Corporate strategy, market intelligence	Industrial firm
6	Global scouting, foresight and technology management	Industrial firm
7	Senior vice president research and advanced engineering	Industrial firm
8	Division management digitalization and IT	Industrial firm
9	Head of foresight	Industrial firm
10	Director of global marketing	Industrial firm
11	Head of global operations	Industrial firm
12	Head of data science	Industrial firm
13	Customer intelligence and human trends	Insurance company
14	Corporate strategy manager	Insurance company
15	VP principal analyst	Consultancy
16	Senior consultant	Consultancy
17 & 18	Principal innovation and strategy managing consultant industrial goods and high tech	Consultancy
19	Senior associate	Consultancy
20	Consultant	Foresight tool provider
21	Director customer innovation success	Foresight tool provider
22	Head of foresight lab	Foresight tool provider

seldomly used by companies in practice. The reason given by the experts in question is that their represented companies are technology followers. In the context of foresight, it is more interesting for those experts to identify innovations that are already available and assess their suitability for the company rather than aiming to develop a new trend. Technology leaders, on the other hand, have the ambition to develop basic technologies, which is why an early-stage DDF is also required for them. For theory, this leads to the realization that in addition to the selection criteria for foresight data sources and methods presented in section three, the positioning of a company as a technology leader or follower also plays an important role. Additionally, the interviews showed that technology followers tend to outsource the aggregation of individual lifecycle-encompassing data sources to external service providers and, in turn, purchase their publications as consolidated data sources. At the same time, technology followers outsource the application of foresight methods to external service providers and only perform manual analyses of the purchased data sources. In this regard, some interviewed experts from technology followers reported that they lack a methodical approach to tapping alternative data sources and that available foresight tools are financially unattractive, especially for technology followers. While this holds potential for digital transformation as such, the question arises whether technology followers are the right target group to introduce a new foresight process for DDF in LCM.

Coming from the challenges and problems in the practical implementation of DDF, the interviews revealed some interesting starting points for developing a novel DDF method in LCM. First and foremost, stands the improvement of effectiveness and efficiency in the further processing of foresight results to downstream departments. This concerns not only the derivation of concrete action measures but also the company-wide strengthening of the understanding of foresight practices and the optimization of knowledge communication and knowledge management. Due to the fact that the qualitative success of foresight activities often is to trigger operational actions in the company, practitioners are always interested in making DDF more suitable for everyday use and accelerating its internal impact. In this context, the interviewed experts also see the potential for optimizing available analysis tools when it comes to automated data collection and analysis. Besides the reduction of false positives, the improvement of usability is also considered urgent. According to the experts, consistent data sources, analyses, and presentation methods could increase the applications' comprehensibility and results. This, in turn, would be beneficial for the further processing of foresight results. Systematizing the selection of data sources and methods could provide an initial remedy and path the way for further digital transformation in foresight processes. For this, the work at hand lays an important foundation with the presented state-of-the-art analysis.

Some generally valid premises can be derived to answer the research question of how companies obtain their data for DDF in LCM and what alternative data sources are recommended. A general premise is to be guided by STEEP perspectives and to cover as many of these perspectives as possible with DDF. The distinction between technology leaders and followers has emerged as an equally valid indicator of how and which data a company obtains for its foresight activities. Technology followers focus their foresight activities on technologies and trends that are already known and can therefore be identified via data sources of the later lifecycle phases (development et seq.). In connection with this, technology followers often outsource the aggregation of individual data to specialized analytics companies and, in turn, purchase their trend reports as foresight data sources. Technology leaders are interested in both mature and emerging technologies and trends as part of their DDF, which is why their data sources cover the entire lifecycle. The aggregation and analysis of individual data are mainly done in-house, which can partly be explained by the fact that technology leaders tend to allocate more human resources to their foresight than it is the case with technology followers. The data sources identified in the systematic literature analysis of this publication are generally recommended as alternative data sources for DDF in LCM. Accordingly, textual as well as numerical or verbal data can be used, either in structured, semi-structured, or unstructured form. To analyze these data sources, different foresight methods are available depending on the type of data. Regarding the specific selection of data, the premise is to be guided by both the perspective- and the lifecycle-related informative value of individual data sources. According to the findings of this work, each STEEP perspective and lifecycle phase relevant to a company should and can be covered by DDF.

By answering the research question, this paper contributes to the current state of research in the field of data-driven foresight in that it identifies the positioning of a company as a technology leader or follower as an additional selection criterion for relevant data sources and foresight methods. Regarding this, the scientific foresight literature focuses mainly on technology-leading companies, and the relevance of the foresight value chain often remains unrecognized. By providing a structured compilation of the state of the art of foresight data sources and methods and describing their typology and perspective expressiveness, this work makes an important contribution to the current state of literature. Together with the positioning of all presented data sources along the life cycle model, which is also an extension to the current state of research. Finally, the work at hand outlines several levers for digital transformation in the fields of DDF and LCM and does not fall short on mentioning that incorporating DDF into LCM holds great potential for the digital transformation of decision processes.

6 Limitations and Future Research

Due to the research methodology and the limited scope of this paper, the present work is based on several limitations that need to be overcome in the context of further research. On the one hand, the classification of DDF data sources along the life cycle model requires quantitative validation. This is because the analyzed literature has isolated gaps in the concrete positioning of known data sources along the life cycle. On the other hand, the state of the art of foresight data sources and methods is subject to constant development and supplementation. Future research should always maintain its openness to alternative data sources and methods. A further limitation of the present work is the qualitative research method used. Although the semi-structured expert interviews deliver valid, transparent, and thus replicable results to answer the research question, this in turn, opens up new research gaps that can only be closed with the help of quantitative methods.

For further research on data-driven foresight in life cycle management, it is, therefore, advisable to conduct quantitative trend analyses using the data sources and methods presented. However, the results should not only be used for pure trend foresight, as it has been the case to date but should also demonstrate the validity of data sources and methods used along the technology or product life cycle. To make this possible, future studies should combine several data sources and methods with each other. Based on these results, further research can focus on developing and manifesting a generally valid approach for lifecycle-encompassing data-driven foresight in industrial companies and thereby exploiting the potential for digital transformation of foresight processes. In this respect, the identified need for research to optimize internal processing of foresight results within a company and the need for further development of foresight tools should also be the focus of future research.

References

Ahlqvist, T., Uotila, T.: Contextualising weak signals: towards a relational theory of futures knowledge. Futures **119**, 102543 (2020). https://doi.org/10.1016/j.futures.2020.102543

Amer, M., Daim, T.U., Jetter, A.: A review of scenario planning. Futures **46**, 23–40 (2013). https://doi.org/10.1016/j.futures.2012.10.003

Balahur, A., Kozareva, Z., Montoyo, A.: Determining the polarity and source of opinions expressed in political debates. In: Gelbukh, A. (ed.) Lecture Notes in Computer Science. Computational Linguistics and Intelligent Text Processing, vol. 5449, pp. 468–480. Springer, Berlin, Heidelberg (2009). https://doi.org/10.1007/978-3-642-00382-0_38

Becker, P.: Corporate foresight in Europe: a first overview. European Commission (2002). https://ams-forschungsnetzwerk.at/downloadpub/2003_st_corporate_foresight_040109.pdf

Blei, D.M., Ng, A.Y., Jordan, M.I.: Latent dirichlet allocation. J. Mach. Learn. Res. **3**, 993–1022 (2003)

Blind, K.: Regulatory foresight: methodologies and selected applications. Technol. Forecast. Soc. Chang. **75**(4), 496–516 (2008). https://doi.org/10.1016/j.techfore.2008.02.004

Blind, K., Cuhls, K., Grupp, H.: Current foresight activities in Central Europe. Technol. Forecast. Soc. Chang. **60**(1), 15–35 (1999). https://doi.org/10.1016/S0040-1625(98)00021-3

Bonaccorsi, A., Chiarello, F., Fantoni, G., Kammering, H.: Emerging technologies and industrial leadership. A wikipedia-based strategic analysis of Industry 4.0. Expert Syst. Appl. **160**, 113645 (2020). https://doi.org/10.1016/j.eswa.2020.113645

Bray, O.H., Garcia, M.L.: Technology Roadmapping: the Integration of Strategic and Technology Planning for Competitiveness, pp. 25–28. IEEE (1997). https://doi.org/10.1109/PICMET.1997.653238

Chang, P.-L., Wu, C.-C., Leu, H.-J.: Using patent analyses to monitor the technological trends in an emerging field of technology: a case of carbon nanotube field emission display. Scientometrics **82**(1), 5–19 (2010). https://doi.org/10.1007/s11192-009-0033-y

Chen, H., Chiang, R.H.L., Storey, V.C.: Business intelligence and analytics: from big data to big impact. MIS q. **36**(4), 1165 (2012). https://doi.org/10.2307/41703503

Costa Dias, M., Norris Keiller, A., Postel-Vinay, F., Xu, X.: Job Vacancies During the Covid-19 pandemic (2020). https://doi.org/10.1920/BN.IFS.2020.BN0289

Cozzens, S., Gatchair, S., Kang, J., Kim, K.-S., Lee, H.J., Ordóñez, G., Porter, A.: Emerging technologies: quantitative identification and measurement. Technol. Anal. & Strat. Manag. **22**(3), 361–376 (2010). https://doi.org/10.1080/09537321003647396

Crehan, P., Elkins, S., Giesecke, S.: The European foresight monitoring network: collection of EFMN briefs. Office for Official Publications of the European Communities (2008)

Daim, T.U., Rueda, G., Martin, H., Gerdsri, P.: Forecasting emerging technologies: use of bibliometrics and patent analysis. Technol. Forecast. Soc. Chang. **73**(8), 981–1012 (2006). https://doi.org/10.1016/j.techfore.2006.04.004

Deming, D., Kahn, L.B.: Skill Requirements across firms and labor markets: evidence from job postings for professionals. J. Law Econ. **36**(S1), S337–S369 (2018). https://doi.org/10.1086/694106

Dransfeld, H., Pemberton, J., Jacobs, G.: Quantifying weighted expert opinion. Technol. Forecast. Soc. Chang. **63**(1), 81–90 (2000). https://doi.org/10.1016/S0040-1625(99)00059-1

Drew, S.A.: Building technology foresight: using scenarios to embrace innovation. Eur. J. Innov. Manag. **9**(3), 241–257 (2006). https://doi.org/10.1108/14601060610678121

Ebener, S., Ebener, M.: Der Einsatz von Text Mining zur Bestimmung des Diffusionsprozesses von Produkten. In: Gansser, O., Krol, B. (eds.) Moderne Methoden der Marktforschung, pp. 247–271. Springer Fachmedien Wiesbaden (2017). https://doi.org/10.1007/978-3-658-09745-5_14

Ehls, D., Polier, S., Herstatt, C.: Reviewing the field of external knowledge search for innovation: theoretical underpinnings and future (re-)search directions. J. Prod. Innov. Manag. **37**(5), 405–430 (2020). https://doi.org/10.1111/jpim.12549

El Akrouchi, M., Benbrahim, H., Kassou, I.: End-to-end LDA-based automatic weak signal detection in web news. Knowl.-Based Syst. **212**, 106650 (2021). https://doi.org/10.1016/j.knosys.2020.106650

Ferragina, P., Scaiella, U.: Fast and accurate annotation of short texts with wikipedia pages. IEEE Softw. **29**(1), 70–75 (2012). https://doi.org/10.1109/MS.2011.122

Freundlieb, M., Teuteberg, F.: Corporate social responsibility reporting—a transnational analysis of online corporate social responsibility reports by market-listed companies: contents and their evolution. Int. J. Innov. Sustain. Dev. **7**(1), Article 52117, 1 (2013). https://doi.org/10.1504/IJISD.2013.052117

Fritsch, M., Titze, M., Piontek, M.: Identifying cooperation for innovation-a comparison of data sources. Ind. Innov. **27**(6), 630–659 (2020). https://doi.org/10.1080/13662716.2019.1650253

Grubmüller, V., Götsch, K., Krieger, B.: Social media analytics for future oriented policy making. Eur. J. Futur. Res. **1**(1) (2013). https://doi.org/10.1007/s40309-013-0020-7

Hamel, G., Prahalad, C.K.: Competing for the Future. Harv. Bus. Rev. **72**, 122–128 (1994). https://hbr.org/1994/07/competing-for-the-future

Hanisch, B., Wald, A.: A bibliometric view on the use of contingency theory in project management research. Proj. Manag. J. **43**(3), 4–23 (2012). https://doi.org/10.1002/pmj.21267

Hirudayaraj, M., Baker, R.: HRD competencies: analysis of employer expectations from online job postings. Eur. J. Train. Dev. **42**(9), 577–596 (2018). https://doi.org/10.1108/EJTD-04-2018-0036

Holler, M., Barth, L., Fuchs, R.: Trustworthy product lifecycle management using blockchain technology—experience from the automotive ecosystem. In: Stark, J. (ed.) Decision Engineering. Product Lifecycle Management: The Case Studies, vol. 4, pp. 13–19. Springer International Publishing (2019). https://doi.org/10.1007/978-3-030-16134-7_2

John, M.: Data Driven Foresight. Fraunhofer-Institut für Naturwissenschaftlich-Technische Trendanalysen INT (2022). https://www.int.fraunhofer.de/de/geschaeftsfelder/kati-lab/data-driven-foresight.html

Jokinen, L., Mäkelä, M., Heikkilä, K., Apostol, O., Kalliomäki, H., Saarni, J.: Creating futures images for sustainable cruise ships: insights on collaborative foresight for sustainability enhancement. Futures **135**, 102873 (2022). https://doi.org/10.1016/j.futures.2021.102873

Kaplan, S.N., Lerner, J.: Venture capital data—opportunities and challenges. In: Haltiwanger, J.C., Hurst, E., Miranda, J., Schoar, A. (eds.) Measuring Entrepreneurial Businesses: Current Knowledge and Challenges (2017)

Keller, J., von der Gracht, H.A.: The influence of information and communication technology (ICT) on future foresight processes—results from a Delphi survey. Technol. Forecast. Soc. Chang. **85**, 81–92 (2014). https://doi.org/10.1016/j.techfore.2013.07.010

Kim, S., Park, H., Lee, J.: Word2vec-based latent semantic analysis (W2V-LSA) for topic modeling: a study on blockchain technology trend analysis. Expert Syst. Appl. **152**, 113401 (2020). https://doi.org/10.1016/j.eswa.2020.113401

Klien, M., Hölzl, W.: Öffentliche Ausschreibungen und Konjunktur. Eine Analyse mit unkonventionellen Daten für die österreichische Bauwirtschaft. WIFO Monatsberichte (monthly reports) (2019). https://www.wifo.ac.at/jart/prj3/wifo/resources/person_dokument/person_dokument.jart?publikationsid=61924&mime_type=application/pdf

Kloptchenko, A., Magnusson, C., Back, B., Visa, A., Vanharanta, H.: Mining textual contents of financial reports. Int. J. Digit. Account. Res. **4**(7), 1–29 (2004)

Kolk, A.: A decade of sustainability reporting: developments and significance. Int. J. Environ. Sustain. Dev. **3**(1), Article 4688, 51 (2004). https://doi.org/10.1504/IJESD.2004.004688

Kortum, S., Lerner, J.: Assessing the contribution of venture capital to innovation. Rand J. Econ. **31**(4), 674 (2000). https://doi.org/10.2307/2696354

Ladegaard, P., Konvitz, J.: Regulatory performance: ex post evaluation of regulatory policies. In: Proceedings from the OECD Expert Meeting on Regulatory Performance, Paris (2003).

Laurell, C., Sandström, C.: Social media analytics as an enabler for external search and open foresight—the case of Tesla's autopilot and regulatory scrutiny of autonomous driving. IEEE Trans. Eng. Manag. **69**(2), 564–571 (2022). https://doi.org/10.1109/TEM.2021.3072677

Leduc, G.: Road traffic data: collection methods and applications. European Commission Joint Research Centre Institute for Prospective Technological Studies (2008)

Lee, C., Jeon, D., Ahn, J.M., Kwon, O.: Navigating a product landscape for technology opportunity analysis: a word2vec approach using an integrated patent-product database. Technovation **96–97**, 102140 (2020). https://doi.org/10.1016/j.technovation.2020.102140

Lee, C., Jeon, J., Park, Y.: Monitoring trends of technological changes based on the dynamic patent lattice: a modified formal concept analysis approach. Technol. Forecast. Soc. Chang. **78**(4), 690–702 (2011). https://doi.org/10.1016/j.techfore.2010.11.010

Lee, C.-H., Liu, C.-L., Trappey, A.J., Mo, J.P., Desouza, K.C.: Understanding digital transformation in advanced manufacturing and engineering: a bibliometric analysis, topic modeling and research trend discovery. Adv. Eng. Inform. **50**, 101428 (2021). https://doi.org/10.1016/j.aei.2021.101428

Li, J., Tao, F., Cheng, Y., Zhao, L.: Big Data in product lifecycle management. Int. J. Adv. Manuf. Technol. **81**(1–4), 667–684 (2015). https://doi.org/10.1007/s00170-015-7151-x

Liew, W.T., Adhitya, A., Srinivasan, R.: Sustainability trends in the process industries: a text mining-based analysis. Comput. Ind. **65**(3), 393–400 (2014). https://doi.org/10.1016/j.compind.2014.01.004

Maarala, A.I., Rautiainen, M., Salmi, M., Pirttikangas, S., Riekki, J.: Low Latency Analytics for Streaming Traffic Data with Apache Spark, pp. 2855–2858. IEEE (2015). https://doi.org/10.1109/BigData.2015.7364101

MacDonald, A., de Civita, P., Downs, A.: Regulatory foresight and change drivers. Government of Canada (2011). https://publications.gc.ca/collections/collection_2011/policyresearch/PH4-78-2011-eng.pdf

Mackieson, P., Shlonsky, A., Connolly, M.: Increasing rigor and reducing bias in qualitative research: a document analysis of parliamentary debates using applied thematic analysis. Qual. Soc. Work. **18**(6), 965–980 (2019). https://doi.org/10.1177/1473325018786996

Maitre, J., Menard, M., Chiron, G., Bouju, A., Sidere, N.: A Meaningful Information Extraction System for Interactive Analysis of Documents, pp. 92–99. IEEE (2019). https://doi.org/10.1109/ICDAR.2019.00024

Martin, B.R.: Foresight in science and technology. Technol. Anal. & Strat. Manag. **7**(2), 139–168 (1995). https://doi.org/10.1080/09537329508524202

Martino, J.P.: A review of selected recent advances in technological forecasting. Technol. Forecast. Soc. Chang. **70**(8), 719–733 (2003). https://doi.org/10.1016/S0040-1625(02)00375-X

Mietzner, D., Reger, G.: Advantages and disadvantages of scenario approaches for strategic foresight. Int. J. Technol. Intell. Plan. **1**(2), Article 6516, 220 (2005). https://doi.org/10.1504/IJTIP.2005.006516

Mikolov, T., Chen, K., Corrado, G., Dean, J.: Efficient estimation of word representations in vector space. Cornell University (2013). https://doi.org/10.48550/arXiv.1301.3781

Mikova, N., Sokolova, A.: Comparing data sources for identifying technology trends. Technol. Anal. & Strat. Manag. **31**(11), 1353–1367 (2019). https://doi.org/10.1080/09537325.2019.1614157

Mühlroth, C., Grottke, M.: A systematic literature review of mining weak signals and trends for corporate foresight. J. Bus. Econ. **88**(5), 643–687 (2018). https://doi.org/10.1007/s11573-018-0898-4

Osswald, M., Ertel, D., Brecht, L., Mahnke, T.: Analysis of intersections between technology and innovation management and product management in B2B. In: Proceedings of the XXVI ISPIM Conference—Shaping the Frontiers of Innovation, Budapest (2015). file:///C:/Users/marie.scheuffele/Downloads/Analysis_of_intersections_betw.pdf

Persson, O.: The intellectual base and research fronts of JASIS 1986–1990. J. Am. Soc. Inf. Sci. **45**(1), 31–38 (1994). https://doi.org/10.1002/(SICI)1097-4571(199401)45:1%3c31::AID-ASI4%3e3.0.CO;2-G

Peter, M.K.:. The evolving approach to strategic corporate foresight at swiss bank post finance in the age of digital transformation. In: Schreiber, D.A. Berge, Z.L. (eds.) Futures Thinking and Organizational Policy, pp. 113–132. Springer International Publishing (2019). https://doi.org/10.1007/978-3-319-94923-9_6

Phaal, R., Farrukh, C.J., Probert, D.R.: Technology roadmapping—a planning framework for evolution and revolution. Technol. Forecast. Soc. Chang. **71**(1–2), 5–26 (2004). https://doi.org/10.1016/S0040-1625(03)00072-6

Piirainen, K.A., Kortelainen, S.: Translating scenarios for management: Use of system dynamics modelling to quantify scenarios. In: ISPIM Conference, Bilbao (2010)

Popay, J., Rogers, A., Williams, G.: Rationale and standards for the systematic review of qualitative literature in health services research. Qual. Health Res. **8**(3), 341–351 (1998). https://doi.org/10.1177/104973239800800305

Porter, A.L.: Technology foresight: types and methods. Int. J. Foresight Innov. Policy **6**(1/2/3), Article 32664, 36 (2010). https://doi.org/10.1504/IJFIP.2010.032664

Porter, A.L., Cunningham, S.W. (eds.): Tech Mining: Exploiting New Technologies for Competitive Advantage. Wiley Series in Systems Engineering and Management. Wiley (2005). http://www.e-streams.com/es0808/es0808_4225.html

Qiu, X.Y., Srinivasan, P., Street, N.: Exploring the forecasting potential of company annual reports. Proc. Am. Soc. Inf. Sci. Technol. **43**(1), 1–15 (2006). https://doi.org/10.1002/meet.14504301168

Reger, G.: Technology foresight in companies: from an indicator to a network and process perspective. Technol. Anal. & Strat. Manag. **13**(4), 533–553 (2001). https://doi.org/10.1080/09537320127286

Remané, G., Hildebrandt, B., Hanelt, A., Kolbe, L.: Discovering New Digital Business Model Types—A Study of Technology Startups from the Mobility Sector. PACIS (2016)

Rohrbeck, R., Battistella, C., Huizingh, E.: Corporate foresight: an emerging field with a rich tradition. Technol. Forecast. Soc. Chang. **101**, 1–9 (2015). https://doi.org/10.1016/j.techfore.2015.11.002

Rohrbeck, R., Gemünden, H.G.: Corporate foresight: Its three roles in enhancing the innovation capacity of a firm. Technol. Forecast. Soc. Chang. **78**(2), 231–243 (2011). https://doi.org/10.1016/j.techfore.2010.06.019

Roper, A.T., Cunningham, S.W., Porter Alan L., Mason, T.W., Rossini, F.A., Banks, J.: Forecasting and Management of Technology, 2nd edn. Wiley, John Wiley [distributor], Chichester (2011)

Rossel, P.: Early detection, warnings, weak signals and seeds of change: a turbulent domain of futures studies. Futures **44**(3), 229–239 (2012). https://doi.org/10.1016/j.futures.2011.10.005

Saritas, O., Aylen, J.: Using scenarios for roadmapping: the case of clean production. Technol. Forecast. Soc. Chang. **77**(7), 1061–1075 (2010). https://doi.org/10.1016/j.techfore.2010.03.003

Saritas, O., Meissner, D., Sokolov, A.: A transition management roadmap for fuel cell electric vehicles (FCEVs). J. Knowl. Econ. **10**(3), 1183–1203 (2019). https://doi.org/10.1007/s13132-018-0523-3

Schallmo, D., Williams, C.A., Boardman, L.: Digital transformation of business models—best practice, enablers, and roadmap. Int. J. Innov. Manag. **21**(08), 1740014 (2017). https://doi.org/10.1142/S136391961740014X

Segev, A., Jung, S., Choi, S.: Analysis of technology trends based on diverse data sources. IEEE Trans. Serv. Comput. **8**(6), 903–915 (2015). https://doi.org/10.1109/TSC.2014.2338855

Starr, M.A.: Qualitative and mixed-methods research in economics: surprising growth, promising future. J. Econ. Surv. **28**(2), 238–264 (2014). https://doi.org/10.1111/joes.12004

Stelzer, B., Meyer-Brötz, F., Schiebel, E., Brecht, L.: Combining the scenario technique with bibliometrics for technology foresight: the case of personalized medicine. Technol. Forecast. Soc. Chang. **98**, 137–156 (2015). https://doi.org/10.1016/j.techfore.2015.06.008

Sterman, J.: Business Dynamics: Systems Thinking and Modeling for a Complex World. Irwin/McGraw-Hill (2000)

Székely, N., vom Brocke, J.: What can we learn from corporate sustainability reporting? Deriving propositions for research and practice from over 9,500 corporate sustainability reports published between 1999 and 2015 using topic modelling technique. PLoS ONE **12**(4), e0174807 (2017). https://doi.org/10.1371/journal.pone.0174807

Tranfield, D., Denyer, D., Smart, P.: Towards a methodology for developing evidence-informed management knowledge by means of systematic review. Br. J. Manag. **14**(3), 207–222 (2003). https://doi.org/10.1111/1467-8551.00375

van Lint, J., Hoogendoorn, S.P.: A robust and efficient method for fusing heterogeneous data from traffic sensors on freeways. Comput.-Aided Civ. Infrastruct. Eng. **25**(8), 596–612 (2010). https://doi.org/10.1111/j.1467-8667.2009.00617.x

Vilares, D., He, Y.: Detecting perspectives in political debates (Palmer, M., Hwa, R., Riedel, S. (eds.)), pp. 1573–1582. Association for Computational Linguistics (2017). https://doi.org/10.18653/v1/D17-1165

Wustmans, M., Haubold, T., Bruens, B.: Bridging trends and patents: combining different data sources for the evaluation of innovation fields in blockchain technology. IEEE Trans. Eng. Manage. **69**(3), 825–837 (2022). https://doi.org/10.1109/TEM.2020.3043478

Zhang, Y., Zhang, H., Zhang, M., Liu, Y., Ma, S.: Do users rate or review? Boost phrase-level sentiment labeling with review-level sentiment classification. In: Geva, S., Trotman, A., Bruza, P., Clarke, C.L., Järvelin, K. (eds.) Proceedings of the 37th International ACM SIGIR Conference on Research & Development in Information Retrieval, pp. 1027–1030. ACM (2014). https://doi.org/10.1145/2600428.2609501

Zhang, Y., Zhang, M., Liu, Y., Ma, S.: Boost Phrase-Level Polarity Labelling with Review-Level Sentiment Classification. Association for Computational Linguistics (2015). https://doi.org/10.48550/arXiv.1502.03322

Zhou, H., Sandner, P.G., Martinelli, S.L., Block, J.H.: Patents, trademarks, and their complementarity in venture capital funding. Technovation **47**, 14–22 (2016). https://doi.org/10.1016/j.technovation.2015.11.005

Marie Scheuffele is a Ph.D. Student at the University of Liechtenstein and Research Associate at the Professorship for Technology and Innovation at Liechtenstein Business School. After receiving her master's degree in Entrepreneurship and Management, she decided to follow her enthusiasm for technology and innovation management by researching recent developments in corporate and technology foresight. Next to developing a new foresight process for product lifecycle management she also works on tapping and analysing new data sources for state-of-the-art trend studies in practical application contexts as well as on combining human- and data-driven foresight methods to improve decision-making processes along the technology lifecycle.

Dr. Niklas Bayrle-Kelso is a Postdoc of Entrepreneurship and Technology at the University of Liechtenstein. In his research, he focuses on the topics of innovation efficiency and technology foresight. Niklas holds a master's degree in physics and management from the University of Ulm. During his doctoral studies, Niklas worked at the Institute of Business Analytics at Ulm University. He is a lecturer for technology and innovation management, digital entrepreneurship, technology foresight, and general management. Besides his academic career, he gained practical experience working for Daimler Buses as a product and innovation manager. Currently, he holds a position as an innovation investment specialist at an asset management firm.

Prof. Dr. Leo Brecht is a full Professor of Entrepreneurship and Technology at the University of Liechtenstein. His main competencies include innovation, technology and product management as well as the relationship to corporate success. Business analytics is one of his most favorable topics. He ran dozens of strategy projects, due diligencies and valuation of technology firms. He combines theory with practical implementation. At the university, he is responsible for a MBA program in Technology and Innovation Management, is the delegate for transfer and runs several research projects mainly with corporates. Leo is an active investor in the fields of FINTECH, SUSTTECH and EDUTECH and works as a serial entrepreneur.

Digital Disruption—How Medical Doctors Employ Influencer Marketing Strategies

Andrea Kanzler

Abstract Digitalization is a major growth driver for the global healthcare market, including increased use of digital communication tools and particularly a new and innovative use of social media by medical doctors. Therefore, this study asks: How can doctors innovate their business model to become successful on social media platforms and what are the perceptions of their followers on key antecedents and outcomes? Based on a survey conducted on medical social media accounts with 703 respondents, this study investigates the impact of 'Trustworthiness', 'Referential Skills', 'Opinion Leadership', 'Hedonism', 'Utilitarianism' and 'Para-social Relationship' on two outcome variables, i.e. the 'Willingness to Offer Positive Word-of-Mouth on Social Media' and the 'Intention to Follow the Advice'. Several theoretical and practical implications are provided.

Keywords Business model innovation · Digital marketing · Social media · Opinion leadership · Para-social relationship · Medical industry · Word of mouth · Influencer · Hedonism · Utilitarianism

1 Introduction

Digitalization is disrupting the healthcare market. The global digital health market is expected to grow with a CAGR of 25% until 2025, by far outperforming overall health market developments (Statista 2019; Businesswire 2019). Digital tools such as smartphones, tablets and particularly social media platforms have become critical for healthcare professionals, since they provide the opportunity for peer-to-peer support and efficient communication between patients and busy doctors. Today, social media platforms like Instagram are a "viable medium for sharing and discussing clinical cases and medical/health knowledge" (Kamel Boulos et al. 2016). Furthermore, doctors use Instagram and other social media platforms for its convenient way of communicating medical data, professional networking, promotion of research and

A. Kanzler (✉)
University of Muenster, Leonardo Campus 1, 48149 Muenster, Germany
e-mail: andrea.kanzler@uni-muenster.de

© The Author(s), under exclusive license to Springer Nature Switzerland AG 2024

D. Schallmo et al. (eds.), *Digital Disruption and Transformation*, Springer Proceedings in Business and Economics, https://doi.org/10.1007/978-3-031-47888-8_8

treatment options, promoting their practice, as well as a learning tool (Rashid and Devaraj 2020). When doctors become more active online and particularly on social media, they are just going where their patients are already searching for healthcare information (Nguyen et al. 2020). For instance, a major medical question during the Covid19 pandemic was whether it was safe for pregnant women to get vaccinated. A family physician potentially could educate his/her online audience and including actual patients through Instagram with one “Live”[1] on this topic, in contrast to having to answer the same question multiple times with each patient in one-on-one consultations. According to Househ (2013) about 60% of physicians favour interactions with patients through social media, since they see strong support for patient education, increased compliance, and better treatment outcomes.

At the same time because of globalization medical tourism is increasing, i.e. going abroad or traveling to a different city or state to get treatments, particularly for cosmetic and dental surgery; cardio, orthopaedic and bariatric surgery or organ and tissue transplantation (Lunt and Carrera 2010; Whittaker 2008). Here as well social media has become an important tool for doctors to build trust since the patients can see the results of the recent treatments the doctor actually did and get in contact with recent patients. Therefore, doctors need to think about new business model innovation to address these changes. Besides being medical professionals, they need to develop skills in creating content for social media, addressing the changing needs of their clients and exploiting new opportunities the digitalization offers in terms of knowledge sharing and promotion/marketing, some of them even become social media influencers (Willis and Delbaere 2022). These changes are considered radical, comparable to the impact that sales teams in new product development have on firm’s capability to understand customer needs (Malshe and Biemans 2014), doctors now can survey their potential clients on Instagram to understand their needs.

While many scholars focus on the risks of doctors discussing health care topics on social media, e.g. violating laws or violating doctor-patient confidentiality (George et al. 2013; Rashid and Devaraj 2020), it is not illegal for doctors to use these social media channels. In fact, even in Germany, a country known for its strict regulations, the journal Deutsches Ärzteblatt published by Bundesärztekammer (German Medical Association) and the National Association of Statutory Health Insurance Physicians, recommends healthcare professionals to familiarize themselves with social media tools (Hartz et al. 2014). Doctors are explicitly allowed to post job related and factual information, furthermore tips for healthy lifestyles are not considered as advertisements (Mediorbis 2021). Particularly, Hartz et al. (2014) name benefits of social media use by doctors, such as creating awareness, building reputation, closer connection to patients, educating their audience on therapy and treatment options.

The concept of influencers is not new. For the past several decades celebrities, famous scientists and other personalities e.g. politicians or religious leaders, have been used as sources of influence in society and communications (Vrontis et al. 2021; Knoll and Matthes 2017). With the growth of the internet today social media users

[1] A “Live” on Instagram is a live video broadcasting where the viewers can ask direct questions to the person who is broadcasting. Every Instagram user has the option to “go Live”.

changed the business model for opinion leaders, who now create content online, can themselves generate a large number of followers and become a source of advice and influence for their audience (Vrontis et al. 2021; Lamberton and Stephen 2016). Thus, they have been termed social media influencers. These individuals excel in creating engaging content for their followers and their online word of mouth is very powerful (Torres et al. 2019).

Social media influencers (SMIs) can also be considered opinion leaders who influence others' behaviours based on their specialized knowledge or authority on a certain topic (Torres et al. 2019; Casaló et al. 2018, 2020; Lin et al. 2018). According to the Digital Marketing Institute about 50% of internet users follow SMIs and believe in their recommendations, and approximately 40% bought a product they saw on Instagram or YouTube (Audrezet and Charry 2019; Digital Marketing Institute 2019; Young 2017). Rahal (2020) found that 86% of marketers and managers incorporated influencer marketing into their strategy and this trend is expected to continue. Medical doctors, like Dr. Mauricio Gonzalez with 879 k followers in NYC (IG: @dr.mauriciogonzalez) or Dr. Cat Begovic with 1.2 million follower (IG: @beautybycat) are seizing this opportunity and adapted to this new and innovative strategy. The marketing innovation, i.e. promoting, distributing or designing a technologically unchanged product (Grimpe et al. 2017), (here for example a medical treatment) in a new way can increase the number of clients and doctor's prices. Furthermore, the data extracted from social networks, e.g. followers' gender and age distribution or questions in direct messages, can further support doctors in innovating their current business model (Sorescu 2017).

While there is literature on influencer marketing—mainly from the perspective of beauty and lifestyle industries (Cuevas et al. 2020; Farivar et al. 2021; Casaló et al. 2018, 2020; Djafarova and Rushworth 2017), there is still a lack of studies on digital transformation and influencer marketing in the healthcare industry so far has not been investigated (Campbell and Farrell 2020; Lanzolla et al. 2020; Zollo et al. 2020; Vrontis et al. 2021). In light of the increasing importance of SMIs in the decision making of consumers, and the fact that four out of five internet users seek health information online additional studies are needed (Groselj 2014; Jami Pour and Jafari 2019). Therefore, this study asks:

How can doctors become successful on social media platforms and what are the perceptions of their followers on key antecedents and outcome variables?

In order to investigate this research question a quantitative survey was sent to followers of 6 doctors' Instagram accounts to further understand followers' perceptions on key antecedents and outcomes of doctors on social media (Instagram). In the following paragraphs the theoretical background and hypotheses are developed. Then the methodology and results are presented. The paper finishes with a discussion of theoretical implications, opportunities for future research and practical recommendations for doctors on social media.

2 Theoretical Background and Hypotheses

Academic literature on SMIs usually focuses on follower intentions and attitudes (Vrontis et al. 2021). Particularly, purchase intentions, intention to follow the influencers recommendation or advice, brand attitude, word of mouth (WOM) or other forms of engagement (more followers, likes, shares, comments) are studied. This makes perfect sense since the idea behind influencer marketing as introduced above is to generate exactly those outcomes. Hence, these constructs can be considered success factors for SMI marketing. For the medical environment, particularly the outcome variables focusing on WOM and intentions to follow the influencers (doctors) advice are interesting. Doctors on social media often give advice on treatment options or health-conscious behaviours. Their purpose on platforms like Instagram is to educate or build trust and reputation with their audience, while expanding their followership and potential patient leads. They are not necessarily promoting products for sale or brands to increase brand attitudes (although this happens, too). However, they are engaging with their audience to get them to schedule a consultation or to get them to consider certain treatment options they are offering. Therefore, for this study the outcome variables '*Willingness to Offer Positive Word-of-Mouth on Social Media (hereafter sWOM)*' and '*Intention to Follow the Advice*' posted by doctors are more suitable.

Among the key antecedents for SMI according to Vrontis et al. (2021) among others are '*Trustworthiness*', '*Opinion Leadership*', communication skills (here '*Referential Skills*'), '*Para-social Relationship*' and hedonic/utilitarian value content. Accordingly, the effects of these antecedents on the selected outcomes are investigated.

Trustworthiness

According to several studies on influencer marketing '*Trustworthiness*' is an important factor in the follower influencer relationship (Ki and Kim 2019; Chapple and Cownie 2017; Martínez-López et al. 2020; Leung et al. 2022; Casaló et al. 2020). '*Trustworthiness*' refers to perceptions of honesty, integrity, and believability of an influencer (Schouten et al. 2020). Hovland et al. (1953) define '*Trustworthiness*' as "the degree of confidence in the communicator's intent to communicate the assertions he considers most valid" (Ohanian 1990). Further, several studies claim that individuals today trust more in the content and opinions of influencers than they do trust in communication of corporate brands (Ki and Kim 2019; Chapple and Cownie 2017; Martínez-López et al. 2020; Reinikainen et al. 2020; Leung et al. 2022). When there is a feeling of '*Trustworthiness*' in relationships, individuals show a higher willingness to engage in social exchange and cooperative interaction (Nahapiet and Ghoshal 1998; Leung et al. 2022).

In an interview study of followers of lifestyle vloggers,[2] Chapple and Cownie (2017) could show that '*Trustworthiness*' towards a vlogger is highly important and

[2] Vloggers defined by Cambridge Dictionary: someone who makes vlogs (= short films that record your thoughts, ideas, or opinions on a subject) and posts them on the internet.

can be a driver for positive word of mouth. They could show that if a follower has had a positive pre-existing relationship with a vlogger *'Trustworthiness'* can lead to followers sharing an endorsement of a vlogger with their friends. Further, they found that "nearly all participants stated that they then bought into the product or service" or had the intent to follow the vloggers advice and purchase the product (Chapple and Cownie 2017). Leung et al. (2022) could demonstrate in their interview study that trust in the influencer can be leveraged to get followers/customers to try out products (e.g. following the advice of the influencer). Furthermore, companies can leverage the 'change in the following'[3] of influencers to reach new customers, since for many influencers the followers are coming and going based e.g. on age or current trends and this helps companies to constantly reach new leads and it creates positive word of mouth online. Sah et al. (2018) could show that followers have greater trust in an influencer, when the influencer discloses conflicts of interest (e.g. giving an honest opinion on something versus the self-interest of getting paid for content) and that the trust in their credibility in turn has a positive effect on persuasion outcomes such as sharing the influencers post or taking the advice of the influencer. Based on previous studies it can be postulated that influencer *'Trustworthiness'* can have two effects, i.e. it can have positive effects on *sWOM* by the followers and it can have positive effects on the *'Intention to Follow the Advice'*.

This is expected to be the case for doctors on social media as well (Hausman 2004; Longoni et al. 2019; Schwartz et al. 2011). A study by López et al. (2012) on patients recommending their doctors showed that *'Trustworthiness'* is a key element why patients speak positive about doctors online. Trust of the patient is also key for "following recommendations, relying on the judgment of physicians, seeking professional medical help, and granting increased control and decision making to the physician" as a study by Trachtenberg et al. (2005) could show. Thus, the following hypotheses can be developed:

Hypothesis 1: trustworthiness has a positive impact on (a) sWOM and (b) the intention to follow the advice.

Referential skills

Another important skill for influencers is the ability to communicate information clearly and unambiguously, which Burleson and Samter (1990) define as *'Referential Skills'*. While literature agrees that influencers have to be able to communicate their content on social media, so far only a few studies exist that actually investigate if *'Referential Skills'* have a positive influence on desired outcomes of influencer marketing.

Lu et al. (2013) find that the comprehensiveness of the content can be a driver for *'Opinion Leadership'* which has positive outcomes in influencer settings, e.g. recommendation intentions and following the advice of the influencer. Huffaker (2010) could show that online leaders influence others through "high communication activity, […] and the use of affective, assertive, and linguistic diversity in their online

[3] This means that some followers will stop to watch the content or unfollow the account and other new followers will start to follow or watch the content of the influencers.

messages." Finally, Pancer et al. (2019) were investigating post readability. They found that in general simple posts are always creating more engagement (likes, comments, shares), long posts when written simple are even better than short simple posts and the worst are long and complex posts, since in their data those generated the least number of likes, shares and comments.

The findings of these studies indicate that the way in which an influencer presents the content is important for their effectiveness. This is particularly true for medical settings as well. Research has shown a positive influence of the quality of doctor-patient communication on patient satisfaction, treatment adherence (following the advice) and outcomes (Farrington 2011; Harrington et al. 2004; Maguire and Pitceathly 2002; Roter and Hall 2006). For instance, Kim et al. (2017) could show that doctors' empathic communication skills significantly and substantially influenced patient satisfaction and patient compliance. Ouschan et al. (2006) could show that an empowering communication style improves the patient-doctor relationship. Further, López et al. (2012) show that clear explanations and answering questions lead to more positive word of mouth for doctors. Barrier et al. (2003) recommend that doctors should keep working on improving their communication skills with the same enthusiasm as they do for their professional medical skills, since communication skills are key for patient satisfaction and compliance. However, these studies have not been conducted in a social media environment where doctors present their content in posts, stories, or lives on Instagram. Still, the findings should hold true for these situations as well, hence the following hypotheses can be developed:

Hypothesis 2: referential skills have a positive impact on (a) sWOM and (b) the intention to follow the advice.

Opinion leadership

The next key asset of influencers is being perceived as opinion leaders (Casaló et al. 2020). Opinion leaders usually have public recognition, are considered experts for a certain product or service, they make substantial and frequent contributions in online communities, they are a role model and thus can be persuasive for others in their purchasing decisions or attitudes towards brands (McCracken 1989; Leal et al. 2014; Godey et al. 2016; Casaló et al. 2020). Casaló et al. (2020) even use the terms influencer and opinion leader interchangeably. Based on the characteristics of opinion leadership, it is likely that social media users will share content posted by an opinion leader with their friends and family because they often have similar needs and interests (Casaló et al. 2020; Djafarova and Rushworth 2017). In fact, in their study with followers of fashion influencers on Instagram Casaló et al. (2020) find positive influences of perceived '*Opinion Leadership*' on intentions to interact with the account in the future, the intention to recommend this account and the '*Intention to Follow the Advice*' posted by the account. Furthermore, Farivar et al. (2021) hypothesize that the higher a social media influencer's perceived '*Opinion Leadership*', the higher followers' intention to purchase based on the recommendation of the influencer. In their online survey with followers from two fashion influencers[4] on Instagram they can show the postulated positive influence (Farivar et al. 2021). Hence, it seems to be likely that '*Opinion Leadership*' has positive effects on followers' sWOM as well as on the '*Intention to Follow the Advice*'.

The concept of '*Opinion Leadership*' is also recognized in the medical field (Locock et al. 2001). Burt (1997) argues that opinion leaders are more often opinion brokers that help in the diffusion of information between groups, and he provides an illustrative example from the medical field, i.e. the adaption of a new drug by doctors through discussing cases with each other and influencing each other in adapting new drugs. Hence, it can be argued that doctors on social media can have the same effect. Due to their expertise in a certain field, they can be considered opinion leaders which then influences their audience for instance to adapt healthier lifestyles by following the advice of physicians. Furthermore, it is likely that if followers receive interesting or new information by doctors, they are likely to further share this information with their peers as well. Thus, the following hypotheses can be developed:

Hypothesis 3: opinion leadership has a positive impact on (a) sWOM and (b) the intention to follow the advice.

Hedonism/Utilitarianism

As discussed above, the form in which the content is presented is highly important for the effectiveness of any influencer. An often-investigated dimension on how products or services are perceived is the hedonism-utilitarianism dimension. Here utilitarian products or services offer benefits in practical functionality (e.g. convenience, saving time or money, or accumulating knowledge, tangible aspects such as product quality) (Locock et al. 2001). Hedonic goods are more about experiential enjoyment or implied social status (e.g. fun and excitement, staying in a luxury hotel). However, hedonism and utilitarianism are not two ends of a linear scale, because products can be low and high in both hedonic and utilitarian aspects (Hirschman and Holbrook 1982; Paul et al. 2009; Chiou and Ting 2011; Lin et al. 2018). For example using an iPhone can be a lot of fun and highly useful from a functional perspective at the same time. The same can be true for content posted on Instagram. Posts can have hedonic and utilitarian (high and low) character at the same time.

A first study that investigated the influences of high hedonic value content on social media engagement was presented by Hughes et al. (2019). They found that posts high in hedonic value positively impact blog platform engagement, i.e. posting comments or liking a brand. Further, they found that on Facebook, posts high in hedonic content are more effective when their intent is to increase trial versus for example to raise awareness about a brand or product (Hughes et al. 2019). Other studies suggest that more informative posts (utilitarian) have a positive influence on brand attitudes and purchase intentions (Ki and Kim 2019; Lou and Yuan 2019).

In advertising often, the categories of storytelling posts (maybe more hedonic) and informational posts (maybe more utilitarian) are used. However, there is still inconsistency in the findings, e.g. some studies find informational ads leading to higher purchase intention (Golden and Johnson 1983; Zebregs et al. 2015), while

[4] One with 30 k, the other with 70 k followers, i.e. micro-influencers.

others find that storytelling has stronger effects on purchasing behaviours (Adaval and Wyer 1998; Kaufman 2003). Hence, influencers should consider balancing hedonic and utilitarian aspects to target both goals engagement and sales outcomes (Leung et al. 2022). Lin et al. (2018) provide a five-step strategy for using online opinion leaders to promote the hedonic and utilitarian value of products and services, where in the best case the influencer is both an opinion leader (utilitarian) and appeal leader (hedonic) that can address both hedonic and utilitarian aspects of a product or service. For doctors on social media this should be similar. Consumers of e-health knowledge particularly feel the utilitarian values of getting useful ideas and not having to go to the doctor's office to get the information needed (Goetzinger et al. 2007; Baum 2004). Hence the following hypotheses can be developed:

Hypothesis 4: hedonism/utilitarianism has a positive impact on (a) sWOM and (b) the intention to follow the advice.

Para-Social relationship

Finally, para-social relationships have been studied in the influencer context (Farivar et al. 2021; Reinikainen et al. 2020). A '*Para-social Relationship*' refers to a one-sided relationship that a follower feels towards an influencer or a media person. By watching the content of the influencer daily, the follower starts to consider the influencer to be their friend, since the follower is virtually participating in the influencer´s life, despite the influencer in many cases not even knowing the individual follower. Previous research has indicated that if followers are feeling a '*Para-social Relationship*' towards influencers, this can impact their behavioural intentions, for instance they are more likely to follow the advice of the influencer or that they have a higher purchase intention. Farivar et al. (2021) show a positive effect of '*Para-social Relationship*' on followers' purchase intention in their online survey of Instagram users, the effect of '*Para-social Relationship*' was even stronger than '*Opinion Leadership*'. Reinikainen et al. (2020) could show for followers of a YouTube vlogger that '*Para-social Relationship*' leads to improved credibility which in turn leads to higher brand trust and purchase intention. Similar findings are presented by Lee and Watkins (2016). Furthermore, Hwang and Zhang (2018) investigated the influence of '*Para-social Relationship*' on electronic word of mouth intensions and found a very strong and positive influence. Their survey results with Chinese participants showed a strong influence on purchase intention by para-social relationship.

Based on these findings, one can postulate that followers of doctors on Instagram will also develop para-social relationships with these doctors, which then result in similar outcomes regarding sWOM and '*Intention to Follow the Advice*' of the doctor. Thus, the following hypotheses can be developed:

Hypothesis 5: para-social relationship has a positive impact on (a) sWOM and (b) the intention to follow the advice.

All hypotheses are summarized in Fig. 1.

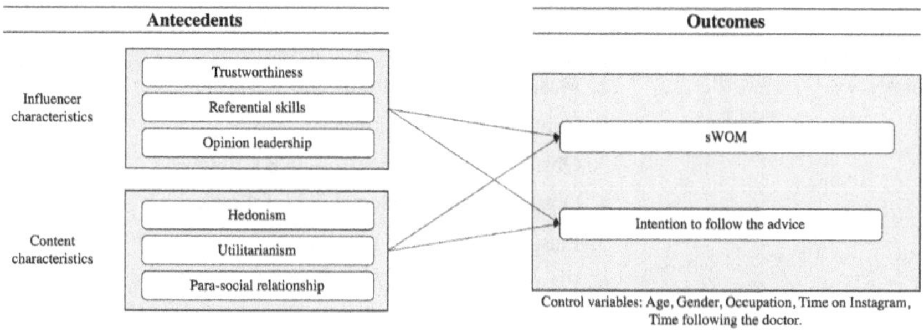

Fig. 1 Summary of the hypotheses

3 Methodology

Survey development and distribution

To test the hypotheses an online survey was conducted. The measures used were adapted from well-established scales published in top journals.[5] The construct *'Willingness to Offer Positive Word-of-Mouth on Social Media (sWOM)'* was taken from Eisingerich et al. (2015). *'Intention to Follow the Advice'* was measured with a construct by Casaló et al. (2020), their paper also provided the construct for *'Opinion Leadership'*.

'Trustworthiness' was taken from Martínez-López et al. (2020). The measure for *'Referential Skills'* was found in Burleson and Samter (1990). *'Hedonism/ Utilitarianism'* was evaluated employing a measure from Koschate-Fischer et al. (2012). Para-social relationships was taken from Reinikainen et al. (2020).

Further two attention control questions were included. A double translation procedure was used to convert the questions from English to Spanish (Torres et al. 2019). Before, sending the questionnaire to the actual respondents, a pre-test with 16 individuals with an academic background was conducted. After considering their recommendations the final version of the survey was reached.

Then, the survey was distributed to Instagram followers of 6 doctor-accounts. Following a recommendation of Farivar et al. (2021) Instagram accounts of doctors with follower numbers between 4,000 and 200,000 followers (at the time of the survey) were chosen, since those accounts mostly fall into the micro-influencer category, which offers the best combination of follower engagement and broad reach. Additionally, it was important to survey a range of accounts with varying follower numbers, to get a broader view on potentially more and less successful accounts. The areas of expertise of the 6 doctors, their follower counts and responses in the survey are listed below in Table 1.

Furthermore, additional criteria for selecting the doctors' Instagram accounts were used (Eisenhardt 1989): (1) The Instagram account had to have at least 100 posts, (2) had to be actively posting at least once a week, and (3) on average posts of the account

[5] Measures were taken from papers published in top level journals of the VHB Jourqual ranking.

Table 1 Doctors participating in the online survey

Doctors name	Respondents
1. Mastologist—5.5 k followers	85
2. Dentists—50.1 k followers	116
3. Obstetrician/gynecologist—35.8 k followers	179
4. Obstetrician/gynecologist—4 k followers	51
5. Plastic surgeon—42 k followers	94
6. Plastic surgeon—167 k followers	178

should have at least 5 comments, 100 likes and 100 unique views. With these criteria a certain degree of engagement with the Instagram account could be implied. At the beginning of each questionnaire the respondents were asked to give the name and the Instagram handle of the doctor they are following. Then the respondents were asked to answer the questionnaire regarding this doctor's Instagram account. The survey was active for one week and received 1856 clicks, resulting in 703 complete cases, after eliminating invalid responses (answers missing, respondents that selected wrong answers to the attention control questions and respondents that gave the same rating to all items). The final response rate[6] was 38%, which can be considered as high once a follower clicked on the survey.[7]

Partial Least Squares method

For the analysis of the data the Partial Least Squares (PLS) method was used. This procedure can be used when the theoretical information is still limited, or the research phenomenon is relatively new (Casaló et al. 2020; Roldán and Sánchez-Franco 2012). The PLS procedure starts with controlling for the validity of the constructs using confirmatory factor analysis. Thresholds for the confirmatory factor analysis are item loadings of 0.7 on their respective construct (Henseler et al. 2009). Second, Cronbachs alpha's above 0.65 (Steenkamp and Geyskens 2006). Third, the average variance extracted (AVE) values should be above 0.5 as an indicator of convergent validity (Fornell and Larcker 1981). Fourth, the Fornell and Larcker criterion must be met, to confirm discriminant validity of all reflective constructs. After confirmatory factor analysis confirmed the validity of the constructs, the PLS method employs 5000 bootstrap iterations estimating the hypothesized model and providing, path coefficients, significance levels for each proposed path and R^2 values (Chin 1998).

[6] Complete and accepted responses divided by number of clicks on the survey link.

[7] Considering that potentially more than 353 k followers (sum of the follower counts of all doctors) could have seen the posts by the doctors, this would bring the response rate to 0.1%, which is still acceptable.

4 Results

Descriptive results of the sample

In the 703 valid respondents 25% were males and 75% females. Regarding the control variable age, about 8% were between 15 and 25 years old; 32% are between 26 and 35 years old; 33% between 36 and 45 years old, 11% between 46 and 55; 9% between 56 and 65 and 7% between 66 and 75 years old. All respondents replied to the Spanish version of the survey and indicated that they are from Colombia. Regarding the occupation 47% stated they were employed, 33% stated to be independent or entrepreneur, followed by about 8% students, 10% pensioned respondents and 2% unemployed respondents.

Regarding the use of social media platforms 655 respondents use Instagram, 445 use Facebook, followed by 390 using YouTube, 234 are on TikTok, 130 use Twitter, 136 are on LinkedIn, 91 respondents use Pinterest, 85 use Snapchat, 37 are on Kwai and 5 on People. Most respondents spend between 2 and 4 h on social media and between 1 and 3 h on Instagram per day. Finally, most respondents have been following the doctor they referred to in the survey for 1–4 years.

Confirmatory factor analysis

During confirmatory factor analysis, factor loadings were checked, and item 2 of '*Utilitarianism*' was eliminated due to a loading below the threshold of 0.7. Furthermore, to fulfil the Fornell Larcker Criterion item 4 and 5 of '*Hedonism*' and item 2 of '*Para-social Relationship*' were eliminated since those items had the lowest loadings in their respective constructs. The final model then fulfilled all requirements and can be used for structural equation modelling. Cronbach's Alphas, Average Variance Extracted and the Fornell and Larcker Criterion are presented below in Tables 2 and 3.

Table 2 Construct reliability and convergent validity—Cronbach's Alphas and Average Variance Extracted

Constructs	Cronbach's Alpha	Average Variance Extracted (AVE)
sWOM	0.960	0.894
Intention to follow the advice	0.974	0.927
Trustworthiness	0.983	0.968
Referential skills	0.984	0.955
Opinion leadership	0.969	0.868
Hedonism	0.946	0.902
Utilitarianism	0.987	0.961
Para-social relationship	0.974	0.867

Table 3 Discriminant validity—Fornell and Larcker criterion[8]

Constructs	1	2	3	4	5	6	7	8
1. Hedonism	0.950							
2. Intention to follow the advice	0.877	0.963						
3. Opinion leadership	0.873	0.938	0.932					
4. Para-social relationship	0.878	0.947	0.928	0.931				
5. Referential skills	0.828	0.907	0.916	0.891	0.977			
6. Trustworthiness	0.888	0.951	0.930	0.920	0.918	0.984		
7. Utilitarianism	0.945	0.900	0.895	0.875	0.868	0.896	0.980	
8. sWOM	0.885	0.946	0.929	0.928	0.893	0.945	0.878	0.945

Table 4 Path coefficients and p-values of proposed structural model

Constructs	Path coefficients	p-values
1a. Trustworthiness → sWOM	0.440	0.000
1b. Trustworthiness → Intention to follow the advice	0.371	0.000
2a. Referential skills → sWOM	0.184	0.007
2b. Referential skills → Intention to follow the advice	0.014	0.806
3a. Opinion leadership → sWOM	0.247	0.000
3b. Opinion leadership → Intention to follow the advice	0.135	0.035
4a. Hedonism → sWOM	0.198	0.000
4b. Hedonism → Intention to follow the advice	−0.114	0.003
4a. Utilitarianism → sWOM	−0.119	0.035
4b. Utilitarianism→ Intention to follow the advice	0.182	0.000
5a. Para-social relationship → sWOM	0.268	0.000
5b. Para-social relationship → Intention to follow the advice	0.428	0.000

Evaluation of the proposed structural model

To estimate the proposed effects the bootstrapping procedure (5000 iterations) in SmartPLS was used. Path coefficients and p-values are summarized in Table 4. The R^2 for sWOM ($R^2 = 0.929$) and '*Intention to Follow the Advice*' ($R^2 = 0.950$) represent a substantial level of explained variance.

For '*Trustworthiness*' the data shows the proposed positive effects, thus hypothesis 1a ($\beta = 0.440$, $p < 0.01$ for sWOM) and 1b ($\beta = 0.371$, $p < 0.01$ for '*Intention to Follow the Advice*') are accepted. '*Trustworthiness*' has the strongest influence on sWOM. '*Referential Skills*' show a positive effect on sWOM ($\beta = 0.184$, $p < 0.01$), but no significant influence on '*Intention to Follow the Advice*'. Therefore, hypothesis

[8] Diagonal elements are the square root of the AVE. Elements below diagonal are the correlations between constructs.

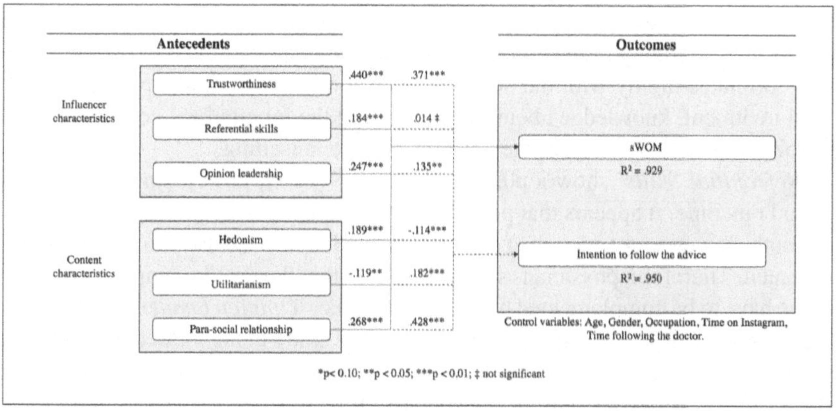

Fig. 2 Summary of results

2a is accepted and 2b rejected. '*Opinion Leadership*' shows both predicted positive effects and thus hypothesis 3a ($\beta = 0.247$, $p < 0.01$) and 3b ($\beta = 0.135$, $p < 0.05$) are accepted.

Regarding the content characteristics '*Hedonism*' and '*Utilitarianism*' show interesting results. While '*Hedonism*' shows a positive effect on sWOM ($\beta = 0.198$, $p < 0.01$) and a negative effect on '*Intention to Follow the Advice*' ($\beta = -0.114$, $p < 0.01$); the effects for '*Utilitarianism*' are reversed ($\beta = -0.119$, $p < 0.05/\beta = 0.182$, $p < 0.01$). However, overall hypothesis 4a and 4b are rejected. Finally, '*Para-social Relationship*' shows both predicted positive effects on sWOM ($\beta = 0.268$, $p < 0.01$) and for '*Intention to Follow the Advice*' ($\beta = 0.428$, $p < 0.01$) this factor has the strongest influence. Thus, hypotheses 5a and 5b are accepted. All results are summarized in Fig. 2.

5 Results

This study set out to answer the question how doctors can become successful on social media platforms and what their follower's perceptions on key antecedents and outcome variables are. The findings of this study reveal several interesting points to answer this research question. For '*Trustworthiness*' the results presented largely confirm the importance of this antecedent for influencer marketing that was pointed out by previous research (Chapple and Cownie 2017; Leung et al. 2022; Sah et al. 2018). Particularly, for generating word of mouth online this construct showed the strongest influence on sWOM. Additionally, '*Trustworthiness*' is the second strongest predictor of '*Intention to Follow the Advice*'. Thus, the findings confirm studies focused on medical settings, which also highlighted the importance of trust, such as López et al. (2012) or Trachtenberg et al. (2005). For a practical recommendation doctors thus should focus on strategies of building trust with their audience. A literature review on trust building by Chandra et al. (2018) found that trust correlates highly with the doctors' level of communication, level of interpersonal treatment, knowledge about the patient and the longitudinal continuity of the doctor-patient relationship, as well as preventive counselling.

'*Referential Skills*' show a positive effect on sWOM, however no effect on the second outcome. It appears that presenting topics clearly is helpful in creating word of mouth, however, not enough to convince the audience to actually follow the advice presented. Therefore, physicians should be aware that flawless communication skills online have to be complemented by other factors, i.e. '*Opinion Leadership*' or '*Para-social Relationship*'. According to the data of this study being viewed as an opinion leader is a key success factor for doctors on social media. This mirrors findings of Burt (1997) who argues that, in a medical setting, opinion leaders are more often opinion brokers that help in the diffusion of information between groups. Future research should investigate indirect effects of '*Opinion Leadership*' as a moderator or mediator variable. From a practical perspective in innovating their business model, doctors that want to become more active online should employ strategies to establish themselves as opinion leaders.

For the content characteristics the effect of '*Hedonism*' and '*Utilitarianism*' is particularly interesting. Hedonic content gets the influencer sWOM, while utilitarian content influences the followers to consider compliance with the advice given by the doctors. Therefore, doctors should plan out their content strategy with a healthy balance of fun and useful content.

Finally, for '*Para-social Relationship*' the second strongest positive effect on the sWOM was found. Further, this factor shows the strongest positive effect on '*Intention to Follow the Advice*'. These findings support prior research of Reinikainen et al. (2020), Farivar et al. (2021), Lee and Watkins (2016) and Colliander and Dahlen (2011) who found similar positive effects on influencer outcomes. Thus, doctors who want to be successful on social media should particularly focus on activities that increases the development of '*Para-social Relationship*', i.e. posting frequently throughout the day, letting their follower participate in their lives, responding to questions and direct messages, sharing personal stories or secrets, besides posting about their professional content.

The key in creating '*Para-social Relationship*' with their followers is to use para-social interaction strategies, which is the illusion of an interaction with conversational give and take (Horton and Wohl 1956). These strategies also involve talking directly to the followers, greeting them, direct eye-contact with the camera and sharing personal, private and informal information, since those behaviours trigger the experience of an actual interaction between follower and influencer (Reinikainen et al. 2020; Hartmann and Goldhoorn 2011). With social media the development of para-social relationships has become easier since they allow for actual interaction via comments, direct messages or live broadcastings, where followers can send in questions that get answered by the influencer. Labrecque (2014) for instance found that addressing the followers by their username improves the feeling of para-social relationship. Additionally, Frederick et al. (2012) showed in an athlete-follower-interactions on twitter that responding to a specific follower also heightens the para-social experience of all other followers that just witnessed the interaction. The data in this study suggests that these strategies should be beneficial for creating desired outcomes for doctors on social media.

This paper also offers several theoretical contributions. Despite the growing body of academic literature on influencer marketing, this study is the first to analyse antecedents and outcomes of influencer marketing in a medical setting. Hereby this study extends the knowledge on influencer marketing in different ways. First, this work extends the current understanding of influencer marketing to a new industry, which several scholars have been calling for, since most work in this area has been done in settings of fashion, beauty, and lifestyle influencers (Campbell and Farrell 2020; Lanzolla et al. 2020; Zollo et al. 2020; Vrontis et al. 2021; Djafarova and Rushworth 2017; Groselj 2014; Jami Pour et al. 2019; Farivar et al. 2021). By investigating the medical industry and doctors in their role as influencers this work contributes to partly closing this research gap.

Second, this study also extends the body of knowledge by investing a non-US country, which was called for by academia as well (Djafarova and Rushworth 2017). The respondents in this study all provided Colombia as their country of origin. The results show some similarities with prior research, however some interesting differences as well, that might be related to the respondents' country of origin and cultural background. However, additional research, e.g. by conducting the survey in other countries would be needed to pinpoint and extract the impact of country and cultural differences on influencer marketing.

Third, this work offers a new combination of antecedents and outcomes called for by Vrontis et al. (2021) and provides a wholistic approach by looking at influencer characteristics and content characteristics. The field of social media influencer marketing is still quite new and needs more structure and theory building. Hence, this work can contribute here as well.

Several limitations of this study must be acknowledged, nevertheless some might be opportunities for future research. First, the sample is dominated by female respondents, due to the specialisations of the doctors in mastology, gynaecology and plastic surgery, which are niches for female patients. Even though gender did not have a significant influence in the data, future studies should investigate a more balanced sample. Second, the study investigates intentions only. This is common practice in academic business research, since intentions have been shown to be a good proxy of actual behaviours. However, future research should try to investigate actual behaviours, e.g. by collaborating with doctors that give access to their Instagram account and their patient records to see if a growing follower number or comments and likes online actually translate over into the real world in terms of an increase of patients scheduling appointments. Third, the doctors distributed the survey to their followers in Instagram, which could have resulted in a bias and respondents rating the items particularly high. Further, the doctors came from a rather narrow field of specializations. Future research could consider other methods of survey distribution where there is no direct link between the respondent and the doctor under investigation. Additionally, other medical specialties, e.g. family doctors, dermatologists, ophthalmologist etc. should be investigated as well.

Fourth, Instagram was used as the target social media platform. While Instagram is one of the most common platform for influencer marketing, other platforms like TikTok, YouTube or upcoming platforms like Kwai should be investigated as well, to check for potential differences among the platforms.

Nevertheless, by investigating this still new and innovative phenomenon of medical doctors becoming social media influencers, this study helped in broadening the body of knowledge on antecedents and desired outcomes of influencer marketing and thus provides a valuable contribution to the academic literature.

References

Adaval, R., Wyer, R.S.: The role of narratives in consumer information processing. J. Consum. Psychol. **7**, 207–245 (1998)

Audrezet, A., Charry, K.: Do influencers need to tell audiences they're getting paid. Harvard Bus. Rev. (2019) https://hbr.org/2019/08/do-influencers-need-to-tell-audiences-theyre-getting-paid

Baum, L.S.: Internet parent support groups for primary caregivers of a child with special health care needs. Pediatr. Nurs. **30**(5) (2004)

Barrier, P.A., Li, J.T.C., Jensen, N.M.: Two words to improve physician-patient communication: what else? In: Mayo Clinic Proceedings, vol. 78, no. 2, pp 211–214. Elsevier (2003)

Businesswire: The $11.9 trillion global healthcare market: key opportunities & strategies (2014–2022) (2019). https://www.businesswire.com/news/home/20190625005862/en/The-11.9-Trillion-Global-Healthcare-Market-Key-Opportunities-Strategies-2014-2022---ResearchAndMarkets.com. Accessed 22 Feb 2022

Burleson, B.R., Samter, W.: Effects of cognitive complexity on the perceived importance of communication skills in friends. Commun. Res. **17**(2), 165–182 (1990)

Burt, R.S.: The contingent value of social capital. Adm. Sci. Q. **42**(2), 339 (1997)

Campbell, C., Farrell, J.R.: More than meets the eye: the functional components underlying influencer marketing. Bus. Horiz. (2020)

Casaló, L.V., Flavián, C., Ibáñez-Sánchez, S.: Influencers on Instagram: antecedents and consequences of opinion leadership. J. Bus. Res. 117 (2020)

Chapple, C., Cownie, F.: An investigation into viewers' trust in and response towards disclosed paid-for endorsements by YouTube lifestyle Vloggers. J. Promot. Commun. **5**(2) (2017)

Chandra, S., Mohammadnezhad, M., Ward, P.: Trust and communication in a doctor-patient relationship: a literature review. J. Healthc. Commun. **3**(3), 36 (2018)

Colliander, J., Dahlen, M.: Following the fashionable friend: the power of social media weighing the publicity effectiveness of blogs versus online magazines. J. Advert. Res. **51**, 313–320 (2011)

Chin, W.: The partial least squares approach to structural equation modeling. In: Marcoulides, G.A. (ed.) Modern Methods for Business Research, pp. 295–358. Lawrence Erlbaum Associates, Mahwah (1998)

Chiou, J.S., Ting, C-C.: Will you spend more money and time on internet shopping when the product and situation are right? Comput. Hum. Behav. **27**(1), 203–208 (2011). https://doi.org/10.1016/j.chb.2010.07.037

Cuevas, L.M., Chong, S.M., Lim, H.: Influencer marketing: social media influencers as human brands attaching to followers and yielding positive marketing results by fulfilling needs. J. Retail. Consum. Serv. **55**, 102133 (2020)

Digital Marketing Institute: 20 influencer marketing statistics that will surprise you (2019). https://digitalmarketinginstitute.com/en-eu/blog/20-influencer-marketing-statistics-that-will-surprise-you. Accessed 22 Feb 2022

Djafarova, E., Rushworth, C.: Exploring the credibility of online celebrities' Instagram profiles in influencing the purchase decisions of young female users. Comput. Hum. Behav. **68**, 1–7 (2017)

Eisingerich, A.B., Chun, H.H., Liu, Y., Jia, H., Bell, S.J.: Why recommend a brand face-to-face but not on Facebook? How word-of-mouth on online social sites differs from traditional word-of-mouth. J. Consum. Psychol. **25**(1), 120–128 (2015)

Eisenhardt, K.M.: Building theories from case study research. Acad. Manag. Rev. **14**(4), 532–550 (1989)

Farivar, S., Wang, F., Yuan, Y.: Opinion leadership vs. para-social relationship: key factors in influencer marketing. J. Retail. Consum. Serv. **59**, 102371 (2021)

Farrington, C.: Reconciling managers, doctors, and patients: the role of clear communication. J. R. Soc. Med. **104**(6), 231–236 (2011)

Fornell, C., Larcker, D.: Evaluating structural equation models with unobservable variables and measurement error. J. Mark. Res. **XVIII**, 39–50 (1981)

Frederick, E.L., Choong, H.L., Clavio, G., Walsh, P.: Why we follow: an examination of parasocial interaction and fan motivations for following athlete archetypes on Twitter. Int. J. Sport Commun. **5**(4), 481–502 (2012). https://doi.org/10.1123/ijsc.5.4.481

George, D.R., Rovniak, L.S., Kraschnewski, J.L.: Dangers and opportunities for social media in medicine. Clin. Obstet. Gynecol. **56**(3) (2013)

Godey, B., Manthiou, A., Pederzoli, D., Rokka, J., Aiello, G., Donvito, R., Singh, R.: Social media marketing efforts of luxury brands: influence on brand equity and consumer behavior. J. Bus. Res. **69**(12), 5833–5841 (2016)

Golden, L.L., Johnson, K.A.: The impact of sensory preference and thinking versus feeling appeals on advertising effectiveness. ACR North Am. Adv. (1983)

Goetzinger, L., Park, J., Lee, Y.J., Widdows, R.: Value-driven consumer e-health information search behavior. Int. J. Pharm. Healthc. Mark. (2007)

Grimpe, C., Sofka, W., Bhargava, M., Chatterjee, R.: R&D, marketing innovation, and new product performance: a mixed methods study. J. Prod. Innov. Manag. 34(3), 360–383 (2017)

Groselj, D.: A webometric analysis of online health information: sponsorship, platform type and link structures. Online Inf. Rev. **38**(2), 209–231 (2014)

Harrington, J., Noble, L.M., Newman, S.P.: Improving patients' communication with doctors: a systematic review of intervention studies. Patient Educ. Couns. **52**(1), 7–16 (2004)

Hartmann, T., Goldhoorn, C.: Horton and Wohl revisited: exploring viewers' experience of parasocial interaction. J. Commun. **61**, 1104–1121 (2011)

Hartz et al.: Social media in der ärztlichen Praxis: Chancen, Risiken, Trends. Deutsches Ärzte Blatt **111**(17) (2014). https://www.aerzteblatt.de/archiv/159365/Social-Media-in-der-aerztlichen-Praxis-Chancen-Risiken-Trends. Accessed 22 Feb 2022

Hausman, A.: Modeling the patient-physician service encounter: improving patient outcomes. J. Acad. Mark. Sci. **32**(4), 403–417 (2004). https://doi.org/10.1177/0092070304265627

Henseler, J., Ringle, C., Sinkovics, R.: The use of partial least squares path modeling in international marketing. Adv. Int. Mark. **20**, 277–319 (2009)

Hirschman, E.C., Holbrook, M.B.: Hedonic consumption: emerging concepts, methods and propositions. J. Mark. **46**, 92–101 (1982)

Horton, D., Wohl, R.R.: Mass communication and para-social interaction: observation on intimacy at a distance. Psychiatry **19**, 185–206 (1956)

Househ, M.: The use of social media in healthcare: organizational, clinical, and patient perspectives. Stud. Health Technol. Inf. **183**, 244–248 (2013)

Hovland, C., Janis, I.K., Kelley, H.H.: Communication and Persuasion. Yale University Press, New Haven, CT (1953)

Huffaker, D.: Dimensions of leadership and social influence in online communities. Hum. Commun. Res. **36**(4), 593–617 (2010)

Hughes, C., Swaminathan, V., Brooks, G.: Driving brand engagement through online social influencers: an empirical investigation of sponsored blogging campaigns. J. Mark. **83**(5), 78–96 (2019)

Hwang, K., Zhang, Q.: Influence of parasocial relationship between digital celebrities and their followers on followers' purchase and electronic word-of-mouth intentions, and persuasion knowledge. Comput. Hum. Behav. **87**, 155–173 (2018)

Jami Pour, M., Jafari, S.M.: Toward a maturity model for the application of social media in healthcare. Online Inform. Rev. **43**(3), 404–425 (2019). https://doi.org/10.1108/OIR-02-2018-0038

Kamel Boulos, M.N., Giustini, D.M., Wheeler, S.: Instagram and WhatsApp in health and healthcare: an overview. Future Internet **8**(3), 37 (2016)

Kaufman, B.: Stories that SELL, stories that TELL. J. Bus. Strat. **24**, 11–15 (2003)

Ki, C.W.C., Kim, Y.K.: The mechanism by which social media influencers persuade consumers: the role of consumers' desire to mimic. Psychol. Mark. **36**(10), 905–922 (2019)

Kim, E., Ratneshwar, S., Thorson, E.: Why narrative ads work: an integrated process explanation. J. Advert. **46**(2), 283–296 (2017)

Knoll, J., Matthes, J.: The effectiveness of celebrity endorsements: a meta-analysis. J. Acad. Mark. Sci. **45**(1), 55–75 (2017)

Koschate-Fischer, N., Stefan, I.V., Hoyer, W.D.: Willingness to pay for cause-related marketing: the impact of donation amount and moderating effects. J. Market. Res. (JMR), **49**(6) (2012)

Labrecque, L.I.: Fostering consumer-brand relationships in social media environments: the role of parasocial interaction. J. Interact. Mark. **28**(2), 134–148 (2014)

Lanzolla, G., Lorenz, A., Miron-Spektor, E., Schilling, M., Solinas, G., Tucci, C.L.: Digital transformation: what is new if anything? Emerging patterns and management research. Acad. Manag. Discov. **6**(3), 341–350 (2020)

Lamberton, C., Stephen, A.T.: A thematic exploration of digital, social media, and mobile marketing: research evolution from 2000 to 2015 and an agenda for future inquiry. J. Mark. **80**(6), 146–172 (2016)

Leal, G.P.A., Hor-Meyll, L.F., de Paula Pessôa, L.A.G.: Influence of virtual communities in purchasing decisions: the participants' perspective. J. Bus. Res. **67**(5), 882–890 (2014)

Lee, J.E., Watkins, B.: YouTube vloggers' influence on consumer luxury brand perceptions and intentions. J. Bus. Res. **69**(12), 5753–5760 (2016)

Leung, F.F., Gu, F.F., Palmatier, R.W.: Online influencer marketing. J. Acad. Mark. Sci. 1–26 (2022)

Lin, H.C., Bruning, P.F., Swarna, H.: Using online opinion leaders to promote the hedonic and utilitarian value of products and services. Bus. Horiz. **61**(3), 431–442 (2018)

Locock, L., Dopson, S., Chambers, D., Gabbay, J.: Understanding the role of opinion leaders in improving clinical effectiveness. Soc Sci Med **53**(6), 745–757 (2001)

Longoni, C., Bonezzi, A., Morewedge, C.K.: Resistance to medical artificial intelligence. J. Consum. Res. **46**(4), 629–650 (2019)

López, A., Detz, A., Ratanawongsa, N., Sarkar, U.: What patients say about their doctors online: a qualitative content analysis. J. Gen. Intern. Med. **27**(6), 685–692 (2012)

Lou, C., Yuan, S.: Influencer marketing: how message value and credibility affect consumer trust of branded content on social media. J. Interact. Advert. **19**(1), 58–73 (2019)

Lu, Y., Jerath, K., Singh, P.V.: The emergence of opinion leaders in a networked online community: a dyadic model with time dynamics and a heuristic for fast estimation. Manage. Sci. **59**(8), 1783–1799 (2013)

Lunt, N., Carrera, P.: Medical tourism: assessing the evidence on treatment abroad. Maturitas **66**(1), 27–32 (2010)

Martínez-López, F.J., Anaya-Sánchez, R., Fernández Giordano, M., Lopez-Lopez, D.: Behind influencer marketing: key marketing decisions and their effects on followers' responses. J. Mark. Manag. **36**(7–8), 579–607 (2020)

Maguire, P., Pitceathly, C.: Key communication skills and how to acquire them. BMJ **325**(7366), 697–700 (2002)

Malshe, A., Biemans, W.: The role of sales in NPD: an investigation of the US health-care industry. J. Prod. Innov. Manag. **31**(4), 664–679 (2014)

McCracken, G.: Who is the celebrity endorser? Cultural foundations of the endorsement process. J. Consum. Res. **16**(3), 310–321 (1989)

Mediorbis: Social-media-marketing: Digitale Stimme der Praxis (2021). https://mediorbis.de/praxismarketing/social-media-marketing-fuer-aerzte. Accessed 22 Feb 2022

Nahapiet, J., Ghoshal, S.: Social capital, intellectual capital, and the organizational advantage. Acad. Manag. Rev. **23**(2), 242–266 (1998)

Nguyen, B.M., Lu, E., Bhuyan, N., Lin, K., Sevilla, M.: Social media for doctors: taking professional and patient engagement to the next level. Fam. Pract. Manag. **27**(1), 19–14 (2020)

Ohanian, R.: Construction and validation of a scale to measure celebrity endorsers' perceived expertise, trustworthiness, and attractiveness. J. Advert. **19**(3), 39–52 (1990)

Ouschan, R., Sweeney, J., Johnson, L.: Customer empowerment and relationship outcomes in health-care consultations. Eur. J. Mark. **40**(9/10), 1068–1086 (2006). https://doi.org/10.1108/03090560610681014

Pancer, E., Chandler, V., Poole, M., Noseworthy, T.J.: How readability shapes social media engagement. J. Consum. Psychol. **29**(2), 262–270 (2019)

Paul, M., Hennig-Thurau, T., Gremler, D.D., Gwinner, K.P., Wiertz, C.: Toward a theory of repeat purchase drivers for consumer services. J. Acad. Mark. Sci. **37**(2), 215–237 (2009)

Rahal, A.: Is influencer marketing worth it in 2020? Forbes, 10 January 2020 (2020). https://www.forbes.com/sites/theyec/2020/01/10/is-influencer-marketing-worth-it-in-2020/#4d26eebf31c5. Accessed 22 Feb 2022

Reinikainen, H., Munnukka, J., Maity, D., Luoma-aho, V.: 'You really are a great big sister'–parasocial relationships, credibility, and the moderating role of audience comments in influencer marketing. J. Mark. Manag. **36**(3–4), 279–298 (2020)

Rashid, A.A., Devaraj, N.K.: Doctors and social media-good, bad or both? A Malaysian perspective. Int. J. Hum. Health Sci. **4**(3), 174 (2020)

Roter, D., Hall, J.A.: Doctors talking with patients/patients talking with doctors: improving communication in medical visits. Greenwood Publishing Group (2006)

Roldán, J.L., Sánchez-Franco, M.J.: Variance-based structural equation modeling: Guidelines for using partial least squares in information systems research. In: Mora, M., Gelman, O., Steenkamp, A.L., Raisinghani, M. (eds.) Research Methodologies, Innovations and Philosophies in Software Systems Engineering and Information Systems, pp. 193–221. IGI Global, Hershey, PA (2012)

Sah, S., Malaviya, P., Thompson, D.: Conflict of interest disclosure as an expertise cue: differential effects due to automatic versus deliberative processing. Organ. Behav. Hum. Decis. Process. **147**, 127–146 (2018)

Schouten, A.P., Janssen, L., Verspaget, M.: Celebrity vs. influencer endorsements in advertising: the role of identification, credibility, and product-endorser fit. Int. J. Advert. **39**(2), 258–281 (2020)

Schwartz, J., Luce, M.F., Ariely, D.: Are consumers too trusting? The effects of relationships with expert advisers. J. Mark. Res. **48**(SPL), S163–S174 (2011)

Sorescu, A.: Data-driven business model innovation. J. Prod. Innov. Manag. **34**(5), 691–696 (2017)

Statista: Projected global digital health market size from 2019 to 2025 (2019). https://www.statista.com/statistics/1092869/global-digital-health-market-size-forecast/. Accessed 22 Feb 2022

Steenkamp, J.B.E., Geyskens, I.: How country characteristics affect the perceived value of web sites. J. Mark. **70**(3), 136–150 (2006)

Torres, P., Augusto, M., Matos, M.: Antecedents and outcomes of digital influencer endorsement: an exploratory study. Psychol. Mark. **36**(12), 1267–1276 (2019)

Trachtenberg, F., Dugan, E., Hall, M.A.: How patients' trust relates to their involvement in medical care. J. Fam. Pract. **54**(4), 344–354 (2005)

Vrontis, D., Makrides, A., Christofi, M., Thrassou, A.: Social media influencer marketing: a systematic review, integrative framework and future research agenda. Int. J. Consum. Stud. (2021)

Whittaker, A.: Pleasure and pain: medical travel in Asia. Glob. Public Health **3**(3), 271–290 (2008)

Willis, E., Delbaere, M.: Patient influencers: the next frontier in direct-to-consumer pharmaceutical marketing. J. Med. Internet Res. **24**(3), e29422 (2022)

Young, K.: How celebrity endorsements influence young consumers. Global WebIndex (2017). https://blog.globalwebindex.com/chart-of-the-day/how-celeb-endorsements-influence-young-consumers/. Accessed 22 Feb 2022

Zebregs, S., van den Putte, B., Neijens, P., de Graaf, A.: The differential impact of statistical and narrative evidence on beliefs, attitude, and intention: a meta-analysis. Health Commun. **30**, 282–289 (2015)

Zollo, L., Filieri, R., Rialti, R., Yoon, S.: Unpacking the relationship between social media marketing and brand equity: the mediating role of consumers' benefits and experience. J. Bus. Res. **117**, 256–267 (2020)

Andrea Kanzler (Ph.D. candidate and research associate from the institute of business chemistry at the University of Münster, Germany) is an economist and marketing consultant. She worked in various multinationals such as VW, BASF, Evonik, Schenker AG. She is the Executive Editor at the Journal of Business Chemistry and at the moment she is teaching innovation management in the business chemistry master program at the University of Münster. Her research focuses on innovation management, digital health, digital transformation, digital marketing, influencer marketing and the impact that physicians and medical influencers are achieving in the last years.

The Transformation of the Accounting Profession Within a Digitalized Economy and the Impact on Accounting Education

Sofia Asonitou

Abstract One of the megatrends in the immediate future of entrepreneurship is the digitalization of production, operations and processes. As accountants stand in the intersection of all functions within a business, they have embraced waves of automation over many years to improve the efficiency and effectiveness of their work. Technological advancements are impacting radically the accounting profession and this should activate transformation policies in the accounting educational sector. The present study aspires to explore the influence of digitalization on the accounting profession and its relation to the readiness of Higher Education Institutions (HEIs) to prepare future accountants.

Keywords Digitalization · Accounting education · Accounting profession · Economy

1 Introduction

The new entrepreneurial era is characterized by digitalization. Digital revolution has brought in the fore new forms and meanings for entrepreneurship in the whole world. Giones and Brem (2017) propose the concept of three different types of digital businesses: technology entrepreneurship, digital technology entrepreneurship, and digital entrepreneurship. Each of them has emerged in diverse environments and produce a range of different opportunities for growth. The main enablers of digitalization are "social" and "mobile" (Legner et al. 2017) while internet-of-things, blockchain technology, "big data", "cloud" and "smart" business intelligence (BI) and business analytics (BA) are the applications associated with them. More enablers include robotics and machine learning, the two main technologies for the automation of processes.

S. Asonitou (✉)
University of West Attica, Athens, Greece
e-mail: sasonitou@uniwa.gr

© The Author(s), under exclusive license to Springer Nature Switzerland AG 2024

D. Schallmo et al. (eds.), *Digital Disruption and Transformation*, Springer Proceedings in Business and Economics, https://doi.org/10.1007/978-3-031-47888-8_9

The unique novelties offered by information technology (IT) seem to be very far away from the agriculture—based economy that humans developed up to mid—nineteenth century. In the following centuries when industry-based economy was established, the accounting profession supported and permitted the creation of multinational industrial businesses. Professional accountants in this period have been valuable members of the management team that leads the globalized operations. However, in the last decades we have passed into the post-industrial, information-oriented economy where "knowledge" is the driving force of the world. This evolution is posing concerns about whether the current accounting profession is in place to remain an indispensable member of the economic engine or it will be replaced by the new technological advancements (Ratnatunga 2018). Technological innovations adopted by companies constitute a new challenge for accounting organizations and accountants who struggle to adapt and keep pace with evolving technologies (Fuller and Markelevich 2020). Accountants need new skills and competences in order to survive and offer valuable services to the companies. These skills include apart from accounting technical expertise, a range of soft skills such as agility, communication skills, interpersonal abilities and certainly strong digital skills (Asonitou and Hassall 2019; IFAC 2006; AICPA 1999). Higher Education is responsible according to employers and managers to provide high quality education to future accountants.

The objective of this study is to depict the interconnectedness between digital technology, the accounting profession and the accounting education.

This study aims to (a) present how the accounting profession has evolved and how it is integrated within the digitalized enterprise and (b) to explore how accounting education is changing in order to accommodate the reforms which happen in the changing business world.

2 Theoretical Framework

Digitalization process is far more complicated than digitization. As Schallmo and Williams explain (2018) digitization is a technical process that allows to transform analogue information to a digital format, making it easier to trace, transmit and communicate. Digitalization on the other hand, involves a deep transformation of the organization, including use of digital technologies, strategy and possibly a new business model to follow. These changes signify an organizational, technical and even cultural shift within a business (Knudsen 2020). A digitalized company uses natively digital data, changes business processes and uses digital information and communication at the core of its operations and strategy (Schallmo and Williams 2018, p. 6). New technology and new business models create a secure environment for enterprises to share valuable data with others within an ecosystem. For example, twenty-eight European automakers and partners in a value chain of key manufacturers, suppliers, and tech companies, joined forces during Covid-19, to launch "Catena-X" platform. This was a data exchange ecosystem that permitted to share information on their own terms with privacy and security guaranteed (Deloitte 2022).

Technology and digitalization are the causes for the creation of new business models (Legner et al. 2017). Enterprises experience huge socio-technical transformation that overturns their organizational structure and strategies (Legner et al. 2017). Technological developments in Business intelligence, Artificial intelligence, robotics, analytics, Blockchain, machine learning and big data, are reshaping the world as we know it already. Digitalization signifies reforms in economies, societies and professions. Covid-19 pandemic crises have accelerated the pace of technological changes.

In this environment, preoccupation has appeared with regards to which professions face extinction and which will survive in the new era. Amongst them is the accounting profession for which inevitably new knowledge horizons and skillset should be designated by stakeholders. Digitalization of enterprises jointly moves with the digitalization of the accounting tasks and the shifting of accountants' duties towards higher demanding roles. Public accounting organizations (PAOs), policy makers, governmental agencies and academics urge to re-invent the profession in order to survive and even thrive in the new digital-oriented world (CGMA 2019). The accountant in its new role as advisor in the management team, participates to systems design, implementation and strategy, while every transaction, either physical or digital, will have to go through the accounting or ERP system. Successful adaptation of accountants to the new technological era presupposes they have acquired the indispensable skills and competences during their studies in Higher Education Institutions (HEIs). Insight on how these fields are interrelated will help both accountants and accounting academics to move in a faster pace towards adaptation of the technology.

Researchers and professionals argue that more research is needed in order to clearly define how the role of accounting professionals is going to change in selected fields.

This leads to the first research question of this study:

Research question 1: How has the accounting profession evolved and how is it integrated within the digitalized enterprise?

This study aims at identifying major current trends and offering an overview of recent research topics. Changes in the accounting profession should activate modifications in the accounting curriculum and the skillset in order to better prepare future accountants in Higher Education Institutions (HEIs). However, there should be concern on the level of readiness of HEIs to accept, organize and implement changes in the curriculum that mirror changes in the accounting profession due to digital business transformation. The leads to the second research question of this study:

Research question 2: How is accounting education responding to the reforms in the digital oriented business world?

The remainder of the paper is structured as follows: Section three presents the methodology while sections four and five provide the results of the review. Conclusions and future research are presented in Sect. 6.

3 Methodology

We conducted a literature review among recent studies and publications which analyse the changes in the accounting profession and the impact on the accounting education. We have used as main key words: "digitalization", "digitization" and "accounting profession", "accounting education" and "information technology". We have identified studies published by the big four auditing and consulting companies and the International federation of accountants (IFAC). The databases we have used are google scholar, research gate, and specific scientific journals such as "accounting education" "international journal of accounting information systems", "journal of accounting education" and "Journal of Emerging Technologies in Accounting".

4 The Accounting Profession

Frey and Osborne (2013) examined how susceptible jobs are to computerization in the light of IT radical advancements. According to this study, bookkeeping, accounting and auditing were among the occupations that should expect to be at risk due to computerization. Since then, this study stimulated a series of articles which reproduced the idea that the accounting and finance professions are in the brink of extinction and their role is redundant in an information driven era. These claims have caused the attention of professionals and authors who explained the misquoted information by the media. Firstly, Frey and Osborn, talked about tasks within jobs—not the jobs themselves and secondly the articles did not recognize that the freed-up time of accountants could be used to perform new insightful tasks within jobs (CGMA 2019). The same perspective of rapidly changing tasks within the finance and accounting industry was given by Accenture (2015): "Transactional tasks will move to integrated business services solutions that use robotics, which will automate or eliminate up to 40% of transaction accounting work by 2020".

Other researchers express the idea that accounting needs to develop a new paradigm in order to keep pace with the new information-based economy. A new theoretical base and proper tools are needed in order to provide digital businesses with (a) strategic and control information (b) future-orientated and historical information (c) financial and non-financial information (d) profit-motivated and socially-responsible information (e) timely and accurate information (Ratnatunga 2018).

Major issues that need attention include a widened accountability focus of accountants towards—customers, suppliers, employees, government and environmental groups, among others, consideration for the recognition and measurement of the extended capital of an enterprise such as "knowledge, innovation, communication, learning, and innovative abilities", contemplation about the timing requirements of information-era given that enterprises now require "real-time" information. Finally, accountants should reconsider all about information stability assumptions by continuous monitoring KPIs and tasks and visualizing reports and trends.

A long-term vision of the finance and accounting profession is generated in which the focus is shifted towards making IT advancements to support accountants' work to become more accurate in forecasting future trends and analyzing real-time digital data. Digitalization increases interconnectedness of customers, business, suppliers, and governmental agencies. As a result, competition becomes tougher, communication becomes faster and ideas are quickly turned into products which are easily copied by competitors (CGMA 2019) Organizations operate in conditions with financial and geopolitical instability, facing rising costs, supply chain and procurement problems, geopolitical instability and an energy crisis. Therefore, the challenges for the businesses are higher in a digital world, and employers turn to accountants and finance professionals to "help them stay afloat and navigate a future pathway to resilience" (IFAC 2022).

The accounting profession includes auditing, taxation, management accounting and control, forensic science and corporate reporting. Accounting is exercised in big and small practices, in the private and the public sector. None of these areas of accounting are left out of the evolutionary digital transformation (Narayan and Stittle 2018; Sorros et al. 2021). Several studies have examined how emerging technologies impact various aspects of accounting (Smith and Castonhuay 2020; Bakarich and O'Brien 2020; Curtis et al. 2009; Mahzan and Lymer 2014; Sutton et al. 2018; Kotb et al. 2019; Al-Htaybat et al. 2018).

Finance and accounting profession should create tighter collaborations and interaction with internal and external stakeholders across organizations and across functions. Digitalization affects management accountants and management control (MC) systems on different aspects. MC is designed to enable an organization to adapt to their environment and to keep organizations reliably on track (Fähndrich 2022). Digitalization has an impact on budgeting and reporting performed by management accountants which can be done more efficiently releasing time for more in-depth analysis of data, better managing risk and increasing the transparency of the activities of management accountants (Appelbaum, et al. 2017). The use of digital tools such as business intelligence, cloud computing, big data and automation allow management accountants to improve operational processes across multiple corporate functions (Fähndrich 2022; Rikhardsson and Yigitbasioglu 2018).

Smaller accountancy practices (SMPs) are influenced by technology also and they seem to have also embraced IT and social media as reported by IFAC (2023). The challenge for SMPs is that their clients do not want or are unable to support their decision for digitalization. The bigger the practice the more digitally advanced are, and the bigger the benefits in productivity, flexibility and overall attractiveness to new recruits and to existing and potential clients.

A recent research by CGMA (2019) revealed the following important points for finance and accounting professionals

- With regards to the time spent with the four basic finance activities, assembling information, analyzing for insights, advising to influence and applying for impact, respondents declared their wish to move towards the three last functions, therefore moving from isolation (accounting) to working in partnership with colleagues across the organization (management). Digital tools allow finance functions to refocus towards insight, influence and impact.

- With regards to the awareness and use of digital tools, the results show a better picture than expected before the research took place, as it is shown in Table 1.

- Cloud computing, process robotics and visualization are categorized as core modernization tools while advanced analytics, cognitive computing and in-memory computing and Blockchain are categorized as exponential technology (Deloitte 2016). From core modernization tools, only cloud technologies have become a mainstream feature, while robotics is included in the "early adopters".
- With regards to the main tools and techniques used by finance professionals the most important cited by respondents have been data, value, costing and business model. All of them need re-evaluation and continuous updating of mastery by finance and accounting professionals in the digital world. Considering data, the focus instead of collection and processing, should be in ensuring the integrity and the proper communication given that it requires much deeper and further analysis than just reporting data.
- Costing systems have not changed dramatically, organizations continue to use activity-based costing (ABC) and management-based costing (ABM). Digital costing is just emerging as a concept but it needs further to be explored.
- Intangibles are becoming more important for organizations therefore measurement rules that ignore them should change. Hence finance professionals who can measure and report intangible value will be in high demand in the future.
- The finance function in the digital world is shaped by five levels. The lowest level concerns systems and technologies of recording. Next level includes technical specialists providing insights and interpretation in their respective areas. Next level consists of systems and technologies of engagement in order to influence and shape how the organization creates and preserves value and finally highest level is about systems and technologies of governance and oversight applying strategic leadership of the organization.

For assurance firms machine learning models and AI developments can complement human intelligence, supporting full data auditing rather a sample of it, enabling

Table 1 Awareness and use of technology (adapted from CGMA 2019)

Technology	Aware of technology (%)	Use of technology (%)
Cloud	91	54
Process robotics	50	11
Visualization	44	18
Advance analytics	68	25
Cognitive computing	33	5
In-memory computing	23	7
Blockchain	48	2

professionals to discover anomalies that may exist without using the resources typically required for traditional audit (Smith and Castonhuay 2020). The whole process will be faster and will take much less effort and will improve the accuracy of the accounting functions. Integrating AI and machine learning in high risk areas improves efficiency while permitting auditing and consultancy firms to regain time for establishing closer and better relationships with clients (Kwarbai and Omojoye 2021; Kokina and Davenport 2017).

Our relationship with technology is not a stable one. All finance and accounting stakeholders, need to continually re-invent this relationship as intelligent systems will undertake gradually more decision-making tasks from professionals. This phenomenon should not threaten the finance community as long as it engages in the optimization, diversification and transformation of the profession to better serve business and investment decisions (CGMA 2019; IFAC 2022; Deloitte 2023). However, this perspective of the finance function within the technology-based society requires new competences and a digital mindset of financial and accounting professionals. Higher Education Institutions have a high share of responsibility to prepare future accountants with digital competences to cope with the new digital world.

5 Educating Future Accountants

Globalization and technology developments have created a skills shortage in the finance and accounting professionals which was anticipated as early as the last quarter of twentieth century (Albrecht and Sack 2000; AECC 1990). Employers were blaming accounting academics for not preparing graduates properly and for the generic skills gap in their training. The market demanded a well-rounded education including hard and soft skills that would create competent professionals for a fast-changing business environment (Pincus et al. 2017; González et al. 2009). Since then many studies explored the range of skills required by the employers and the importance assigned to skills and competences (Roepen 2017; Asonitou 2015; Hassall et al. 2003). Digital skills were found to be highly appreciated by employers and academics in the required competences of accounting graduates. ERP systems became increasingly more and more important to employers moving from position 12 in importance to position 7 within ten years (Tan et al. 2004). Three major challenges were reported by Hood (2015) which preoccupied the profession (1) technology-induced changes that devalue core services of the profession, (2) finding new employees with the right mix of skills and retraining current employees who need new skills, and (3) keeping up with the pace of technology change.

Digitalization, the megatrend in the new era, apart from technical skills requires advanced analytical skills and business acumen from accountants so they can understand business operations, perform operational analysis, provide real-time reports and facilitate accounting decisions (Wang 2021). Therefore, a solid academic preparation is necessary and accounting curricula should be directed towards integrating these types of technology within studies.

Academia has started long ago to include digital skills and new technology into the accounting curricula however in different pace and speed in each country. Wang (2021) refers to an example of introducing data analytics program into the accounting curriculum and how rewarding it has been for the students. The study refers also to some major challenges such as time and talent requirement as this is a very demanding course compared to routine offered courses. Students need extensive practice to be able to perform an analysis, interpret the findings and provide recommendations.

Faculty considers the most important topic to include in a data analytic topic, is to develop student's data analytics mindset and give emphasis on data-driven critical thinking skills (Dzuranin et al. 2018). It is very important to develop students' ability to ask questions that can be answered using data and train them to effectively communicate process and outcome of data analytics processing.

The above challenges should be added to a number of barriers which have been explored already about skills introduction into the accounting curricula (Asonitou 2021; Arquero et al. 2022). Timing seems to be also a major challenge. Most HEIs are slow to adjust curricula to reflect changes in the IT environment and to integrate such analytical tools. It seems that there is a delay in HEIs responsiveness to adapt to changing conditions in comparison to the great acceleration of digital technology in the real world (Spraakman et al. 2015; Asonitou 2021).

Other researchers state that given the complexity of technology, no single stakeholder is sufficient to satisfy labor demands in digital skills. Accounting educators in HE are equally important as managers and employers in strengthening new accountants skills (Jackson et al. 2023). Projects and case studies are outlined as the most appropriate methods for delivering data analytics content to students.

6 Conclusions, Implications and Limitations

The aims of this study were to present the digital evolution of the accounting profession and the efforts of the accounting education to prepare well rounded future accountants.

Employers within this digital world require from accountants a range of skills including critical thinking, communication skills, agility, problem solving and well-developed ICT skills. Universities should develop accounting programs that have the proper balance of technical and generic skills to prepare future accountants to compete in a digital-oriented world.

Educators can achieve their goal by integrating various analytical tools and other advanced technology platforms for training of students. However other methods should also be followed such as: (a) promoting apprentices in business which have adopted and use such tools (b) promote synergies between different departments in HEIs, and promote also combined projects between students from different departments (c) promote synergies between HEIs and society for example with associations with related expertise (d) cooperate with organizations which can provide resources to faculty to include in data analytics course (e) creation of hubs within universities which can attract talents and become knowledge resources for students.

Moreover, more collaboration initiatives between HEIs and enterprises will support an upgraded preparation of the next generation of accountants-advisors. In this way the accounting profession will be in place to serve the companies and face the challenges of the rapid pace of technological change.

This study offers an insight into the future of accounting education and the accounting profession in relation to the digital new world. This is not an exhaustive literature review but rather an interpretation of the current trends. A systematic literature review can offer a deep perspective on the issue under investigation.

References

Accenture: Death by digital: good-bye to finance as you know it (2015). https://www.cfo.com/technology/2015/10/death-digital-good-bye-finance-know/. Accessed 21 Feb 2023

AECC (Accounting Education Change Commission): Objectives of education for accountants: position statement number one. Issues Account. Educ. **5**(2), 307–312 (1990)

AICPA (American Institute of Certified Public Accountants): The AICPA core competency framework for entry into the accounting profession. AICPA, New York (1999)

Albrecht, W.S., Sack, J. R.: Accounting education: charting the course through a perilous future. American Accounting Association. Accounting Education Series, vol. 16 (2000)

Al-Htaybat, K., Alberti-Alhtaybat, L.V., Alhatabat, Z.: Educating digital natives for the future: accounting educators' evaluation of the accounting curriculum. Account. Educ. **27**(4), 333–357 (2018)

Appelbaum, D., Kogan, A., Vasarhelyi, M., Yan, Z.: Impact of business analytics and enterprise systems on managerial accounting. Int. J. Account. Inf. Syst. **25**(2), 29–44 (2017)

Arquero, M.J.L., Fernandez-Polvillo, C., Hassall, T.: Non-technical skills and students' overconfidence in accounting. Educ. Train. (2022). https://doi.org/10.1108/ET-08-2021-0309

Asonitou, S.: Employability skills in higher education and the case of Greece. Procedia-Soc. Behav. Sci. **175**, 283–290 (2015). https://doi.org/10.1016/j.sbspro.2015.01.1202

Asonitou, S.: Impediments and pressures to incorporate soft skills in higher education accounting studies. Account. Educ. **31**(3), 243–272 (2021). https://doi.org/10.1080/09639284.2021.1960871

Asonitou, S., Hassall, T.: Which skills and competences to develop in accountants in a country in crisis? Int. J. Manag. Educ. **17**(3) (2019). https://doi.org/10.1016/j.ijme.2019.100308

Bakarich, K.M., O'Brien, P.: The robots are coming ... but aren't here yet: the use of artificial intelligence technologies in the public accounting profession. J. Emerg. Technol. Account. **18**(1) (2020)

CGMA: Re-inventing finance for a digital world, the future of finance (2019). https://www.cgma.org/resources/reports/re-inventing-finance-for-a-digital-world.html. Accessed 18 Feb 2023

Curtis, M.B., Jenkins, J.G., Bedard, J.C., Deis, D.R.: Auditors' training and proficiency in information systems: a research synthesis. J. Inf. Syst. **23**(1) (2009)

Deloitte: Crunch time: Finance in a Digital World (2022). https://www2.deloitte.com/content/dam/Deloitte/global/Documents/Finance/gx-ft-crunch-time-finance-in-a-digital-world.pdf. Accessed 15 Apr 2023

Deloitte Tech Trends (2016). https://www.deloitte.com/global/en/our-thinking/insights/topics/technology)-management/content/tech-trends.html. Accessed 21 Feb 2023

Deloitte Tech Trends (2023). https://www2.deloitte.com/us/en/insights/focus/tech-trends.html. Accessed 15 Apr 2023

Dzuranin, A.C., Jones, J. R., Olvera, R.M.: Infusing data analytics into the accounting curriculum: a framework and insights from faculty. J. Account. Educ. **43** (2018).
Fähndrich, J.: A literature review on the impact of digitalization on management control. J. Manag. Control. (2022). https://doi.org/10.1007/s00187-022-00349-4
Frey, B.C., Osborne, A.M.: The future of employment how susceptible are jobs to computerization? Technol. Forecast. Soc. Chang. **114**, 254–280 (2013)
Fuller, S., Markelevich, A.: Should accountants care about blockchain? J. Corp. Account. & Financ. **31**(2), 34–46 (2020). https://doi.org/10.1002/jcaf.22424
Giones, F., Brem, A.: Digital technology entrepreneurship: a definition and research agenda. Technol. Innov. Manag. Rev. **7**(5) (2017)
González, J.M., Montano, J.L., Hassall, T.: Bologna and beyond: a comparative study focused on UK and Spanish accounting education. High. Educ. Eur. **34**(1), 123–135 (2009)
Hassall, T., Joyce, J., Montano, A.J.L., Donoso, J.A.: The vocational skills gap for management accountants: the stakeholders' perspectives. Innov. Educ. Teach. Int. **40**(1), 78–88 (2003)
Hood, D.: Losing sleep: leaders of the profession on its biggest nightmares. Account. Today **29**(10), 1+ (2015). https://www.accountingtoday.com/news/losing-sleep. Accessed 25 Apr 2023
IFAC: International Education Standard 8, competence requirements for audit professionals, International Accounting Education Standards Board (2006). http://www.ifac.org/Education. Accessed 15 Apr 2023
IFAC: Professional accountants as finance and business leaders. PAIB-Finance-Business-Leaders_2022.pdf. Accessed 21 Feb 2023
IFAC: The benefits and challenges of smaller accountancy practice digitisation (2023). https://www.ifac.org/knowledge-gateway/developing-accountancy-profession/discussion/benefits-and-challenges-smaller-accountancy-practice-digitisation. Accessed 21 Feb 2023
Jackson, D., Michelson, G., Munir, R.: Developing accountants for the future: new technology, skills, and the role of stakeholders. Account. Educ. **32**(2), 150–177 (2023). https://doi.org/10.1080/09639284.2022.2057195
Knudsen, D.R.: Elusive boundaries, power relations, and knowledge production: a systematic review of the literature on digitalization in accounting. Int. J. Account. Inf. Syst. **36**, 100441 (2020). https://doi.org/10.1016/j.accinf.2019.100441
Kokina, J., Davenport, T.H.: The emergence of artificial intelligence: how automation is changing auditing. J. Emerg. Technol. Account. (2017)
Kotb, A., Abdel-Kader, M., Allam, A., Halabi, H., Franklin, E.: Information technology in the British and Irish undergraduate accounting degrees. Account. Educ. **28**(5), 445–464 (2019). https://doi.org/10.1080/09639284.2019.1588135
Kwarbai, J.D., Omojoye, E.O.: Artificial intelligence and accounting profession. Babcock J. Account. Financ. **1**(1), 1–26 (2021)
Legner, C., Eymann, T., Hess, T., Matt, C., Böhmann, T., Drews, P., Mädche, A., Urbach, N., Ahlemann, F.: Digitalization: opportunity and challenge for the business and information systems engineering community. Bus. Inf. Syst. Eng. **59**(4), 301–308 (2017)
Mahzan, N., Lymer, A.: Examining the adoption of computer-assisted audit tools and techniques: cases of generalized audit software use by internal auditors. Manag. Audit. J. **29**(4), 327–349 (2014)
Narayan, A., Stittle, J.: The role of accounting in transforming public tertiary institutions in New Zealand. Account. Audit. & Account. J. **31**(7) (2018). https://doi.org/10.1108/AAAJ-09-2016-2722
Pincus, K.V., Stout, D.E., Sorensen, J.E., Stocks, K.D., Lawson, A.R.: Forces for change in higher education and implications for the accounting academy. J. Account. Educ. **40**, 1–18 (2017)
Ratnatunga, J.: Globalisation: A paradigm shift for the accounting profession. J. Appl. Manag. Account. Res. Institute of Certified Management Accountants (Australia) & Swinburne University (2018)
Rikhardsson, P., Yigitbasioglu, O.: Business intelligence & analytics in management accounting research: status and future focus. Int. J. Account. Inf. Syst. **29**, 37–58 (2018)

Roepen, D.: Australian business graduates' perceptions of non-technical skills within the workplace. Educ. + Train. **59**(5), 457–470 (2017)

Schallmo, D.R.A., Williams, C.A.: History of digital transformation. In: Digital Transformation Now!, pp. 3–8. Springer (2018)

Smith, S., Castonhuay, J.: Blockchain and accounting governance: emerging issues and considerations for accounting and assurance professionals. J. Emerg. Technol. Account. **17**(1), 119–131 (2020)

Sorros, J., Lois, P., Charitou, M., Theofanis, A., Karagiorgos, N.: Belesis: improving competitiveness in education institutes—ABC's neglected potential. Compet. Rev.: Int. Bus. J. **32**(3), 302–325 (2021). https://doi.org/10.1108/CR-01-2021-0008

Spraakman, G., O'Grady, W., Askarany, D., Akroyd, C.: Employers' perceptions of information technology competency requirements for management accounting graduates. Account. Educ. **24**(5), 403–422 (2015). https://doi.org/10.1080/09639284.2015.1089177

Sutton, S.G., Arnold, V., Holt, M.: How much automation is too much? Keeping the human relevant in knowledge work. J. Emerg. Technol. Account. **15**(2) (2018)

Tan, M.L., Fowler, B.M., Hawkes, L.: Management accounting curricula: striking a balance between the views of educators and practitioners. Account. Educ. **13**(1), 51–67 (2004)

Wang, T.: The impact of emerging technologies on accounting curriculum and the accounting profession. Pac. Account. Rev. 0114–0582 (2021). https://doi.org/10.1108/PAR-05-2021-0074

Sofia Asonitou is Associate Professor at the Department of Business Administration, University of West Attica in Greece. She holds a BSc in Economics from NKU Athens, an MBA from VUB-SOLVAY in Brussels while her Ph.D. is on Accounting Education, SHU, U.K. Her teaching interests include Management Accounting and Financial Statements Analysis. Her research interests are on accounting scholarship.

She has published in *The International Journal of Management Education, The International Journal of Sustainability in Higher Education and Accounting Education.* She is Deputy Scientific Coordinator in the Centre for Teaching and Learning and the Director of the "Accounting, Economics and Financial Research Lab".

SMEs Innovation Leveraged by Digital Transformation During Covid-19

Elaine Mosconi and Caroline Blais

Abstract The Covid-19 pandemic of the last few years has affected many enterprises, especially SMEs. Difficult market access, supply issues, and labor problems have characterized their business environment. Despite these challenges, some SMEs decided to stand out by innovating and investing in digital technologies to develop a new way of doing business during this period. However, little is known about the benefits that these initiatives have had in creating value for these SMEs. To answer this question, we studied two SMEs that have successfully developed new products and simultaneously implemented technological initiatives to significantly improve their processes and counter the challenges related to the pandemic. Inspired by the "S^4" integrated digital transformation framework, we demonstrated that the numerous benefits that emerged from these innovations contributed to creating value for these SMEs in a COVID-19 context.

Keywords Digital transformation · Product innovation · Digital innovation · Value creation · Small and Medium Enterprises (SMEs)

1 Introduction

The Covid-19 pandemic has affected all economic sectors, including small and medium enterprises (SMEs) (Adam and Alarifi 2021). Government policies in many countries have resulted in temporary or even permanent closures for enterprises that have not been able to deal with the challenges of this period, including those related to supply chain disruption (Baig et al. 2020). To survive and respond to new market demands, some SMEs have chosen to innovate (Clauss et al. 2022) and seize new opportunities (Wenzel et al. 2021). A recent survey of 711 Canadian SME managers

E. Mosconi (✉) · C. Blais
Université de Sherbrooke, 2500 Boul. de l'Université, Sherbrooke, QC J1K 2R1, Canada
e-mail: elaine.mosconi@usherbrooke.ca

C. Blais
e-mail: caroline.blais@usherbrooke.ca

© The Author(s), under exclusive license to Springer Nature Switzerland AG 2024
D. Schallmo et al. (eds.), *Digital Disruption and Transformation*, Springer Proceedings in Business and Economics, https://doi.org/10.1007/978-3-031-47888-8_10

revealed that half revised their business model during the pandemic. In addition, for 16% of the SMEs surveyed, this period led to the development of new products, services, markets or customers (Québec Innove 2020). Also, more than half (55%) of these SMEs carried out accelerated digitization projects during the pandemic. As a result, new business models and processes have emerged to adequately respond to the COVID-19 pandemic challenges (Cukier et al. 2021), and digital technologies that would typically take five years to implement were adopted in only eight weeks by accelerating digitalization and digital transformation (DT) (Baig et al. 2020). These initiatives have propelled SMEs to innovate and rethink their business entirely to face crises and help them develop a significant advantage in a post-COVID-19 recovery (Roper and Turner 2020).

DT is used interchangeably with digitization (digitization or digitalization) (Gong and Ribiere 2020). Both are important for businesses. Nonetheless, DT is different from digitization since digitization strengthens the value proposition and the identity of companies by supporting existing activities. DT aims to transform them, changing the dynamics driving businesses' value proposition and identity (Wessel et al. 2021). DT is based on superior connectivity and an explosion of available data, changing the way enterprises do business (Mosconi et al. 2019). DT goes beyond technical or technological aspects, which frequently implies the development of new strategies, new business models, and new capabilities helping organizations to become more sustainable, integrated, efficient, agile, and adaptable to the market and to fierce competition based on innovation around value creation (Bordeleau et al. 2021).

Although innovation appears to be a winning strategy, it also brings challenges (Perin et al. 2017). A significant number of projects do not reach completion, leading to loss of resources and financial distress. In a context of high uncertainty, risk-taking increases, and rates of failure in innovation projects are high (D'Este et al. 2016; Jenson et al. 2016; Maslach 2016). Rhaiem and Amara (2021) indicate that 40–90% of innovation projects end in failure. In addition, accelerated DT opens many occasions for digitization of innovation processes, and outcomes can disrupt existing innovation management practices since it becomes difficult for a business to separate the relationship between innovation processes and products (Nambisan et al. 2017, 2019). However, few studies describe how the DT journey can create value for SMEs related to digital innovation. In addition, we argue that SMEs need to allocate their resources to innovation and DT projects with a better chance of success. And, the potential benefits are achievable in the short term, allowing them to optimize these resources and strive for successful innovation initiatives and value creation, especially in a COVID-19 context.

This gap requires attention since SMEs have a smaller margin of error due to their more limited resources (Astrini et al. 2020). In this context, our research objective is to understand how SMEs that have successfully innovated during the recent health crisis have evolved technologically and how DT has enabled value creation. Our research question is: what are the benefits of DT in SMEs that successfully innovate in a COVID-19 context?

The contributions of this research help understand how certain SMEs conducted innovation initiatives to survive crises by creating new products, reinforcing links between DT and digital innovation. Finally, the acceleration of DT initiatives has enabled digital innovation as products, processes, and managerial innovation for SMEs. Our research also contributes to applying the theoretical S^4 DT framework (Bordeleau et al. 2021) to the analysis of these SMEs' respective journeys. We concluded that technologies worked as triggers that required new capabilities and skills to carry out transformation and innovation in value creation for customers, stakeholders, and society in the COVID-19 context.

2 Theoretical Background

2.1 Innovation and Digital Innovation

Innovation is defined in academic and professional literature, highlighting the innovation process or outcomes. The Oslo Manual (2018) presents two major types of innovation: innovations that change the firm's products (product innovations) and innovations that change the firm's business processes (business process innovations). A product innovation "is a new or improved good or service that differs significantly from the firm's previous goods or services and that has been introduced on the market" (OECD 2018, p. 21). A new product (goods or services) can require business process innovation. It is defined as a "new or improved business process for one or more business functions that differ significantly from the firm's previous business processes and that has been brought into use by the firm" (OECD 2018, p. 21).

Digitalization can "entail the application of digital technologies to a wide range of existing tasks and enables new tasks to be performed" and "has the potential to transform business processes" (OECD 2018, p. 37). Digital innovation refers to the "use of digital technology during the process of innovating" (Nambisan et al. 2017, p. 223) and "the creation of (and consequent change in) market offerings, business processes, or models that result from the use of digital technology" (Nambisan et al. 2017, p. 224).

Digital innovation and DT are two related concepts because they require changes in business processes and lead to value creation using emerging technologies. Emerging technologies can be digital, physical, and biological technologies that are ubiquitous in our daily lives as well as in organizations, leading to a robust technological convergence that should change the modus operandi of all productive sectors in an unprecedented way (Schwab 2016). As mentioned by Nambisan et al. (2017), the properties of digital technologies offer new opportunities for creating infrastructure, products, and business models and, thus, can reshape the ways in which firms organize for innovation (Nambisan et al. 2017) with what is known as DT. DT changes the nature and structure of new products and services, creates novel value creation, and transforms industries propelled by emerging technologies.

2.2 Digital Transformation

DT is crucial for businesses, and it is gaining attention worldwide. Digital technologies do not create value per se, but it is their use in a particular context that allows organizations to discover novel ways to create value in a new and constantly changing environment; technologies are the spark enabling DT (Bordeleau et al. 2021; Wessel et al. 2021). Technology is one piece of the complex puzzle in an organizational context since creating value requires rethinking the strategy, structure, and processes that call for mindset and cultural changes within the organization (Vial 2019). Otherwise, DT could amplify the gaps in the organization and make them visible, generate employee disengagement, and more (Tabrizi et al. 2019). Managers and researchers are still struggling to conceptualize both the DT journey and its end goal for value creation. DT is complex to manage in a real setting, and the need to understand how to support businesses in their transformation remains (Bordeleau et al. 2021).

Business managers and senior executives have pointed out that DT is a concern because 70% of DT initiatives do not reach their goals (Tabrizi et al. 2019). DT has both intended and unintended opportunities and challenges that emerge in different levels and contexts since it is related to social and technical shifts in organizational contexts (Bordeleau et al. 2021). Socio-technical system theory considers human and technological and organizational issues in technology deployment (Bostrom and Heinen 1977).

The "S^4" integrated framework of DT presents an interdependent vision of socio-technical elements for value creation (Bordeleau et al. 2021). The authors have presented a DT journey that stems from a technology-push perspective to help people to understand this complex phenomenon. It begins with technology convergence or triggers, and its building blocks consist of capabilities (human, organizational and technological) and innovations around value. This journey results in a meaningful understanding of DT for future organizations (Bordeleau et al. 2021).

2.3 DT S^4 Framework

The S^4 framework proposes that emerging technologies from the digital (e.g., artificial intelligence or cloud computing), physical (e.g., advanced materials), and biological (e.g., advanced genetics) worlds are the triggers for digital transformation, especially through their potential to converge into sophisticated systems (e.g., 3D printing of human tissue). These triggers need capabilities or skills, such as the ability to work in real-time, among others. These capabilities are organized into three groups: human capabilities (e.g., humans have enhanced visualization capabilities with the use of augmented reality), technological (e.g., data processing will be much faster with quantum computing), and organizational (e.g., organizations can have a direct channel with almost all customers through social media). Furthermore, these capabilities can be combined and enable value creation differently, driving innovation (Bordeleau et al. 2021).

The capabilities supported by DT principles are building blocks that are essential to the proposition, creation, delivery, and management of value. According to Bordeleau et al. (2021), the notion of value takes a central place in the DT journey. Three types of innovation around value are proposed: the notion of value may be different (e.g., the value of a smartwatch goes beyond providing the time), the way value is created and distributed may be different (e.g., the production of super-customized parts through additive manufacturing and drone delivery), and finally the way the value creation chain is managed may be different (e.g., a supply chain in a 3D printing platform, such as 3DHubs or Thingverse, may include thousands of suppliers, instead of hundreds, forcing managers to rethink how to develop and evaluate suppliers). Together or separately, these three types of innovation around value have the potential to create the next-generation enterprise which undertakes DT with a broader ambition than just being technology-oriented.

Innovations around value allow a business to become more "sensing," as it can better sense or understand its internal and external environment, thanks to the enormous amount of data available. Using available data analyzed with artificial intelligence algorithms (e.g., deep learning) makes businesses smarter since the quality of decisions is better. Moreover, companies can be more sustainable in these actions since their decisions are more data-driven and holistically analyzed. Finally, businesses have the chance to propel the adaptation and evolution of the social beings that we are, i.e., supporting collective intelligence and cooperation ("social"). Businesses, humans, and objects, e.g., the Internet of Things, are connected now like never before (Bordeleau et al. 2021). Then, the four main aspects (triggers, ingredients/principles, innovations, and intentions) interact cyclically to guide the DT journeys of organizations, leading to greater intended impact as well as to a better awareness of their impact at different levels, including organizational and societal. By doing so, businesses have the opportunity to become more intended-impact and conscious organizations. The value creation for these businesses is limited to business performance in terms of financial and productivity indicators, but it is created for the business ecosystem (Bordeleau et al. 2021). The authors mention that "sensing", smart, sustainable, and social business enables business and mindset intentions for the transformation of the following generation of organizations, called "S^4" organizations. The integrative S^4 framework is shown in Fig. 1.

All these considerations are important for SMEs because they are known to have less resources than large enterprises to innovate and integrate the latest technology (Blais 2023) nor unlimited access to information on the most up-to-date technology (Hassani and Mosconi 2022). This can explain why some SMEs are slow to invest in new technology and struggle to rethink their value creation by redefining strategic, structural, process-based, and cultural aspects of the business (Wessel et al. 2021). SMEs are more likely to improve their readiness and their capability to innovate successfully, using digital innovation as a lever for value creation. The S^4 framework proposes a vision for a DT journey for value creation that we will adopt to analyze the journey of SMEs during the COVID-19 pandemic.

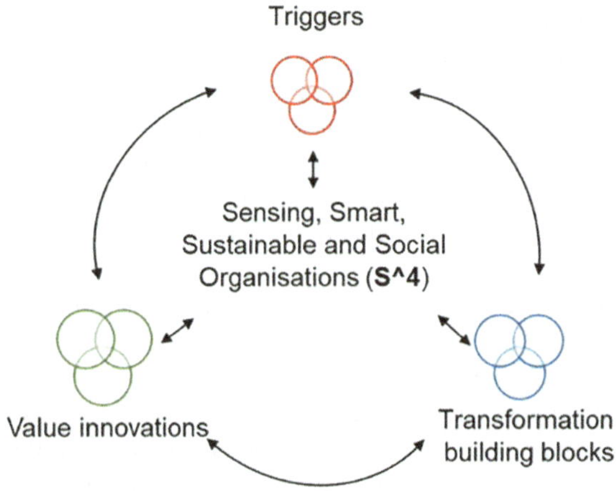

Fig. 1 S^4 Framework for the DT journey—adapted from Bordeleau et al. (2021)

3 Research Methodology

DT and its value creation on SMEs as well as digital innovation are topics currently underdeveloped in the literature in terms of case and field studies. Then, exploratory research through a multiple case study approach seems appropriate to investigate this phenomenon in SMEs (Yin 2017).

3.1 Case Selection and Description of SMEs and Respondents

Two Canadian SMEs were selected (SME A and SME B1) because the recent COVID-19 pandemic led them to adopt an innovation strategy based on emerging technologies. These two SMEs were known to the researchers from a previous collaboration. A new set of data was collected during the global pandemic, providing an in-depth and longitudinal understanding (2019–2020) of their innovation practices and DT strategy.

These SMEs are the only enterprises in a previous sample of five enterprises to have innovated and implemented technologies during the pandemic. Not all SMEs had the same leadership in innovation in this period, so it becomes essential to focus on those that stood out and to learn more about their innovation strategy and innovative practices.

The two SMEs innovated by developing protective equipment to ensure the safety of thousands of employees in the agri-food (SME A) and health (SME B) sectors. They have been widely cited in the media for their innovative capacity and success during this period. Considered "nonessential" businesses at the beginning of the

Table 1 Information about the SMEs and characteristics of respondents

	Number of employees	Sales (Canadian $)	Position within the SME	Education	Years of experience in innovation
SME A	85	14 million	CEO and owner	MBA	28
			R&D Director	Engineer	15
SME B	265	40 million	VP Operations and Engineering	Plastic technician	6
			Business Development Director	Engineering technician	2

pandemic lockout, these SMEs temporarily ceased their activities following the policies imposed by the Canadian government. Table 1 presents information about the SMEs and certain characteristics of their respondents.

3.2 *Data Collection and Analysis*

Once an agreement was reached on the respondents' participation, the data collection consisted of a 90-min semi-structured interview with two managers in each SME. Other data sources were also analyzed: internal reports, the companies' websites, and social and traditional media featuring their activities. The use of multiple sources increases the quality of data collected and allows triangulation (Yin 2017).

The data were then transcribed, classified, and coded under different previously identified themes as well as new themes that emerged during the analysis using NVivo software. The principles of thematic analysis were applied (Paillé and Mucchielli 2008). The themes used to code the data include technology implementation projects (triggers), resources and skills (capabilities—building blocks), innovation initiatives, and DT benefits and challenges for future development.

4 Results

During the recent pandemic, the two SMEs identified an opportunity to rethink their business value proposition by innovating and integrating digital technologies. This period allowed SME managers to step back and think about how to develop and market their new products adequately. We found that the low level of technological implementation before the pandemic was, at least in part, improved and compensated for during the pandemic. These initiatives enabled SMEs to meet their need to reach the market quickly. It also allowed both SMEs to reemploy most of their staff to produce their protective equipment during a difficult moment of the pandemic supply chain disruption.

We adopt the S^4 framework to understand and analyze the data collected on the DT journey of the SMEs studied. SME A and SME B experimented with digital innovation and DT at the same time since their managers decided to innovate by integrating a new product into the market. We use the S^4 to study their implemented technologies (digital, physical, and biological—triggers of DT); the explored and exploited as capabilities (building blocks); the innovation outcomes (product/service, processes or managerial) and what they get from this journey in terms of benefits and challenges. Finally, our aim was to study how these benefits and challenges could be related to becoming an intelligent organization, an organization of the new generation, which is S^4 or an intelligent organization (sensing, smart, sustainable, and social).

4.1 Technology Implementation Projects (Triggers)

During the recent pandemic, the two SMEs conducted technology implementation projects to meet their needs and quickly meet the market to face supply chain disruption and business opportunities. We found that the low level of technological implementation before the pandemic was, at least in part, improved and compensated for during the pandemic. This period accelerated the implementation of technology initiatives. To illustrate this acceleration,

> In the past, we had discussions about 3D printing: are we investing in it? We didn't see the possibilities. However, the need to manufacture certain components in-house to deal with the inability to purchase them externally [during the pandemic] led to the purchase of 3D printers. So overnight, the first deal I did, was to order a 3D printer. We started developing [the new product], learning about 3D printing and how it works. But not long after that, we bought a second [3D] printer. Then not long after, we bought a third [3D] printer with a different technology [VP Operations and Engineering—SME B].

Table 2 shows the technology implementation projects (digital and physical technologies) conducted before and during the pandemic in each of the SMEs.

Like many enterprises, before the health crisis, both SMEs were connected to the Internet and used cloud computing to host data, advanced software, and an ERP system. Teleworking was already present. The use of these technologies allowed access to enterprise data everywhere and facilitated distance working. However, SME B differs from SME A by implementing more pre-pandemic technology initiatives. The automotive field of SME B explains in part its greater technological advancement because it had to invest more to meet the needs of major clients of the industry. SME B is known for its avant-gardism in terms of robotization and automation of its production line on several sites, including a plant in Mexico. SME B has camera-based control systems (with sensor and distance control) to monitor the quality of the products manufactured, allowing it to react more quickly if a defect occurs. Better quality control and more stability in production are then noted. All of SME

Table 2 Technology implemented in SMEs before and during the pandemic

Technologies implemented	SME A		SME B	
	Before	During	Before	During
Digital				
Advanced software	x	x	x	x
Automation of tasks (paperless)		x		x
Cloud computing	x	x	x	x
Connected sites (plants)			x	x
Distance control			x	x
Integrated system/ERP	x	x	x	x
Internet connection	x	x	x	x
Internet of things		x	x	x
Sensor		x	x	x
Technology platform—e-commerce		x		x
Teleworking	x	x	x	x
Physical				
3D printing				x
Robotic—automation		x	x	x

B's factories are connected to the same information systems, and key performance indicators (KPI) are output in real-time from the production sites.

4.2 Resources Used to Deploy These Initiatives (Capabilities—Building Blocks)

The availability of a recently hired marketing resource has helped SME A deploy a transactional platform. As mentioned by the CEO: "We are developing marketing tools because we now have a full-time marketing resource. We are creating a transactional platform and technological tools to support sales. We are also more active on social media [because of this staff]".

By integrating a transactional platform, SME A needed to invest in technical capabilities to support the connectivity and the dematerialization of the sales business process. This decision is a digitization decision that helped it to respond to business needs to improve sales and business performance.

For SME B, the availability of an in-house resource skilled in IT helped in the deployment of all digital initiatives. The VP Operations and Engineering mentions that "We are fortunate to have someone in IT who is forward thinking and believes in it, so initiatives are often put in place ahead of time [compared to other enterprises in the sector]."

4.3 Innovation Initiatives

To survive and seize an opportunity in a new market, SME A and SME B conducted innovation initiatives that allowed them both to develop innovative products. The lockdown and the ceased activities allowed them to take the available time to figure out how to innovate and restart their activities. They identified an opportunity to rethink their business value proposition by innovating and integrating digital technologies, which gave them several benefits and brought challenges but also opened their eyes to future developments.

4.4 Digital Transformation Benefits

During the pandemic, both SMEs innovated and implemented new technologies (Table 2) to satisfy multiple requirements in their innovation process for developing their new products. However, these initiatives differed from each other, as their needs were also divergent, even if their new products were, in both cases, a piece of protective equipment.

SME A identified technologies and acquired new digital production equipment promoting the automation of the cutting function (with sensors) and established a transactional website (e-commerce). The digital production equipment allowed:

- to improve production capacity by reintegrating operations previously done by subcontractors,
- to manage client demand by better-controlling production,
- to reduce product development and commercialization time by making more prototypes in less time,
- to reallocate its workforce to more profitable products,
- to obtain real-time data to support decision-making,
- to increase productivity and operations effectiveness,
- to raise the quality level of the developed product, and
- to increase control over costs, deadlines, and quality.
- The transactional website benefits were meeting clients' needs within three days, and
- increasing sales for products already in inventory.

For SME B, the need to manufacture specific components internally led to the purchase of three 3D printers. This investment brought some benefits:

- solving technical problems more quickly,
- providing better guidance on corrections to be made before the "real" component became available,
- offering greater flexibility,
- accelerating product development,
- facilitating iterations during product development,

- having more possibilities to validate certain mechanical concepts,
- better managing technical risks, and
- generating innovation in the processes that were beneficial to the manufacturing of other products.

Other technology implementation projects included the creation of a transactional website (e-commerce), integration with customer systems, and the implementation of an Amazon Store. These initiatives allowed SME B to:

- meet the requirements for doing business with clients, and
- generate sales faster.

The integration of these technologies required improvements in technical, human, and organizational capabilities to reach innovation on the product and on the process and culminated in DT's impact on the value proposition of the SME.

4.5 Challenges for Future Technology Development

The implementation of digital technologies has led managers of both SMEs to focus more on this aspect for the future development of their enterprise. Managers are wondering about artificial intelligence. The challenges (or unknowns) regarding the possibilities of implementing new technology relate to two main aspects:

- the approach to integrating this technology:
- "I don't know exactly how to get there" [R&D Director—SME A]
- the balance of effort to ensure that the desired results are achieved by implementing this technology:
- "We started hearing the word (artificial intelligence). It brought us a certain level of curiosity. I read a lot about it, and I ask myself, what can we do with it? What are we going to get in terms of contracts with clients? What are we going to put effort into? We have limited resources with engineering. We are very few people. At the end of the day, it's about knowing, the time we put in. Does it pay off?" [VP Operations and Engineering—SME B].

5 Discussions

The objective of this paper is to understand how SMEs that have successfully innovated during the COVID-19 pandemic have evolved through DT and how it leveraged value creation. Case studies were conducted in five SMEs to learn more about the topic. However, only two corresponded to the research criteria: successfully innovating at the product, process, and managerial levels by using emerging technologies during the recent pandemic. We observed that during the COVID-19 pandemic, some

SMEs decided to innovate by introducing new products in a new market and implementing new technology initiatives to help them achieve their innovation project. However, during this period, uncertainty was high because many enterprises had to shut down their activities, the supply chain was disrupted, and the usual way of doing things was no longer useful. It was, therefore, necessary to integrate new ways of doing things (Cukier et al. 2021).

The two SMEs invested in technology initiatives to compensate for the lack of internal resources and for the inability of external suppliers to adequately meet their needs in a changing environment. These innovation initiatives were mainly associated with digital and physical triggers and helped SMEs accelerate technology integration in their activities and processes. This accelerated digitization and DT allowed them to counterbalance the slow and late adoption of technologies and implementation of technological projects. It also contributed to generating product innovation more efficiently and launching new products faster, thus reducing the potential loss of resources. These decisions were crucial in helping SMEs achieve success in innovation initiatives during the pandemic and in reducing the potential risk of failure in projects. In the context of SMEs, because they are known to have more limited access to resources than larger enterprises, it is essential to identify possibilities that can help use the resources efficiently.

As DT goes beyond technological aspects (Bordeleau et al. 2021), the technology initiatives implemented need to create value for the business to make the DT journey useful. The two SMEs in our study used the pandemic context to rethink their business model and to invest in innovation initiatives with the integration of new technologies. By using internal capabilities to exploit these technologies, they were able to transform their value proposition (product innovation), their business process (process innovation), and their relationship with partners in the supply chain (managerial innovation).

Following the S^4 DT framework, we observed that SME A and B's journeys required improvements of their building blocks based on technical, human, and organizational capabilities to innovate in their products, services, and processes, culminating in DT impacts on their respective value proposition (Bordeleau et al. 2021). The technology implementation projects and the innovation initiatives led to changes in business practices and strategies and encouraged the SMEs to review their business processes and their innovation and digital strategy.

6 Theoretical and Practical Contributions

The contributions of this research help understand how SMEs conducted innovation initiatives to survive COVID-19 pandemic challenges by creating new products. Also, in the two cases under study, DT accelerated and enabled new products and processes since technologies worked as triggers that required new capacities and generated innovation around value creation for customers and other stakeholders, and society in the COVID-19 pandemic context.

As theoretical contributions, we clarify the value created by digital technology initiatives undertaken by two SMEs that innovated in a COVID-19 context. The innovation leveraged by these SMEs' DT journey provides a meaningful understanding of how these decisions were beneficial and how they became resilient and improved their readiness for the next generation of business.

In summary, we propose that DT and digital innovation in SMEs are deeply linked. Digital innovation is generated by an innovation initiative: most innovation projects use emerging technologies (triggers) that are currently integrated into products, processes, and managerial practices that create digital innovation; that is sparks for DT.

DT is also guided by innovation initiatives: most redefinitions of business lead to digital innovation as an integrated outcome of the journey based on the convergence of emerging technologies explored and exploited by organizational, technical, and human capabilities in organizations. They are interrelated and interdependent. Our study observed that both DT and digitization are founded on the building blocks of transformation, as suggested by Wessel et al. (2021), and that they also contribute to catalyzing digital innovation.

For the practical implication, our results show that the DT journey is difficult to navigate for SME managers, who are not always able to perceive and anticipate its impacts and challenges. All businesses, including SMEs, are experiencing paradoxical choices. On the one hand, with difficulties and challenges related to digitalization, disruption of the supply chain, and rapid changes in customer needs, companies need to improve their processes and think about how they need to change to remain competitive. At the same time, they must invest in DT initiatives even as they struggle to capture the full potential of their transformation efforts or deliver a satisfactory return on investment (Bordeleau et al. 2020; McKinsey 2022).

On the other hand, our results showed that the DT journey generates digital innovation that creates opportunities and advantages for SMEs, all while generating huge amounts of data. These advances will require new innovations to deploy artificial intelligence to benefit from the data available, pushing businesses to invest in skilled people and new organizational capabilities to absorb this new game changer across many industries (Gröger 2021). By understanding this dynamic, we recommend practitioners and managers embark on continuous innovation. Therefore, our study's conclusions can motivate managers to implement digital technology initiatives like those undertaken by the participating SMEs because they may better understand their potential benefits and increase the organization's resilience.

7 Conclusion, Limitations, and Future Research

Our research objective led us to document product-related, process-related, and management-related innovations as well as the technology implementation projects that culminated in a DT journey. We also observed their benefits and challenges to better understand the value creation of innovation initiatives in two SMEs during a pandemic.

The COVID-19 pandemic challenges led these SMEs to rethink their business model by investing in new technologies that helped them innovate faster and in a way that used their limited resources more efficiently (Clauss et al. 2022). The two SMEs had to compensate quickly for the changes in the environment: almost every business was closed, disrupting the supply of components, even internationally (Baig et al. 2020; Wenzel et al. 2021). These SMEs innovated in a hurry to survive in this context but also to be in a better position (new market, new customers) after the pandemic. The accelerated technology implementation projects allowed them to counterbalance the low technological maturity level they had before the pandemic (Baig et al. 2020; Cukier et al. 2021). The technology implementation benefits of these initiatives create short-term value in these SMEs and hopefully for a longer period since businesses have had no choice but to embrace emerging technologies, new capabilities and skills and value innovation to become more sensing, smart, sustainable, and social (Bordeleau et al. 2021). Doing so will help them to face significant challenges and develop opportunities linking DT and digital innovation, with no regard to the activity sector or business size.

Our study was conducted on only two SMEs, and the conclusions cannot be generalized to the broader SME population. The exploratory nature of our research helps to better understand the impacts and benefits of a DT journey. Conducting the study in other contexts and with other SMEs (that experienced failure instead of success in innovation, for example) could have led to other conclusions. For future research, it may be interesting to document the benefits of emerging technologies such as artificial intelligence, for example, implemented in SMEs as a spark for digital innovation. It could also be interesting to follow a DT journey in a longitudinal study to better identify trigger mechanisms, such as emerging technologies, to document the challenges, failures, and benefits related to digital innovation. In this paper, there was little discussion of how a DT journey can be helpful for businesses of the following generation, as suggested by the DT S^4 framework. Further research could explore the contribution of innovation around value to become more sensing, smart, sustainable, and social. Finally, DT appears to be necessary for today's companies, including SMEs that wish to innovate, stand out and survive in the current business context.

References

Adam, N.A., Alarifi, G.: Innovation practices for survival of small and medium enterprises (SMEs) in the COVID-19 times: the role of external support. J. Innov. Entrep. **10**(1), 15 (2021). https://doi.org/10.1186/s13731-021-00156-6

Astrini, N.J., et al.: Innovativeness, proactiveness, and risk-taking: corporate entrepreneurship of Indonesian SMEs. IOP Conf. Ser.: Mater. Sci. Eng. **722**(1), 012037 (2020). https://doi.org/10.1088/1757-899X/722/1/012037

Baig, A., et al.: Digital adoption through COVID-19 and beyond. McKinsey Digital (2020). https://www.mckinsey.com/business-functions/mckinsey-digital/our-insights/the-covid-19-recovery-will-be-digital-a-plan-for-the-first-90-days. Accessed 27 Apr 2022

Blais, C.: Innovation in SMEs in Times of Crisis: The ability to reconcile formality, agility and speed. Int. J. Innovat. Tech. Manage. 2342002 (2023). https://doi.org/10.1142/s0219877023420026

Bordeleau, F.-E., Mosconi, E., de Santa-Eulalia, L.A.: Business intelligence and analytics value creation in industry 4.0: a multiple case study in manufacturing medium enterprises. Prod. Plan. & Control **31**(2–3), 173–185 (2020). https://doi.org/10.1080/09537287.2019.1631458

Bordeleau, F.-È., Santa-Eulalia, L.A., Mosconi, E.: Digital Transformation Framework: Creating Sensing, Smart, Sustainable and Social (S^4) Organisations, p. 4610 (2021). http://scholarspace.manoa.hawaii.edu/handle/10125/71176. Accessed 20 Jan 2021

Bostrom, R.P., Heinen, J.S.: MIS problems and failures: a socio-technical perspective, part II: the application of socio-technical theory. MIS Q. **1**(4), 11–28 (1977). https://doi.org/10.2307/249019

Clauss, T., et al.: Temporary business model innovation—SMEs' innovation response to the Covid-19 crisis. R&D Manag. **52**(2), 294–312 (2022). https://doi.org/10.1111/radm.12498

Cukier, W., et al.: The mother of invention: skills for innovation in the post-pandemic world. Toronto (2021). https://ppforum.ca/publications/mother-of-invention/. Accessed 27 Apr 2022

D'Este, P., Amara, N., Olmos-Peñuela, J.: Fostering novelty while reducing failure: balancing the twin challenges of product innovation. Technol. Forecast. Soc. Chang. **113**, 280–292 (2016). https://doi.org/10.1016/j.techfore.2015.08.011

Gong, C., Ribiere, V.: Developing a unified definition of digital transformation. Technovation 102217 (2020). https://doi.org/10.1016/j.technovation.2020.102217

Gröger, C.: There is no AI without data. Commun. ACM **64**(11), 98–108 (2021). https://doi.org/10.1145/3448247

Hassani, A., Mosconi, E.: Social media analytics, competitive intelligence, and dynamic capabilities in manufacturing SMEs. Technol. Forecast. Soc. Chang. **175**, 121416 (2022)

Jenson, I., et al.: Innovation system problems: causal configurations of innovation failure. J. Bus. Res. **69**(11), 5408–5412 (2016). https://doi.org/10.1016/j.jbusres.2016.04.146

Maslach, D.: Change and persistence with failed technological innovation. Strateg. Manag. J. **37**(4), 714–723 (2016). https://doi.org/10.1002/smj.2358

McKinsey: Reaching scale in the fourth industrial revolution(2022). https://www.mckinsey.com/business-functions/operations/our-insights/capturing-the-true-value-of-industry-four-point-zero. Accessed 16 Apr 2022

Mosconi, E., Packmohr, S., Santa-Eulalia, L.A.: Making digital transformation real. In: Proceedings of Hawaii International Conference on System Sciences. Maui, Hawaii, p. 3 (2019)

Nambisan, S., et al.: Digital innovation management: reinventing innovation management research in a digital world. MIS Q. **41**(1), 223–238 (2017). https://search.ebscohost.com/login.aspx?direct=true&db=bth&AN=121204229&lang=fr&site=eds-live (Accessed: 13 June 2021).

Nambisan, S., Wright, M., Feldman, M.: The digital transformation of innovation and entrepreneurship: progress, challenges and key themes. Res. Policy **48**(8), 103773 (2019). https://doi.org/10.1016/j.respol.2019.03.018

OECD (2018) Oslo Manual 2018: Guidelines for Collecting, Reporting and Using Data on Innovation, 4th edn. Organisation for Economic Cooperation and Development, Paris. https://www.oecd-ilibrary.org/science-and-technology/oslo-manual-2018_9789264304604-en. Accessed 28 Apr 2022

Paillé, P., Mucchielli, A.: L'analyse qualitative en sciences humaines et sociales (2e édition ed.). Armand- Colin (2008)

Perin, M.G., et al.:Network effects on radical innovation and financial performance: an open-mindedness approach. BAR—Braz. Adm. Rev. 13 (2017).https://doi.org/10.1590/1807-7692bar2016160057

Québec Innove: Grande enquête sur les PME et l'innovation en temps de pandémie. Québec Innove, Montreal (2020). https://www.quebecinnove.com/enquete2020/. Accessed 27 Apr 2022
Rhaiem, K., Amara, N.: Learning from innovation failures: a systematic review of the literature and research agenda. RMS **15**(2), 189–234 (2021). https://doi.org/10.1007/s11846-019-00339-2
Roper, S., Turner, J.: R&D and innovation after COVID-19: what can we expect? A review of prior research and data trends after the great financial crisis. Int. Small Bus. J. **38**(6), 504–514 (2020). https://doi.org/10.1177/0266242620947946
Schwab, K.: The Fourth Industrial Revolution, 1st edn. Crown Business, New York (2016)
Tabrizi, B., et al.: Digital transformation is not about technology. Harv. Bus. Rev. **13**, 1–6 (2019)
Vial, G.: Understanding digital transformation: a review and a research agenda. J. Strateg. Inf. Syst. **28**(2), 118–144 (2019). https://doi.org/10.1016/j.jsis.2019.01.003
Wenzel, M., Stanske, S., Lieberman, M.B.: Strategic responses to crisis. Strateg. Manag. J. **42**(2), O16–O27 (2021). https://doi.org/10.1002/smj.3161
Wessel, L., et al.: Unpacking the difference between digital transformation and IT-enabled organizational transformation. J. Assoc. Inf. Syst. **22**(1) (2021). https://doi.org/10.17705/1jais.00655.
Yin, R.K.: Case Study Research: Design and Methods (6 ed.). Sage Publications (2017)

Elaine Mosconi is an Associate Professor at the Université de Sherbrooke, Business School, Department of Information Systems and Quantitative Methods, Canada. Elaine is the scientific director of the Createch Research Center on Intelligent Organizations and the head of IntelliLab, a research group on emerging digital technologies. Professor Elaine has coauthored papers published in peer-reviewed journals TFSC, IT&People, Journal of Decision Systems, Production Planning Control and selected conferences as AoM, HICSS and ICIS. Her current research interests are related to digital transformation, digital literacy, digital innovation, business intelligence, Industry 4.0 and decision performance.

Caroline Blais is a professor of management accounting in the Department of Accounting Sciences at the Business School of University of Sherbrooke, Canada. She holds a CPA (chartered professional accountant) designation and a doctorate in business administration. Her research interests include performance management and measurement, innovation process, project management, digital transformation and small and medium enterprises. Her work has been published in International Journal of Project Management, International Journal of Innovation and Technology Management and Innovations: Journal of Innovations Economics and Management. She is a member of the Createch Research Centre on Intelligent Organisations and IntelliLab at University of Sherbrooke.

SPRINGER NATURE

GPSR Compliance

The European Union's (EU) General Product Safety Regulation (GPSR) is a set of rules that requires consumer products to be safe and our obligations to ensure this.

If you have any concerns about our products, you can contact us on ProductSafety@springernature.com

In case Publisher is established outside the EU, the EU authorized representative is:

Springer Nature Customer Service Center GmbH
Europaplatz 3
69115 Heidelberg, Germany

The manufacturer's authorised representative in the EU is Springer Nature Customer Service Centre GmbH, Europaplatz 3, 69115 Heidelberg, Germany. If you have any concerns regarding our products, please contact ProductSafety@springernature.com

Printed and bound by CPI Group (UK) Ltd, Croydon, CR0 4YY
28/09/2026
02224086-0002